AF541460

AATMANIRBHAR

AATMANIRBHAR

A SWADESHI PARADIGM

Edited by **ASHWANI MAHAJAN**

RUPA

Published by
Rupa Publications India Pvt. Ltd 2023
7/16, Ansari Road, Daryaganj
New Delhi 110002

Sales Centres:
Bengaluru Chennai
Hyderabad Jaipur Kathmandu
Kolkata Mumbai Prayagraj

P-ISBN: 978-93-5702-524-9
E-ISBN: 978-93-5702-526-3

First impression 2023

10 9 8 7 6 5 4 3 2 1

Printed in India

CONTENTS

FOREWORD
By Dr Mohan Bhagwat

Aatmanirbharta is a much-discussed term nowadays in the economic and developmental discourse of modern Bharat. After 75 years of independence, at this juncture of our historical evolution, we needed a deep resolve to be a powerful and responsible nation along with the confidence in our own ability to perform this task successfully. This resolve is very apparent in the present government, administration and all the stakeholders of the society alike.

The word aatmanirbharta, is a combination of two Sanskrit words—*aatma* and *nirbharta*—which roughly translates to 'self' and 'reliance'. The reliance or sufficiency here does not rule out having economic relations including trade with other economic entities. The word 'self' however does need a clearer description because each nation has its own specific notion of 'self'. This specificity or meaning of self, dictates the vision and concept of development, economy and ethics of the nation.

The prevalent Western discourse regarding the progress of humanity relies on a materialistic, fragmentary and consumerist approach to everything that exists. Following this discourse, naturally, happiness is sought from various objects in the world which are scarce. The desires of human beings are unlimited and according to Western discourse, the only way of satisfying those desires is through increased consumption. However, the very satisfaction of desires fuels them to increase further, like the offering of *ghee* in fire. Therefore, there will be no end to these desires. In such a case, there has to be a competition to gain control over consumables in which only the fittest will naturally survive. The unfit either perish, or live at the volatile mercy of the fit who dictate over them. The system of conduct of economy and development prevalent today, in which various experiments have been done in the last 200 years, held the fort of happiness and peace but ultimately and unquestionably failed. This system has no solution or succour to guide the stumbling human society to a brighter, peaceful and prosperous future. Despite huge progress in science and technology, humanity is now riddled with various rifts and clashes; destruction of families; psychological disorders; psychosomatic diseases; and irreversible damages to the environment, ecology and stratosphere on which human life depends. The situation is rather alarming.

In Bharatiya tradition, it is universally acknowledged that it is the state of mind and not objects of gratifications that give happiness. This happiness is not only of the body but also of the mind, intellect and inner essence of existence. This inner essence connects everyone and everything. So, simply the fulfilment of desires or having the means to fulfil them cannot bring the quest for happiness to a successful and sustainable end. You have to realize and experience the inner essence which connects everything and for that you have to observe a disciplined regimen in life. All these things are *purusharthas* (pursuits of life) which have to be undertaken to obtain happiness, contentment and fulfilment. Fulfilling one's desires is *kama* purusharth and the acquirement of means to do so is *arth* purusharth. These have to be conducted within the *dharma* purusharth which directs these endeavours to everlasting happiness or *moksha* purusharth. It is the final quest for moksha purusharth which we need to devote our lives to.

Generally, most Bharatiyas understand this vision. But we need to express this Bharatiya vision and thought into a concrete plan of conduct of human society in general, and Bharatiya society in particular. This reshaping must happen in the context of changed times; the scientific and technological knowledge added to the accumulated repository of human knowledge; the needs and expectation of the society of the day; and the need to continue the protection and practise of the Dharma values and Sanskriti.

Aatmanirbhar: Making India Self-Reliant is a collection of thoughts in this direction venturing further into the details of policy, planning and execution of this Bharatiya vision in resurgence of modern Bharat. Eminent scholars and luminaries, presently working and helping in this field, have contributed to this collection and therefore this introduction need not dwell or elaborate on the subject matter further. The editor Prof. Ashwani Mahajan and the publishers deserve hearty congratulations and best wishes for a very timely publication of this book which is at once a guide as well as a thought-provoking, brainstorming session of ideas. These ideas should kindle new debates out of which will emerge the pathway that will lead us to a new aatmanirbharta, one which will bring all round happiness to all Bhartiyas.

—Dr Mohan Bhagwat
Sarsanghchalak, Rashtriya Swayamsevak Sangh

INTRODUCTION

Ashwani Mahajan

Aatmanirbharta or self-reliance is not a new word for policymakers in India. After independence, the policy of planned economic development adopted under the leadership of Pandit Jawaharlal Nehru was also called the policy of self-reliant India. But the strategy adopted then for this planned development, called Mahalanobis Strategy, was to establish large and basic industries. It was a strategy of machines for producing machines and also had the stated objective of making India self-reliant, primarily by keeping the commanding heights of the economy with the public sector. Along with this, there was talk of building big dams and a strong industrial infrastructure. Although the strategy was aimed at achieving self-reliance, in reality, the dependence on foreign countries increased due to the huge requirement of resources and foreign exchange. In such a situation, when economic sanctions were imposed by the United States (US) and European countries on India due to the Indo–Pak War (1965), uncertainty regarding economic resources forced us to give a break to our planning for no less than three years.

The politicians of that time believed that the Mahalanobis Strategy was the only good path for the development of the country. It was said that in order to achieve the objectives set forth in this strategy, the public sector will have to play a major role. The thinking was that the private sector neither had the resources, nor the long-term vision and ability to take risks. In such a situation, the public sector became dominant in every segment of the economy, and the private sector was reduced to a secondary status. Although the private sector was allowed to operate in some arenas, the licence quota raj prevailed there as well. Every entrepreneur who wanted to set up industry was required to obtain a licence from the government and a quota for raw materials. Not only this, if an entrepreneur produced more than the licenced capacity, then there was a provision for monetary penalties and/or jail.

Due to the dominance of the public sector; licence quota raj; inspector raj; restrictive regulations; and a closed economy (in which the country's industries enjoyed complete protection) where heavy import duties were imposed on goods coming from abroad, our industries lagged behind in competition at the international level. The domestic industries had no incentive to improve efficiency, make quality goods or improve competitiveness. They had no incentive to develop technology or create new models. Both in private and public sectors, domestic industries had developed vested interests in controls like licence and quota raj—as they were living in the 'safe zone'—due to tariff walls and non-tariff measures, especially those like quantitative restrictions (QRs).

In this situation, where the imports were controlled either by way of tariffs or by imposing quantitative restrictions, the demand for foreign exchange in the country was also controlled. Therefore, the government could keep the exchange rate fixed as per its wish. It may be noted that till 1966 the exchange rate was ₹4.76 per US (United States) dollar. After 1966, when there was a devaluation of the rupee, the exchange rate was kept around only ₹6.36 per US dollar, and later it was further devalued from time to time before it reached ₹22.74 per US dollar in 1991. Through this, it can be said that Pandit Nehru's policy was to ensure self-reliance through restrictive measures, in which, along with private sector development remaining constrained, technological development and research and development (R&D) too remained strangulated. Victims were production and gross domestic product (GDP).

Low rate of growth, caused by these restrictive policies, was mischievously termed as 'Hindu Rate of Growth', which should actually be termed as 'Nehruvian Rate of Growth'. Though, there was reasonable expansion of educational institutions in the public sector during this time, people's participation in nation building through research and development was almost negligible. The efficiency and competitiveness of Indian exports was at its bottom. Therefore, the contribution of Indian exports at global level was low and also continued to decline.

When Prime Minister (PM) Narendra Modi presented the concept of self-reliant India to the nation, critics tried to dismiss it saying that it would be a return of the Nehruvian era. They argued that if we stop or curb imports to build a self-reliant India, then it will impact the competitiveness and efficiency and the economy will turn inward. But as the AatmaNirbhar Bharat Abhiyan (2020) of the present government is progressing, it is becoming clear that it is totally different from the 1950s self reliance policy of Pandit Nehru. It's all about bringing efficiency and competitiveness. It is a policy aimed at producing things which are currently being imported, and in the process building the capacity to produce for the world.

In this book, various renowned writers have presented the concept of self-reliant India in their own way. Almost all the writers have explained that the present government's policy of self-reliant India is completely different from the policy of self-reliant India of Pandit Nehru. They have spoken about how, due to the increasing presence of Chinese goods in the country's markets (in the last two decades), the country's industrial ecosystem has suffered immensely. Under these circumstances, it is essential to revive domestic industry, as it is imperative to provide gainful employment for our large army of youth. The Covid-19 pandemic has exposed the hollowness of misleading terms such as 'global cooperation' and 'global value chain'. The Russia–Ukraine war ongoing since February 2022 has also affected the global supply chain. In the changing geopolitical environment, the US and European countries have started weaponizing globalization, payment systems etc. It has become necessary for India to move forward not only in rebuilding industries, but in every field including electronic, telecom, textiles, machinery, chemicals, APIs (active pharmaceutical ingredients), toys, defence equipment and other manufacturing; along with payment systems and services (including software, banking, designs and consultancy).

Prof. Sachin Chaturvedi, the director general at Research and Information System (RIS) for Developing Countries, in his paper, reminds us of the beginning of *swadeshi* as a political and economic movement. He writes about its rise as a political movement from August 1905, when formal proclamation of the Swadeshi Movement was made. The call for boycotting foreign goods became part of the swadeshi thought process. He writes that this was a practical manifestation of the idea of Swadeshi, but the original idea extended far beyond this. Gandhi ji believed in non-violent industrial development of India. However, after independence the Swadeshi Movement soon embraced socialism and entered into a phase where terms like 'self-reliance' emerged to discredit private sector and move ahead with the celebration of state-led development, with nationalization of private enterprises. Centrality of State replaced the swadeshi spirit of encouraging local enterprises and their vibrancy.

He writes:

> The widespread balance of payment crisis, which eventually forced opening of the economies in the 1990s, discredited the development model of self-reliance and swadeshi. In India, economic reforms and opening up led to severe stress for local enterprises which again saw a rise of swadeshi, but without any reference to the elements of self-reliance. The new initiative of AatmaNirbhar Bharat has further expanded the frontier.

While tracing the evolution of the Swadeshi Movement, he further provides exposition to the efforts of self-reliance and swadeshi and cooperation among the developing or the third-world countries at the international level, prior to neoliberalism.

In India, the efforts towards self-reliance between 1950 and 1990 were marred with the problem of minimized role of private sector. This was the major cause of losing international competitiveness. However, the policies of LPG (liberalization, privatization and globalization) also couldn't do much to make the Indian industrial sector develop. This was due to excessive reliance on foreign capital and premature opening up of the economy. Prof. Chaturvedi notes that these policies were vehemently opposed by the Swadeshi Movement from 1990s onwards, led by Dattopant Thengadi.

The new approach of AatmaNirbhar Bharat includes protecting industry from unfair competition; using a judicious mix of tariff and non-tariff measures (that are World Trade Organisation [WTO] compliant with signing of FTAs [fair trade agreements] etc.); along with improving efficiencies and reducing transaction costs. According to Prof. Sachin Chaturvedi:

> Several policy reforms like work from home (WFH) added new advantage to firms, particularly Information Technology (IT) sector to deliver new opportunities and capture new horizons. Addressing conceptual, technical and operational elements of swadeshi through inclusive development plans such as, Aspirational Districts and Blocks Programme provided a new impetus coupled with initiatives like Sagarmala, Bharatmala Pariyojna and BharatNet. More inclusive approaches with focus on financial inclusion (JAM [Jandhan Aadhar Mobile] Trinity, DBT [direct benefit transfer], payment gateways, NPCI [National Payments Corporation of India]), provide a new dimension for the rise of India, in the areas hitherto reserved for Western and Chinese companies.

Devinder Sharma, an expert on Indian agriculture, while showing concern about large-scale migration of rural population to urban areas just to live under miserable conditions, highlights the importance of absorbing them back in rural areas with remunerative income. To transform the lives of people in rural areas in general and farmers in particular, he suggests making a historic correction. He makes the case for 'ease of doing farming'. According to him, India should formulate an 'ease of doing farming' index. He notes that just like several steps are taken to make it easier to do business, we should adopt a similar kind of policy initiative for farming. Apart from reforms in agricultural marketing, he suggests replicating the 'Amul Model' for pulses, fruits and oil seeds as well. Devinder Sharma argues that since 86 per cent of the land holdings are less than 5 acres, cooperatives alone can be an effective way to aggregate the smaller landholdings. Claiming that the Green Revolution has outlived its utility, he makes a case for chemical-free farming and suggests shifting the focus to agro-ecological farming system. This is what constitutes aatmanirbharta, he claims.

Sridhar Vembu, CEO of Zoho Corporation, has written his paper expressing concern about imbalances in the rural economy and its high dependence on agriculture. He says that the agricultural income is not enough to fund the needs of the rural people, which includes gas stoves, tractors, motorcycles, cell phones, etc. This persistent rural trade deficit can be bridged only by equipping rural people with low-cost technology, and making them capable of producing simple goods to reduce their dependence on big companies. He says that rural entrepreneurs can be provided with standardized designs for marketable products, that can be produced with low-cost machines (for example, basic electronic components, household goods like fans, scissors, power tools etc.). 'If needed, government and corporations can employ soft loans or a profit- sharing model, privately or through a rural development bank, to help establish these factories,' he suggests.

Nagesh Kumar, the director of the Institute for Studies in Industrial Development (ISID), in his paper notes that while moving from an agriculture-dominated economy, India has achieved significant growth with the help of the service sector. However, the manufacturing sector has failed to grow along expected lines. This makes India lag behind its peers from East Asian economies that include Japan, the Republic of Korea, Thailand, Malaysia, Vietnam and China, who have done extremely well in creating a mark in the manufacturing sector. He notes that failure to grow its manufacturing sector has caused enormous loss to the Indian economy, as it fails to provide gainful employment to its ever-growing workforce. He notes that, 'Neglect of manufacturing has cost the country in terms of creation of productive jobs for nearly 12 million workers that join the workforce every year especially because the manufacturing sector has the highest backward and forward linkages of any productive sector.'

Nagesh Kumar talks at length about opportunities for industrialization in India, which include making for India as well as for the rest of the world. He further emphasizes on sunrise industries which include digital as well as green industrialization. He claims that strategic import substitution, export promotion and digital and green industrialization has the potential to lift India's manufacturing value added from the current $450 billion to $1 trillion by 2025.

While fully endorsing the concept of AatmaNirbhar Bharat, Prof. Shamika Ravi (non-resident senior fellow of the Governance Studies Program at the Brookings Institution Washington DC) writes about how Covid-19 has exposed the hollowness of global cooperation. In this environment, self-reliance has worked to save Indian people and make India stand apart and proud amidst the ongoing pandemic. Almost all contributors of this anthology, including Prof. Shamika, have opined that self-reliance is not autarky and the Modi government's resolve for AatmaNirbhar Bharat is quite distinct from Nehru's vision. Though, most of the authors have opined that the policies from 1960s have been the major cause of Indian industries losing competitiveness, some—including Shamika Ravi—have talked about the darker side of neoliberal policies, apart from the worst inequalities caused by these policies.

Prof. Shamika thinks that neoliberal idea of trade liberalization has brought many good results. However, she says that it could displace many people leading to political and social disruption (as witnessed in some of the world's leading economies). She underlines the need for expansion of social safety nets to address the concerns of those displaced due to trade liberalization. She says that market efficiency and privatization should be encouraged, but with sufficient safeguards ensuring that economic power is not concentrated in the hands of a few. Unfortunately, the neoliberal economic models that focus exclusively on efficiency do not address political and social issues arising from the concentration of wealth.

Dr V. Anantha Nageswaran's (the chief economic advisor to the Government of India) opinion is that integration vis-à-vis self-reliance need not be an either–or choice. Being self-reliant has its own merits but that does not necessarily imply that open trade and integration reflect an adverse policy choice. He writes:

> Formulating and implementing economic policy in a globally intertwined world comes with its share of costs and benefits. There are gains to be made from being integrated into the form of large foreign investments, knowledge and R&D exchange and efficiency gains via comparative trade advantages. At the same time, a high degree of association also has costs that are amplified in times of crisis. Countries are exposed to volatilities of trade and foreign capital outflow shocks, besides episodes of unwarranted imported inflation.

Dr Nageswaran suggests that in order to achieve self-reliance, we also need to integrate our policy levers with the global economy.

He says, 'The design and effective implementation of self-reliance measures with emphasis on performance and productivity are key determinants of sustainable growth going forward, while also acting as a buffer against any unforeseen global shocks.'

Prof. Ashima Goyal, emeritus professor at Indira Gandhi Institute of Development Research, starts her paper by talking about the fear expressed by the critics of AatmaNirbhar Bharat. The fear is that it means a reversal of liberalization and a closing of the economy once again. Dispelling these fears, she argues in her paper that the objectives of aatmanirbharta is strengthening domestic capacity. 'Achieving this requires pragmatism and diversity, both of which entail more, not less, openness while staying away from policy extremes of fully-open or fully-closed market. It also requires coordination between governments and producers. We illustrate these principles with India's recent export drive,' she opines.

She argues that the post-Independence import substituting policy regime led to high-cost–low-quality outcome for Indian manufacturing in a protected market. However, in the import competition regime, in the post-1991 period, manufacturing found it difficult to survive given high costs and unfair government-subsidized competition from China. She calls both these policy regimes unproductive and suggests that the more sustainable current regime can be called 'export competition'. 'Manufacturing has to compete internationally and therefore, become efficient in order to export. But it will be protected from unfair competition and helped to develop economies of scale under a broad set of policies that lower costs of doing business,' she argues.

Sanjeev Sanyal, a member of the Prime Minister's Economic Advisory Council, in his paper, makes clear that AatmaNirbhar Bharat is not a return to the socialist era import substitution, and the licence permit raj that accompanied it. He further says that it is not an attempt to close India from the global supply chain, foreign technologies or international investments. He joins other contributors in criticizing the pre-liberalization era, that led India into a minefield of inefficiency, bureaucratic hurdles, rent-seeking and low economic performance, which continued to haunt Indian economy because of the aftermath of that short-sighted approach. He says that AatmaNirbhar Bharat is about leveraging India's internal strengths to encourage indigenous entrepreneurship, innovation and risk-taking to compete in an evolving competitive world. While we should not be blind to the advantages of certain trade deals, one should also not be accepting of any and every FTA. What matters is that the policymakers do a realistic assessment of the advantages and disadvantages of such deals. What Sanjeev Sanyal opines is a very powerful argument about the imperative of AatmaNirbhar Bharat.

Otherwise a staunch supporter of globalization, Dr Sanjaya Baru (distinguished fellow, United Service Institution of India and former media advisor and chief spokesperson PMO [Prime Minister's Office]) in his paper makes a case for increasing the share of manufacturing in India's GDP. He suggests that to achieve aatmanirbharta in manufacturing, we need institutional reforms aimed at enhancing total factor productivity. Amending his earlier thoughts on globalization, he says that many developed economies have become increasingly protectionist and India should not be an exception.

Though developed countries claim to be supporters of globalization, while negotiating on the FTAs with India they insist on inclusion of non-trade issues (which they also term as fair trade) aimed at making it difficult for our goods to get entry into their respective countries. Concerned about the emerging geopolitical atmosphere and how the US and other Western countries weaponized economic and financial links (including payment system and imposing other sanctions), Dr Baru now calls for greater self-reliance in economic development and defence preparedness. He says, 'India's "Make in India" programme for defence equipment manufacturing gains greater urgency given these new global developments. Equally, a more cautious approach towards global finance; global financial integration; and the management of balance of payments is warranted. The external economic environment has become uncertain and has been destabilized by recent events and actions. All this only reinforces the relevance of the AatmaNirbhar Bharat Abhyan,' he opines.

Dr Rajiv Kumar (former vice chairman of NITI Aayog) and his co-author Shashank Shah (senior specialist at NITI Aayog), in their paper, emphasized on increasing India's share in global manufacturing. This was for two reasons: one, for generating good quality jobs for the next few decades; and two, because India cannot afford to depend upon imports of manufacturing product indefinitely. They argue that India needs to become self-reliant in non-fossil energy to reduce its dependence on imported fossil fuels, especially oil. They also talk about encouraging exports from India, especially exports of manufactured product.

Prof. Abhijit Das, former head and professor, Centre for WTO Studies, Indian Institute of Foreign Trade, writes that AatmaNirbhar Bharat is understood to include boosting the production of goods and services for domestic consumption and exports. He further states, 'It also envisages enhancing technological capabilities and encouraging investment, including from foreign sources, to propel Indian economy to a higher growth trajectory. However, AatmaNirbhar Bharat must not be misunderstood as restricting imports and seeking to produce most of the goods domestically. Instead, this initiative must be viewed from the perspective of using international trade strategically for securing its objectives.'

He believes that international trade agreements can have a significant impact on the objective of AatmaNirbhar Bharat. Prof. Das observes that FTAs are in the pipeline with Canada, European Union (EU) and the United Kingdom (UK). He opines that if some of the provisions in the past FTAs of Canada, EU and the UK are also included in their FTA with India, then India would be required to comply with certain onerous obligations, particularly the following: prohibition on imposing export duties and taxes; prohibition on imposing any restrictions on imports of re-manufactured goods; eliminating import tariffs on a large number of information technology (IT) products and consumer electronic goods; and eliminating import tariffs on environmental goods. These provisions, along with many others that are to be included in India's FTA with these countries, may be detrimental to India's resolve towards self-reliance or AatmaNirbhar Bharat.

Prof. Ashok Kumar Lahiri, former chief economic advisor to the Government of India, in his paper traces the history of the Swadeshi Movement and how it led to the infant industry argument during British India (which ultimately led to the policy of discriminating protection). He further argues that protection should not continue infinitely. He says, 'The failure of the extremely protectionist policies of the first four decades of Independence manifested in the country's recurrent balance of payment problems until the early 1990s.' Citing the mutual dependence of different countries with regard to global supply chain, he argues in favour of free trade. He opines that India stands to gain by trading with other countries and that there is no need to fear dominances of the foreigners given ever-increasing incomes and other indicators of human development (especially education).

As a note of caution he writes, 'A policy of not limiting imports does not mean that there is no need to monitor whether India is becoming too dependent on a particular country or a few suppliers for keeping the domestic industry, including the export sector, running.' In this context he further writes, 'Trying to produce everything within the country without imports is not the right lesson to derive from the Covid-19 pandemic and US–China trade war. But it is important to be vigilant that India is not becoming too dependent on China or any other single country for raw materials or processed inputs.'

Gopal Srinivasan, who is deep into the capital sector as CEO of TVS Capital, writes about how by promoting the domestic capital we can make India a $10 trillion economy by 2047. He lists several measures in the long-, medium- and short-term to achieve this objective. He argues for the need to encourage domestic capital, in investing and harvesting from venture capital and start-ups in a more robust manner. Taxation parity between listed and private markets, and between domestic and overseas investors are both important reform measures. He opines that capital and stock markets have gained maturity. Therefore, the government should not consider allowing overseas listing of the shares of Indian start-ups without their parallel listing in India, and it should also encourage rupee investors.

Bibek Debroy (chairman of the Economic Advisory Council to the Prime Minister) along with his co-author Aditya Sinha (public policy professional working with the Economic Advisory Council to the Prime Minister), argues that AatmaNirbhar Bharat does not imply protectionism, isolation or autarky. They say:

> One can argue that there are some similarities between AatmaNirbhar Bharat and the 'neo-mercantilist' conception of economic nationalism, which Georg Friedrich List had advanced in the nineteenth century. Autarky is all about minimizing international linkages whereas neo-mercantilism, aims for outward-oriented targeted trade restrictions. The government's economic activism is aimed to make domestic industries compete on the global stage. The stress is on promoting domestic manufacturing rather than just the domestic industries. There is a distinction. India aims at attracting investors and manufacturers to manufacture in India. The aim is to reduce import dependence and promote exports. The logic of a market economy is to locate economic activities in geographical regions where they are most productive and profitable. Production linked incentive

(PLI) schemes are doing precisely that. PLIs have aided the relocation of the manufacturing units to India.

Ashish Kumar Chauhan, CEO of National Stock Exchange and former CEO of Bombay Stock Exchange, in his paper traces the history of development of financial and capital markets in India. He explains how, over the last 147 years, organized share market has led to the promotion of investment culture among Indians. He lists the achievements of Bombay Stock Exchange and explains how it has helped the wealth creation in the country. He further states how technology adoption can drive India to the next stage of development. He opines that stock market automation in early 1990s made India the pioneer in automation of stock market infrastructure at a global level, and also provided impetus to the development of IT prowess—for which India is now well known.

Sanjiv Puri, chairman and managing director for ITC (India's largest Fast Moving Consumer Goods [FMCG] company), pins hopes on creating world class products and services, from a clarion call for an aatmanirbhar Bharat. He equates AatmaNirbhar Bharat Abhiyan with calls of 'Jai Jawan Jai Kisan' by former PM Lal Bahadur Shastri and 'Give me blood, I will give you freedom' by Subhas Chandra Bose. He further writes that creating world-class brands is the way forward. Listing the brands that India has been able to create so far, he says that there is great hope for creating more based on indigenous R&D and digitalization. As we are making great strides in both, he foresees that creating more world-class brands and making the best products for the world over is no longer a distant dream. With this we shall be able to create a downstream value chain, making lives better for people, including the rural population.

Shri N.K. Singh—the chairman of the 15th Finance Commission, Government of India—in his paper, elaborates on the historical experience of international financial architecture, and emphasizes on the need to initiate reforms in the light of present geopolitical and economic changes. In view of global economic crises and upheavals; the ongoing Ukraine–Russia war; tensions in other parts of the world; declining faith in Global Value Chain (what he termed as broken psyche of GVC); declining mercantilism; weaponization of money by the West; and changing geopolitical dynamics on finance and trade, he advocates rethinking on the Washington Consensus based on globalization. He calls for a new world order with greater degree of self-reliance, with special emphasis on self-reliance in defence and reduced dependence on fossil fuels. 'Nations have to increasingly address their security concern and enhance resilience amidst uncertainties even while being cognizant of maintaining competitiveness with factor endowments,' he opines. Given his vast and long experience in economic and geopolitical affairs, his advice assumes a special significance for the policymakers.

Saji Narayanan, the leader and past president of the Bhartiya Mazdoor Sangh (India's largest labour organization), in his paper highlights the pains of labour in recent times. 'In the name of disruptive technologies and business models, a new category of workers has emerged, namely "gig workers". As India is making strides towards self-reliance, it is natural for the labour to get a better treatment than what was meted out to them in the past,' he says.

He argues that the pandemic has exposed a big migrant labour crisis in India. He further highlights the importance of 'family model' in labour relations, shunning conflict between labour and management. He propagates that cooperation and confluence should replace conflicting and antagonistic approaches in labour relations. He explains the importance of non-exploitative labour relations and emphasizes that as per India's traditional labour culture, surplus should belong to the 'nation and not just the capitalist in capitalism or to the state in communism'.

It is natural that due to competition from cheap imports for a long time, the affected industries have either closed down or are on the verge of closure. The relentless reduction in import duties due to obsession towards globalization has caused huge damage to India's manufacturing sector. Governments remained insensitive towards the closing industries and no effort to save them has been visible in the yesteryears. Rather, the situation was made worse by the UPA (United Progressive Alliance) government by constantly reducing tariffs. The deindustrialization trend was clearly visible in most of the industries including APIs, electronics and telecom, chemical, machinery, toy industries and many more. Manufacturing sector as a whole saw a downturn, as visible from the fact that share of manufacturing in the GDP declined from 19 per cent in 2006–07 to only 16.35 per cent in 2018–19. This decline of registered manufacturing's share in GDP was evenly spread across different industries. The policymakers continued to advance the argument of making goods cheaper for the consumers, and there was no visible effort by them to arrest the decline of manufacturing in the country. On the one hand, the country's trade deficit was reaching intolerable levels and on the other, due to continuous decline in manufacturing the opportunities for employment generation in the country were also fast eroding. Between 2010–11 and 2019–20 (a decade before Covid-19), the index of industrial production increased at an extremely slow pace—0 and 4 per cent in the first nine years and ultimately at -0.8 per cent in 2019–20.[1]

Understanding this precarious situation in 2014, the Narendra Modi government announced the policy of 'Make in India', under which various measures were adopted to promote manufacturing in the country. One of the major measures was preferential treatment to Make in India items in government procurement. Encouragement was given to enterprises to produce in India and efforts were made to facilitate production

[1]'Table 28 : Index Numbers of Industrial Production', *Handbook of Statistics on Indian Economy, Reserve Bank of India*, 15 September 2022, https://tinyurl.com/3xcb7z2c. Accessed on 11 July 2023.

in the country, including products from foreign companies. But even after that, the flood of Chinese goods in the country could not be stopped. In 2018, to protect Indian industries, the process of increasing tariff was started. This was the first time after the economic policy of 1990s that the government decided to increase the import duty to protect domestic industries. Supporters of free trade in the country and economists opposed raising tariffs for protection of domestic industries, but the government remained firm in its resolution.

After the pandemic broke out in 2020, it became clear that due to the youth's excessive dependence on China there was an intolerably deficient production capacity in various sectors. As the country could not depend on China any longer, the Modi government made a major policy shift and initiated the policy of AatmaNirbhar Bharat. We can see several dimensions in this policy of self-reliant India announced by PM Narendra Modi.

The first and most important dimension is that in this concept of self-reliant India, encouragement has been given to the production of those items in which India had excessive dependence on foreign countries (especially China). For the last 20 years or so, ever since China joined the WTO, the dumping and dominance of Chinese goods in the country's markets increased to such an extent that our existing industries started shutting down fast. A list of 14 such industries was prepared which needed rehabilitation. These industries included electronics, medical equipment, bulk drugs, pharmaceuticals, telecom products, food products, air conditioners (ACs), LEDs, high-efficiency solar PV Modules, automobiles and auto equipment, textile products, special steel, drones etc.

The second dimension of this policy was that in order to promote production in the identified sectors, a plan was made to give PLIs. To that end, a targeted PLI of ₹1.97 lakh crore in the next few years for such industries was announced. Later, a provision of additional ₹19,500 crore for solar PV modules and

₹76,000 crores to boost semi-conductor production was made.[2]

In the third dimension, the import duty was increased to prevent the import of these goods from abroad. It is believed that through all these efforts, the GDP growth in the country can be increased by 2–4 per cent.

Finally, the policy also includes self-reliance of villages. Self-reliance of the country cannot be imagined without self-reliant villages. Integrated farming and promotion of different kinds of activities—animal husbandry, poultry, fisheries, food processing and other rural industries like bamboo production, mushroom production, etc.—is the key to increase income of the villagers. We must understand that the adoption of AatmaNirbhar Bharat, keeping the objectives of enhancing incomes with employment generation; environmental protection; and equality in distribution of income and wealth in mind is the mantra for rebuilding the nation. With this we can add a new chapter of happiness in our country.

Because of the past experience of perverted experimentation with self-reliance during the first 40 years after independence, there are some natural fears about adopting the policy of AatmaNirbhar Bharat. This book is an attempt to collect ideas and analyses from some of the best minds in the country in the fields of economics, industry and social science about how to deal with the present situation, and make this historic effort successful. Almost all the authors have supported this idea of self-reliance to bring back the glory of this nation, and have discussed in their own ways, the contours of AatmaNirbhar Bharat.

---

[2]'PLI Schemes Contribute to Increase in Production, Employment Generation, and Economic Growth', *PIB Delhi*, 13 June 2023, https://tinyurl.com/38p4wuy4. Accessed on 11 July 2023; Dutta Mishra, Ravi, and Rituraj Baruah, 'Centre Approves ₹19500 CR PLI for Solar PV Modules', *mint*, 22 September 2022, https://tinyurl.com/2s44vuc3. Accessed on 11 July 2023; 'Cabinet Clears Rs 76,000-Cr Incentive Scheme for Semiconductors', *The Economic Times*, 16 December 2021, https://tinyurl.com/2pxcwf4w. Accessed on 11 July 2023.

Respected Dr Mohan Bhagwat ji has extended his blessings for the book by writing the foreword and has given the philosophical basis of the idea of aatmanirbharta, as manifestation of the self. He says that given the limited supply of objects, we can't fulfil the greed and only India's philosophical tenets of contentment and discipline can give us real happiness. According to him our efforts towards AatmaNirbhar Bharat, therefore, should be within the ambit of *dharma purusharth*, aimed at survival of all and not within the Western thought of 'survival of the fittest'.

1

SWADESHI AND AATMANIRBHAR BHARAT: CONTRADICTIONS, COMPLEMENTARITIES AND THE WAY FORWARD

Prof. Sachin Chaturvedi

Director General, Research and Information System for Developing Countries (RIS)

During the colonial and post-colonial reconstruction phase, trade and investment linkages within developing countries acquired large importance in national economic policies, and even greater political significance in the pursuit of national space for local actors contributing to a reformed global economic architecture. Immediately after the Second World War, when reconstruction began, the developing world (often described as the 'third world') in those years realized that the huge resource and skill gaps, coming out of poverty and widespread deprivations were a major impediment to survival.

In some countries, like India, leveraging political movements for opposing produce from the industrial revolution—with the idea of protecting local livelihoods and space for local produce—led to initiatives like *swadeshi*. It was a natural connect with *swaraj* (freedom). The Swadeshi Movement had its roots in the anti-partition movement initiated to oppose Lord Curzon's decision of dividing the then province of Bengal. In August 1905, at Calcutta (now Kolkata) Town Hall, a massive meeting was held, and the formal proclamation of the Swadeshi Movement was made. The message to boycott goods such as Manchester cloth and Liverpool salt was propagated. After the partition of Bengal, widespread opposition was shown by the people of Bengal by singing Bankim Chandra Chatterjee's, 'Vande Mataram'. Rabindranath Tagore also composed the song, 'Amar Sonar Bangla'. In Andhra Pradesh, the Swadeshi movement was launched as the Vande Mataram Movement.

With mass mobilization and people coming together in solidarity and complementarity, the idea seized the public imagination. The power of being together, and the ability to constitute an insurmountable strength augmented the people's collective capability to withstand local damages done by colonial masters. The calls for boycotting foreign goods thus became part of the swadeshi thought process. This was a practical manifestation of the idea of swadeshi but the original idea was far beyond this. Gandhi believed in non-violent industrial development of India. His emphasis on redistribution of wealth was consistent with the kind of moral framework of *dharma* that he talked about. His simplicity and awareness of the masses played an important role in making swadeshi part of a popular discourse, on independence and economic progress.

However, within a brief span of time this Swadeshi Movement soon embraced socialism. It got into a phase where terms like 'self-reliance' emerged to discredit private sector and move ahead with the celebration of state-led development, with nationalization of private enterprises. The intertwining was so intense and deep that down the years, the centrality of State replaced the swadeshi spirit of local enterprises and their vibrancy. It was seen as a new trajectory for an equitable society which, however, eventually led to crippling of the private sector and the rise of economic inefficiency at the domestic level. The widespread 'balance of payment' crisis, which eventually forced opening up of the economies in the 1990s, discredited the development model of self-reliance and swadeshi. In India, economic reforms and opening up led to severe stress for local enterprises. This again saw a rise of swadeshi, but without any reference to the elements of self-reliance. The new initiative of AatmaNirbhar Bharat has further expanded the frontier.

This paper explores the contours that define the ideas of the Swadeshi Movement and AatmaNirbhar Bharat, and places them in the backdrop of global debates and relevant initiatives.

FEATURES OF SWADESHI AND ITS PRE-INDEPENDENCE DISTANCE FROM SELF-RELIANCE

The elements of swadeshi have only been analysed with the approaches of self reliance and self-sufficiency, while the key constituents also come from swaraj and *swabhiman* (self-respect). The early commentators focussed more on these facets of swadeshi and placed greater emphasis on documentation and analytical reasoning for arguing out a case in the Indian context.

The idea of development was delineated in its wider context by Dadabhai Naoroji and Justice Madhav Govind Ranade. Dadabhai articulated the theory of wealth drain, while Justice Ranade emphasized on manufacturing and its importance in an agrarian economy. As Justice Ranade explained: 'Every nation which desires economical advance has to take care that its urban population bears an increasing ratio to its rural masses with every advance it seeks to make.'[1]

Robert Gallagher in his article, 'M.G. Ranade and the Indian System of Political Economy' in the *Executive Intelligence Review*, has mentioned: 'In the Poona Quarterly Journal, he documented the sorry truth, how from 1871 to 1891, the percentage of the labor force

[1]Grewal, Kairvy, 'MG Ranade—The "Father of Indian Economics" Who Also Fought for Widow Remarriage', *The Print*, 16 January 2020, https://tinyurl.com/2xfvuvrb. Accessed on 3 April 2023.

involved in agriculture and production of livestock increased from 56% to 66%, while the percentage involved in manufacturing trades decreased from 30% to 21%. This he described as a "retrograde movement" in his Deccan College address.'[2]

Gopal Krishna Gokhale as the Congress President in 1905 announced 'the true Swadeshi Movement as both a patriotic and an economic movement. The idea of Swadeshi or one's own country is one of the noblest conceptions that had ever stirred the heart of humanity'.[3] Subsequently, the Congress appealed to the people to boycott British goods.

While mentoring Gandhi, Gokhale shared his ideas on swadeshi and the importance of local production. Gandhi's ideas of swadeshi evolved with time. In a speech delivered at the Missionary Conference in Madras on 14 February 1916, he said:

> Swadeshi is that spirit in us which restricts us to the use and service of our immediate surroundings to the exclusion of the more remote. Thus, as for religion, in order to satisfy the requirements of definition, I must restrict myself to ancestral religion. That is the use of my immediate surroundings. If I find it defective, I should serve it by purging it of its defects. In domain of politics, I should make use of the indigenous institutions and serve them by curing them of their proved defects. In that of economics, I should use only things that are produced by my immediate neighbours and serve those industries by making them efficient and complete where they might be found wanting.[4]

---

[2]Gallagher, Robert, 'M. G. Ranade and the Indian System of Political Economy', *Executive Intelligence Review*, Vol. 15, No. 22, 27 May 1988, https://tinyurl.com/3u2nbeu3. Accessed on 3 April 2023.

[3]Priyadarsi, S., 'Causes and Consequences of Swadeshi Movement in India', *HistoryDiscussion.net*, https://tinyurl.com/2p8st6s9. Accessed on 3 April 2023.

[4]'Self-Reliance and Self-Sufficiency', *Egyankosh*, https://tinyurl.com/nhkde4aw. Accessed on 3 April 2023.

His idea was to leverage the concept of swadeshi, not for closing the markets but for enhancing quality and efficiency of products. He also linked it up with moral obligation and non-violence. Unfortunately, these linkages were missed out in the industrial policy documents, where machines were given more importance than the morality of Indians. Later in 1926, Gandhi ji articulated space for foreign trade. He said: 'To reject foreign manufactures, merely because they are foreign and to go on wasting national time and money in the promotion in one's country of manufactures for which it is not suited would be criminal folly and a negation of the Swadeshi spirit.'[5]

In *Hind Swaraj*, Gandhi captures the sentiment of swadeshi beautifully:

> Before I leave you, I will take the liberty of repeating:
>
> 1. Real home-rule is self-rule or self-control.
> 2. The way to it is passive resistance: that is soul-force or love-force.
> 3. In order to exert this force, Swadeshi in every sense is necessary.
> 4. What we want to do should be done, not because we object to the English or because we want to retaliate but because it is our duty to do so. Thus, supposing that the English remove the salt-tax, restore our money, give the highest posts to Indians, withdraw the English troops, we shall certainly nor use their machine-made goods, nor use the English language, nor many of their industries. It is worth noting that these things are, in their nature, harmful; hence we do not want them. I bear no enmity towards the English but I do towards their civilization.[6]

---

[5]'Meaning of Swadeshi', *MKGandhi.org*, https://tinyurl.com/5n99xwsk. Accessed on 19 July 2023.

[6]'Hind Swaraj or Indian Home Rule: Chapter-20: Conclusion', *Gandhi Sevagram Ashram*, https://tinyurl.com/kvzscr3k. Accessed on 3 April 2023.

With the gazette notification of the partition of Bengal in 1903, the Swadeshi Movement gained much greater momentum. Insights and guidance from Gurudev Rabindranath Tagore shaped the evolution. His 1904 speech for a 'swadeshi samaj' called for self-reliance in several diverse fields like agriculture, commerce and business, art, literature, etc. His emphasis was on people-to-people connect at micro-levels (at the level of villages). In his speech, he also pointed out that the State and the society should function independently of each other. The State should target for 'minimum state', and allow each individual to be left free to pursue their chosen vocation and lifestyle.[7]

Before we close this section, it is important to mention that the Swadeshi Movement in India had an impact beyond boycotts and burning of clothes. Its contents and impact were evident across various walks of life (as seen in the section below, titled, 'Multifaceted Outcomes of the Swadeshi Movement'). It triggered a rise of local industries, banks, insurance agencies, academic institutions. It also led to popular movements for promotion of vernacular languages and literature. The Swadeshi Movement led to blocking of imports and triggered development in various domestic industries, bringing back local livelihood security and scope for skill development. Several important policy works emerged during the evolution of this movement.

Multifaceted Outcomes of the Swadeshi Movement (1850 onwards)[8]

New Institutions by Indians for Better Domestic Options

The National Council of Education, formed in 1906 (established to promote science and technology as part of the Swadeshi

---

[7]'Swadeshi Samaj by Rabindranath Tagore', *Digital District Repository Detail, Azadi ka Amrit Mahotsav*, https://tinyurl.com/4em8zjpu. Accessed on 3 April 2023.

[8]Compiled by the author. This is just a representative collation.

Industrialization Movement), founded the Bengal National College and Bengal Technical Institute (which later merged to form Jadavpur University). The institutions which were functioning under the national council were considered to be hotbeds of swadeshi activities.

Industry

Many industries were formed during the evolution of the Swadeshi Movement. The names of a few have been added below:

- Prafulla Chandra Ray's Bengal Chemical Works (Prafulla Chandra Ray)
- Tata Iron and Steel Company (Jamshedji Tata)
- Bengal Luxmi Cotton Mills Ltd
- Mohini Mills Ltd
- Many new banks from 1906–11: Bank of India, Corporation Bank, Indian Bank, Bank of Baroda, Canara Bank and Central Bank of India
- Insurance companies
- Ship-building Industries
- Swadeshi Steam Navigation Company
- Khadi spinning centres (organized by Mahatma Gandhi to revive the Indian Cottage Industry)

Trade

Foreign goods including clothes, sugar, salt and various other luxury items were not only boycotted, but were also burned (most symbolic burning was of 150,000 English clothes at Elpinstone Mill Compound, Parel, Mumbai on 31 July 1921). Imports were declined between 1906–08.

Social Initiatives

Satguru Ram Singh founded the Namdhari Sect on 12 April 1857 and asked his followers to boycott everything which bore the stamp of the British Government. There was a rise in the popularity of vernacular languages and literature owing to the Swadeshi Movement.

Table 1
Key Conceptual and Policy Work on Swadeshi and Related Themes[9]

Book or Policy Work	Person	Year
Poverty and Un-British Rule in India	Dadabhai Naoroji	1901
Deposition before the Welby Commission	Gopal Krishna Gokhale	1897
Played a leading role in bringing about Morley-Minto Reforms		1909
Swadeshi Samaj	Rabindranath Tagore	1904
Hind Swaraj	Mahatma Gandhi	1909

SWADESHI: THE INTERNATIONAL CONTEXT

Since the Second World War, the Southern economies tried to rebuild themselves with local resource mobilization and capacity-building. During this period, the economies from the South helped each other and facilitated collective growth. At the same time, the UN (United Nations) institutions were also prompted to support the rebuilding effort of these erstwhile colonial economies. In some cases, the UN blocked proposals of underdeveloped economies—like Special UN Fund for Economic Development (SUNFED)—and in some cases it was allowed to prevail.

The idea of self-reliance in the 1950s and 1960s, particularly during the reconstruction phase and due to the collective efforts by the South through platforms like the UN Conference on Trade

[9]Ibid.

and Development (UNCTAD), emerged in a major way. India already had its own take on development strategy, many decades before it became independent. Swadeshi was very much at the centre of this framework since it meant development through local and indigenous resources.

It is in this respect that theoretical support from Raúl Prebisch (Argentine economist and former executive director for the Economic Commission for Latin America), proved to be extremely beneficial in shaping the narrative of the UN institutions. His idea of centre–periphery relationship provided the necessary basis for additional development support for the South. His contributions facilitated conceptualization of the theory of dependency and the resulting policy options for the Southern countries to opt for import substitution strategies for industrialization, and achieve a higher degree of self-reliance for themselves. The theoretical framework elaborated the idea of peripheral capitalism, which also shaped the agenda for the Bandung Conference (1955). The argument focussed on terms of trade that was against the exporters of primary commodities, vis-à-vis the importers who were then exporting finished products using their technological advantage. The final draft outcome document of BAPA+40 (Buenos Aires Plan of Action Plus 40) released on 6 March 2019, and emphasized on linking South-South Cooperation (SSC) with the 2030 Agenda to leave no one behind. It also carries the spirit of Prebisch's call to establish an inclusive global order, and does away with the distinction between centre and periphery.

This work enunciated and motivated multilateral organizations, as Prebisch joined the UNCTAD as its director general (1964–69). At all stages, India extended full support to this wider community at the UNCTAD, in debates involving the set of proposals put forward in the 1970s by developing countries called the New International Economic Order (NIEO). This proposal was essentially aimed at improving their terms of trade. The UNCTAD and the Economic Commission for Latin America and the Caribbean (ECLAC) produced several papers and documents that provided the basis for UN institutions to lead capacity-building programmes to support domestic development endeavours.

At the UN, the Economic Cooperation among Developing Countries (ECDC) appeared in 1974—in light of the debate on the NIEO through the General Assembly Resolution 3201. It identified the limitations of the global development strategies; its imperatives for an interdependent world; and the exclusions that it was leading to. They were defined most elaborately in the BAPA on TCDC (Technical Cooperation among Developing Countries) adopted in 1978; the Fourth Ministerial Meeting of G-77 in Arusha in 1979; and the Caracas Programme of Action on ECDC adopted in 1981.

It is in this way, that the international cooperation of the South motivated several national governments and other actors for country-specific strategies. Several countries initiated their own programmes to move towards self-reliance. In Tanzania, the Arusha Declaration (*Azimio la Arusha* in Swahili), bringing forward TANU's (Tanganyika African National Union) Policy on socialism and self-reliance (1967) came out as the most prominent documents. However, in the recent past, other strategies have evolved and the proposal of the African Continental Free Trade Area (AfCFTA) talks about self-reliance more in the context of trade cooperation and local linkages. These linkages would be through value chains, as the inflow of additional resources has not improved. In the last 10 years, India's development assistance on an average has remained at 2.3 per cent to 2.8 per cent of the gross national income. In the next section of the chapter, we explore how India's strategy on swadeshi evolved over the years and how best this reconciled with other global approaches.

The initial success of the G-77 movement was clearly backed by a clear sense of solidarity among the Southern countries, even though the operational principles developed over time lacked this spirit of solidarity and began giving it lip service over the years. This, perhaps, gives a new direction to India's expected perspective on operationalizing solidarity, not just at the global level but within the domestic domain as well. The need for embracing new approaches at the global level under the rubric of solidarity requires greater emphasis on people-to-people connect as the fundamental driver for SSC, rather than government-to-government cooperation alone. Localization of cooperation beyond national borders is the desired way forward.

SWADESHI AND POST-INDEPENDENCE JOURNEY

It is largely surprising to realize how quickly after Independence the expected role of the private sector, within the framework of swadeshi, dimmed under the consensus of a mixed economy. The post-Independence journey of the idea of swadeshi has probably gone through three distinct phases. First, from 1950s to 1990s, second during the post-reforms period (1991–2019) and third in the phase of AatmaNirbhar Bharat (2020 to present).

First Phase (1950s to 1990s)

The historical legacy of broad and inclusive economic development in India somehow quickly moved towards foreclosing of external linkages. Swadeshi as self-reliance chased out entrepreneurship development, and the vibrancy of domestic and local production trajectories. The nationalization of banks and blocking of private-sector entry in insurance and coal gave a major blow to the idea of Swadeshi Samaj that Tagore talked about. Madras's *Swarajya* magazine worried that India would be starved of the entrepreneurial spirit and take the road to serfdom.[10]

[10]Balasubramanian, Aditya, 'Contesting "Permit-and-Licence Raj": Economic Conservatism and the Idea of Democracy in 1950s', *Past & Present*, Vol. 251, No. 1, May 2021, pp. 189–227.

The approaches dispossessed the private sector of all its decorum and dignity, and reduced them to being applicants—genuflecting down and seeking favours. Shri Chakravarti Rajagopalachari had firmly opposed it owing to its potential for political corruption and economic stagnation. He coined the phrase 'permit licence raj' and blessed the launching of the Swatantra Party with Minoo Masani and B.R. Shenoy.

Instead of declining, the tendency to control went up. Several legislations, like the Monopolies and Restrictive Trade Practices Act (MRTP, 1969), and the Foreign Exchange Regulation Act (FERA, 1973) were introduced for creating an inspector raj. Among the institutions, the Planning Commission was the most visible manifestation of the command economy.

The smaller legislations then gradually got added to the list of restrictions. For instance, seeking no objection certificate from the fire department; safety clearance from the chief of electrical inspector general; MSME (Micro, Small and Medium Enterprises) registration; permission under the Contract Labour (Regulations and Abolition) Act, 1970; and permission to set up an office under the Shops and Establishment Act, 1953.

Eventually in 1991, the government led by Prime Minister (PM) P.V. Narasimha Rao freed India from the shackles of the rent-seeking system. Gurucharan Das described this saying, 'We were going to be free from a rapacious and domineering state.'[11]

Second Phase (Post 1991)

The first and foremost step launched under the reforms process was to abandon all kinds of industrial licensing. All processes were abolished for almost all product categories; except for alcohol, tobacco, hazardous chemicals, industrial explosives, electronics,

[11]Panagariya, Arvind, 'India in the 1980s and 1990s: A Triumph of Reforms', *IMF.org*, 6 November 2003, https://tinyurl.com/42z7bscj. Accessed on 3 April 2023.

aerospace and pharmaceuticals. The sweeping reforms pushed the pendulum towards the other end. Without any sequencing and bare opening as the end objective, a huge challenge for domestic enterprises was created.

This was the time Dattopant Thengadi launched the Swadeshi Jagaran Manch (SJM) and placed swadeshi back on the national agenda. A new phase for Swadeshi was again launched with substantive studies and publications. *Third Way* by Dattopant Thengadi; *The Menace of Multinationals* by Shri Dayakrishna; and *Hindu Economics* by Dr M.G. Bokare were the first ones to be launched, apart from several other smaller publications for people to grasp what SJM was all about.

Thengadi evolved a unique approach of large-scale connect, and sharp and intellectually-rich articulation of the idea and philosophy of national reconstruction. Like in the Independence struggle, boycott was the message from the earlier armoury of swadeshi legacy. At Nagpur on 15 November 1993, in the National Council Meeting, it was decided to boycott the products of multinational corporations like Pepsi, Coke and Colgate. This was also extended to the opposition on global connect through the Dunkel Draft at General Agreement on Trade and Tariffs (GATT).

This trend of swadeshi also emphasized internal accountability and transparency. A major movement was launched against the Enron Corporation for an expansive and confidential deal with the Maharashtra government. Eventually the state government had to cancel the deal. Thengadi also opposed Sankhya Vahini, a high-speed data network project given to Sankhya Vahini India Ltd (SVIL). The SVIL was a joint venture between government organizations and IUNet, a body wholly owned by the Carnegie Mellon University (CMU).

At the intellectual articulations, writings from Thengadi delineated elements of swadeshi beyond goods and services positioned, and focussed on the need of international cooperation by achieving effective national strategies. His writings on SSC and reforms of WTO inspired a new trend that later Bharatiya Mazdoor Sangh (BMS), other trade unions and social organizations also followed.

One quote that will help us understand the impact of SJM-led swadeshi campaign is from when Dr Manmohan Singh suggested having a positive approach to swadeshi. In 2009, at Sewa Gram, Wardha, he said:

> I am not unambiguously attached to reforms. I feel that India has to compete with the rest of the world on its own strength. I am not enamoured of India copying the western consumption style. The challenge for us is how to pursue a growth strategy and prosper and become a modern self-sufficient country even at a per capita income of $1,500.[12]

Third Phase (2020 to Present)

The Swadeshi Movement was taken to another level when AatmaNirbhar Bharat was launched by PM Narendra Modi on 12 May 2020, with a special economic and comprehensive package of ₹20 lakh crore (equivalent to 10 per cent of India's GDP) to fight the Covid-19 pandemic in India. The five pillars of AatmaNirbhar Bharat are economy, infrastructure, system, vibrant demography and demand.

Accordingly, the government announced reforms and enablers across seven sectors, apart from taking some bold reforms such as Supply Chain Reforms for Agriculture, Rational Tax Systems, Simple & Clear Laws, Capable Human Resource and Strong Financial System to give a boost to the Make in India campaign. Deciphering various strategic components of self-reliance and

---

[12]"'Swadeshi Is about Positive Self-Reliance'", *The Economic Times*, 22 May 2009, https://tinyurl.com/y8pjxyey. Accessed on 3 April 2023.

their incubation through operative components and technical provisions required immense conceptual clarity, which was duly addressed as per the modern challenges.

In India, the current policy choices are coherently evolving as building blocks. This is evident through various enabling provisions like inclusive development plan, financial inclusion and a new approach to the external sector covering trade and investment.

The idea of swadeshi permits gains from increased domestic production, with a built-in mechanism to link it with consumption. The idea of AatmaNirbhar Bharat seems to take it further, with emphasis on due specialization, economies of scale and scope for reduced transaction costs. As a result, it seems to be leading to restructuring pressures as well as growing imports from third-world countries which may also lead to inter-firm cooperation, mergers and consolidations. It also addresses imperfections in factor and product markets such as wage rigidities and labour immobility; monopolistic and oligopolistic market structure; positive and negative external effects; public goods, etc., that are not only affecting approach and orientation on external trade but also free trade agreements (FTAs). In order to address the distortions caused by such imperfections, trade policy measures such as import restrictions and export subsidies are being used along with AatmaNirbhar Bharat. These measures are often criticized for being anti-competitive and introducing distortions with non-competitive market structures, government intervention and other imperfections.

THE WAY FORWARD

'The corona virus pandemic has taught a lesson to the world that globalisation is important but being self-reliant is also necessary,' said PM Narendra Modi.[13] The Covid-19 crisis enabled the nation to cope with deficits and disruptions in supply chains.

Several policy reforms like work from home (WFH) added new advantage to firms, particularly in the IT (information technology) sector, to deliver new opportunities and capture new horizons. Addressing conceptual, technical and operational elements of swadeshi through inclusive development plans—such as, Aspirational Blocks Programme—coupled with initiatives like Sagarmala, Bharatmala Pariyojna and BharatNet provided a new impetus. More inclusive approaches with focus on financial inclusion (JAM [Jandhan Aadhar Mobile] Trinity, DBT [direct benefit transfer], payment gateways, NPCI [National Payments Corporation of India]) provide a new dimension for the rise of India, in the areas hitherto reserved for Western and Chinese companies.

New swadeshi approaches are going beyond the freedom struggle specific features like boycotts, etc. It has further evolved and adapted new features essential to safeguard against the modern invasion techniques and approaches. These invasive techniques range from weaponizing monsoons and economies to financial transactions and data, all requiring new and time-bound responses. For several of them, interconnectedness is as crucial as self-reliance. Challenges from Islamabad, Beijing and others require partnerships that are across the board and bring in new policy choices for efficacy and effectiveness. As Thengadi emphasized, India has to go from a norm-taker to a norm-setter. PM Modi has actually got on to that track with several of his initiatives at the G20 Summit COP27 (27th Conference of the Parties), and such other global fora.

AatmaNirbhar Bharat is swadeshi with the spirit of *Vasudev*

---

[13]'COVID-19 Has Taught the World Self-Reliance Is Necessary: PM Modi', *The Times of India*, 7 November 2020, https://tinyurl.com/w3n9kt4e. Accessed on 3 April 2023.

kutumbakam (the world is one family). It reflects our new realities and builds on our rich and time-tested legacy of swadeshi. Those who think swadeshi is an inward-looking strategy should spend some time studying the trade and investment policies of those who preached the Washington Consensus. Current Indian policies advocate for AatmaNirbhar Bharat, but at the same time we are also getting in the new set of FTAs, with full confidence of global competitiveness.

One element that Gandhi emphasized and that is still relevant today is ethics in economic development. Indian development and particularly swadeshi ethos should nurture this, going beyond corporate social responsibility. At the same time, it needs to be ensured—as emphasized by PM Narendra Modi—that there is sustainable consumption of production with minimum carbon footprint.

2

MAKING OUR VILLAGES AATMANIRBHAR

Devinder Sharma
Expert on Indian Agriculture

Two years after an estimated 100 million daily-wage workers trudged home, walking hundreds of kilometres on foot after lockdown was imposed owing to the pandemic, I was reminded of what the World Bank had stated several decades ago. Way back in 1996, I was attending an international conference at the M.S. Swaminathan Research Foundation in Chennai. I vividly recall the then vice-president for environmentally sustainable development at the World Bank, Ismail Serageldin, in his presentation, saying that the Bank estimates the number of people likely to migrate from rural to urban areas of India in the next 20 years (which then meant by 2015) would be equal to twice the combined population of the UK (United Kingdom), France and Germany.

The combined population of UK, France and Germany then stood at 200 million. So, the World Bank's estimate was that 400 million people would be migrating from the rural areas of India. That was quite a staggering number, a population bigger than the size of the US was expected to migrate to the urban areas. I initially thought that the World Bank was trying to warn India, alert us, expecting the government to take adequate measures to stem the tide. But after a number of years, I understood that the bank was not trying to alert us to the negative consequences emanating from this huge population shift, but it was a kind of a directive that successive governments were expected to follow.

The 400 million that the World Bank was asking India to move out of the villages in a span of 20 years were, in my opinion, agricultural refugees. These were victims of a flawed economic thinking that relied more on sacrificing agriculture for the sake of industry. Like climate change is driving millions from the coastal areas as a result of the rise in sea levels, these millions were pushed out by deliberately keeping agriculture impoverished. It is not as if agriculture was unproductive, but by denying the rightful income to farmers and by reducing the public sector investments it became easy to convert agriculture into an uneconomical activity.

Successive governments did follow what the World Bank prescribed. This was ad nauseam reiterated by the credit rating agencies and international financial institutions, as well as by a dominant class of Indian economists. A 2020 study by McKinsey Global Institute is often quoted, which says that India needs to create another 90 million jobs by 2030.[1] In my opinion this is an outdated economic thought, a narrative built during the era when neoliberal economics began to dominate. Pushing people out of agriculture remains an unwritten economic policy, and there is a huge backing for policy decisions that point in that direction. Newspapers openly endorse it.

Several reports indicate the rising proportion of unemployment in the country, which stood at 7.71per cent of labour force in 2021.[2] But instead of deliberating on the reasons that led to a crisis of such a huge magnitude, we simply ignored it. Perhaps it suited us. After all, in a country where job creation

---

[1]*India's Turning Point: An Economic Agenda to Spur Growth and Jobs*, McKinsey Global Institute, August 2020, https://tinyurl.com/y997y3xt. Accessed on 3 April 2023.

[2]'India: Unemployment Rate from 1999 to 2022', *Statista*, 1 June 2023, https://tinyurl.com/yc5crf2t. Accessed on 20 June 2023.

tops the country's political agenda, you will agree that 7.71 per cent of labour force remaining out of employment is a worrisome phenomenon. The bigger tragedy however, is that we have failed to acknowledge where we went wrong.

Using the purchasing power parity (PPP) norms and writing in the *Hindustan Times*, author Janmejaya Sinha makes his point abundantly clear using economic parameters that people can easily understand. He says there is a Europe of about 50 million people with a per capita of $45,000 per annum existing in India; an Indonesia of 425 million people with a per capita income of $9,500 per annum; and the remaining 900 million people of India he equates to a Sub-Saharan Africa with a per capita income of $3,300 per annum, including about 300 million people whose income is even below that of Sub-Sahara. These 900 million are, in reality, the abandoned people. They seem to have fallen off India's growth trajectory.[3]

In a quest to become a $5 trillion economy, the focus has so far been largely on an India aspiring to live in the urban centres. It is generally believed that trickle-down will help reach the benefit to the masses.

'The State of Inequality in India', another study commissioned by the Economic Advisory Council to the Prime Minister and prepared by the Institute for Competitiveness, found that people earning ₹25,000 per month or more formed part of the top 10 per cent bracket of the country. Between 2017–18 and 2019–20, the income of top 1 per cent grew by 15 per cent whereas the income of the bottom 10 per cent declined by 1 per cent, thereby indicating 'the failure of the trickle-down approach to economic growth'.[4] While the dominant economic thinking still

---

[3]Sinha, Janmejaya, 'Focus on the Base of the Pyramid', *Hindustan* Times, 10 August 2022, https://tinyurl.com/44ahy5zb. Accessed on 3 April 2023.

[4]Kapoor, Amit, and Jessica Duggal, *The State of Inequality in India Report*, Institute for Competitiveness, 2022, https://tinyurl.com/36wnsnbx. Accessed on 20 June 2023.

clings to the outdated concept of trickle-down, the US (United States) President Joe Biden has publicly acknowledged trickle-down to be a failure.

The study rightly cautioned: 'If an amount like this comes to the top 10 percentile, the bottom-most condition cannot be imagined.'[5] This is a question that the *Hindustan Times* article too had posed when it compared the bottom 900 million with Sub-Saharan Africa. Driving people out to join the temporary workforce in the cities is not the solution. The challenge should be to make farming a viable proposition, creating more sustainable livelihoods thereby reducing the dependence for menial employment in the cities.

Now, let's look at estimates put out by the Centre for Monitoring Indian Economy (CMIE). It says that in March 2022 industrial jobs alone fell by 16.7 million. Agriculture made up for the job losses, adding another 15.3 million to the already existing workforce. CMIE did talk about a percentage of workers returning to the cities. In addition, millions who traversed on foot after the lockdown were comfortably absorbed in agriculture. With their household food security taken care of, they may be engaged in other part-time activities. Instead of still hoping that someday the manufacturing sector will be back on track—and the higher economic growth projections that we continue to make (9 per cent and above)will provide for additional non-farm jobs—the right challenge that policymakers need to take up now is to shift the focus to rebuilding agriculture.[6]

But still the dominant economic thinking relies on the revival of non-farm activities, and not on agriculture, to create ample employment opportunities. With roughly 50 per cent of India's population, a little more than 600 million, dependent

[5]Ibid.

[6]Sharma, Devinder, 'How Agriculture Could Resolve India's Unemployment Crisis', *Bizz Buzz*, 28 April 2022, https://tinyurl.com/k3f6yzxu. Accessed on 20 June 2023.

on agriculture, the challenge should be how to make farming a viable enterprise. Instead of pushing people out of the villages, the better option would be to make the villages prosperous. This is where the promise of aatmanirbharta comes into play. Since nearly 70 per cent of the rural households are dependent on agriculture, the answer lies in making farming a viable and profitable enterprise. Just because the US and the Europian Union (EU) have relentlessly pushed farming population to move to the cities does not mean that we too have to blindly follow that outdated prescription.

Actually, this is what 'Economics 101' had programmed us to believe—to achieve higher economic growth, the number of people dependent on agriculture has to be brought down. Some of the best brains, including economists, academicians and writers, are unable to look beyond what they studied in their graduation courses. Times have changed, and so have the employment dynamics, but our economic thought process is still stuck there. Even now when the world is witnessing a job-loss growth (moving ahead of the jobless growth encountered in the late 1990s) and automation and artificial intelligence is now taking over business and industrial production, our economic thinking—howsoever irrelevant it may be in the times we are living in—hasn't changed.

The economic thinking that when the number of people in farming goes down, farm income will automatically increase is not borne by facts. Even in the US where only 1.5 per cent of the population remains in farming, incomes have steadily been on the decline. Subsidies provide nearly 40 per cent of the average farm income in the US, and about 50 per cent in the EU. The controversy around the massive subsidy support for agriculture in the OECD (Organisation for Economic Cooperation and Development) countries, the richest trading bloc, continues to hog the negotiations at the WTO. Even in these countries, despite the big businesses controlling agriculture, farming is in a terrible state of distress. To borrow the same flawed market-oriented agriculture into India therefore, is not the kind of reform that Indian agriculture needs.

Let's first try to see what we are missing. In both the cases—first the lockdown period and then the slump in labour force participation rate—the underlying message is that agriculture, despite the neglect and apathy over the decades, alone has the potential to absorb large sections of the population. Instead of pushing small farmers to migrate to the cities in search of menial jobs, revitalizing agriculture can easily turn the tables and provide gainful employment. Give farmers a guaranteed price, along with enhanced public sector investments, and agriculture can easily turn into a powerhouse of economic growth. And let me reiterate, agriculture alone has the potential to reboot the economy.

Let us not forget that a farmer is also an entrepreneur. Despite having small landholdings (86 per cent owning less than 5 acres), they still continue to produce a record harvest year after year. With a continuous decline in public sector investments in agriculture—which the RBI had in a study calculated to be around 0.4 per cent of the GDP between 2011–12 and 2017–18—we can't expect the small farmers to perform a miracle.[7] But still, they continue to provide a strong economic base for the country to rely on. If only we gave farmers their right due, and provided them with the right kind of public infrastructure, I am sure they would be able to convert farming into a favoured economic enterprise for the future.

Denial of rightful income to farmers has been the easiest way to make them abandon agriculture and migrate. An OECD–ICRIER (Indian Council for Research on International Economic Relations) study has shown that Indian farmers suffered a monumental loss of ₹45 lakh crore in 16 years, between 2000 and 2016. Although the study itself was an underestimate since it compared domestic

[7]'Pocket Book of Agricultural Statistics 2017', *Government of India, Ministry of Agriculture and Farmers Welfare*, https://tinyurl.com/syy68a6j. Accessed on 20 June 2023.

prices with international ones—which is heavily depressed because of the massive subsidies that are doled out in the rich developed countries—it still gives us an idea about the extent of loss that farmers continued to incur year after year. The 2016 Economic Survey further acknowledged the depravity that persisted in the farming sector, when it admitted that the average income of a farming family in 17 states of India (roughly half the country) stood at less than an appalling ₹20,000 a year.[8] In other words, farmers in almost half the country were living on less than ₹1,700 per month. Since it is not possible to rear a cow in less than ₹2,000 a month, I shudder to think how these farmers survive.

The iconic farmers protest at the doorsteps of New Delhi in 2021 was a clarion call for setting the economic imbalances right, and in the process taking a leap to building aatmanirbharta. Besides the demand for the repeal of the three controversial laws (which eventually the government did withdraw), the bigger challenge that still remains to be addressed is how to make farming a viable proposition.

Before we make an attempt to see how farming can be turned into a cheerful economic activity, our policymakers must first and foremost acknowledge the historical blunder in treating agriculture as an economic burden or a laggard. For long, I have maintained that the policy of sacrificing agriculture for the sake of industrial growth is only helping in building a strong army of agricultural refugees. These refugees are being deliberately driven out of agriculture to swarm into the cities in need of cheap labour. The over-emphasis on the industrial sector turned the focus away from the agrarian community. That was a mistake.

It is time to make a historic correction. Instead of worrying about the lack of non-farm employment, let us shift the attention to making farming a viable enterprise.

[8]'Agriculture: More from Less', *Economic Survey 2015–16*, https://tinyurl.com/bdd4y8ah. Accessed on 20 June 2023.

EASE OF DOING FARMING

On the lines of the 'Ease of Doing Business', proposed by the World Bank and since discontinued, India should formulate an 'Ease of Doing Farming' index. This will help strengthen the existing infrastructure, create efficiency by removing the usual snarls and hiccups that farmers encounter at every step. Given that lack of governance adds to the prevailing agrarian distress, an Ease of Doing Farming index will make the system operate without any inconvenience to farmers. If 7,000 steps can be taken to make it easier for the industry, there is no reason why a similar kind of policy initiative will not unleash the entrepreneurial ability of the farming community.

AGRICULTURAL MARKETING

Real freedom for farmers can be ensured when adequate marketing infrastructure is made available closer to the farms. History has shown how crucial is the need for regulated *mandis* (markets) for farmers. India has, at present, nearly 7,000 regulated mandis under the Agricultural Produce Market Committee (APMC) Act. If farmers are to be provided with a market within a 5 km radius of their farms, India will need a total of 42,000 mandis spread across the country. Over the years, certain discrepancies have emerged in the APMC structure. The need is to reform these mandis and also invite the private sector to set up private mandis (but all operating under the same rules and regulations).

COOPERATIVE FARMING

Given the success of the Amul dairy cooperative, it is time to replicate the cooperative model for pulses, fruits and oilseeds along similar lines. Considering that 86 per cent of the land holdings of farmers are less than 5 acres, cooperatives alone can be an effective way to aggregate them. This will require appropriate public sector investments and also hand holding at various steps. Moreover, as the Amul Model has shown, it is possible to provide farmers with 80 per cent of the end consumer price. This needs to be replicated in case of agricultural commodities, where the proportion of the end consumer price going to farmer is very low, thereby exacerbating agrarian distress.

AN EVERGREEN REVOLUTION

The Green Revolution has outlived its utility. With climate emergency knocking at our doors—with the massive destruction of natural resources and agriculture playing a significant role in adding to the greenhouse gas (GHG) emissions—the world is realizing the need to move away from chemical-farming. The focus is shifting to agro-ecological farming systems. Agriculture is in need of a transformation and, as the Prime Minister has repeatedly emphasized, natural farming forms the basis for aatmanirbharta. This will require a shift in the mindset and calls for framing appropriate policies to usher in an evergreen revolution.

LIVING INCOME

To move from income disparity to parity, agriculture all over the world is desperate for an assured and guaranteed income. In the developed, as well as in the developing countries, farmers continue to be denied a living income by way of a rightful price. All products available in the market—pen, spectacles, furniture and automobiles, to name a few—come with a price tag. Only agriculture comes without a price tag and farmers are left to face the vagaries of the markets. This has to change. Farm produce too needs a price tag. Minimum Support Price (MSP) is a mechanism that, if properly implemented, can ensure that no trading is allowed below that benchmark price. Farmers need the assurance of a guaranteed price. That will be the real freedom for farmers.

THE WAY FORWARD

Taking these corrective steps will usher in a new revolution, based on the underlying principles of aatmanirbharta. This will make agriculture undergo a much-needed transformation, to turn it into an engine of economic growth. If we can restore the focus on resurrecting agriculture, it would be the most appropriate way to achieve '*Sabka Saath Sabka Vikas* (joint effort helps in joint growth)'.

3

AATMANIRBHAR VILLAGES: ELIMINATING RURAL POVERTY WITH TECHNOLOGY

Sridhar Vembu

CEO, Zoho Corporation

RURAL POVERTY AND LACK OF BALANCE

Why is a rural district poor? It has wants and needs that it is not able to fulfil from what it produces, which are mostly agricultural commodities. In the past, our rural areas did not consist only of farmers. They had an entire ecosystem of weavers, potters, *ghee* makers, masons, iron and gold smiths, midwives, *vaidyas* (physician) and so on. We had balanced and self-reliant rural economies that produced a wide range of goods.

Today, the descendants of these rural craftsmen are landless labourers, or have migrated away to cities and towns. The rural economy has become very unbalanced and exclusively dependent on agriculture. Agricultural income is not enough to fund the needs of the rural district—which today includes gas stoves, tractors, motorcycles, cell phones and more. This leaves a rural area with a persistent 'trade deficit', where the value of what they sell is below the value of what they buy.

How is that 'rural trade deficit' bridged? In one of four ways:

1. Borrowing money
2. Selling assets such as land

3. Receiving remittance from migrant workers in cities
4. Receiving government transfer payments

None of these four approaches are sustainable, and that is why we see rural areas continuing to decline.

In order to revive rural areas culturally and spiritually, we have to restore balance to the rural economy. How do we restore balance? We come to the idea of symmetry.

SYMMETRY OF TECHNOLOGY CAPABILITIES

If we want to consume complex technological goods, we must be able to produce such complex technological goods. A farm labourer—with few tools beyond his hands, feet and a bullock—cannot match the rupee value produced by industrial factories. It is not sustainable for a rural district to export rice and vegetables, and import motorcycles and smartphones.

We can see the consequences of technological asymmetry in Sri Lanka, where it has happened on a national scale. Sri Lanka relied largely on exports like tea and tourism. It imported complex goods like synthetic materials, locomotives, medicine, computers and other electronics, lacking the capacity to build these themselves. When agriculture and tourism suffered, the country was pushed to the brink. A more diversified economic base, with balance and symmetry as its core principles, would have been much more resilient.

It's clear that we must build manufacturing know-how in rural districts in India. The path to do so is given in the last section of this paper. Then, once we can produce complex goods, the next step is to master the technology used to produce those goods. We must learn to design better factories; build new machinery; and eventually build machines that will then make our factory machines. This is the ladder to a strong manufacturing base.

INTERNAL HARMONY

Even as we strive to achieve balance and symmetry externally, we must also preserve internal harmony. Internal harmony is the idea that balance and symmetry apply even within various segments of society. Even if we have external balance, if some communities become highly unbalanced with respect to other communities, that lack of internal balance will lead to social disharmony and destroy the external balance as well. Hence, harmony is social justice expressed as an economic principle.

CONTENTMENT

It is only in the presence of economic balance, symmetry and harmony that we can talk about contentment. This is a crucial notion because prosperity can be destroyed by its own excess, when the quest for 'more and more' drives people towards reckless consumption.

With balance, comes freedom. People are free from debt and dependence. With symmetry, comes confidence. They are self-reliant, skilled and no longer feel hopelessly behind. There is an even playing field, and a clear path forward for steady improvement. With harmony, there is a healthy community life. People work together without social stress, jealousy or excessive competition. They feel good and rooted in their home, and not anxious to leave for somewhere 'better'. The district moves forward as a healthy whole, rather than in fragmented parts. Finally, with contentment, we are at peace with ourselves.

THE PATH FORWARD

Harmony comes from culture, which is more difficult to shape through policy. But establishing balance and symmetry is entirely under our control. Here are some policy recommendations:

1. Landholders in rural districts must be encouraged to establish small- to mid-sized factories. Surplus agricultural productivity should be invested back in the rural area as factories. This is a win-win. Factory owners with low-cost land will get higher margins from manufactured goods than only from agriculture, and rural workers will be trained for factory work which commands higher wages.
2. These factories must start with simple, low-cost machinery—machinery that is easy to take apart and understand. Only when the machines are understandable can we repair, customize and improve them. It is in this way that we build industrial know-how. This model, of a humble start followed by continuous learning and improvement, is the one South Korea employed to great success with POSCO (formerly Pohang Iron and Steel Company) and Hyundai Motor Company.
3. Both government and private companies should invest in producing these low-cost machines. An old report from the MSME, titled 'Project Profiles for Small Enterprises', outlines each step and machine needed to build an electric fan.[1] (This should give unfamiliar readers an idea of the kinds of machines needed.) We should target machines that are necessary for a wide range of goods.
4. They should then release standardized designs for marketable products that can be produced with this low-cost machinery (e.g. basic electronic components, household goods like fans, scissors, power tools). We can see the Arduino microcontroller and its surrounding ecosystem as a model of this. The Arduino is an easy to understand, modular machine. Many different products

[1]'Table Fan', *The Development Commissioner (SSI), Ministry of SSI*, New Delhi, https://tinyurl.com/v4z957nc. Accessed on 11 July 2023.

can be built on top of the Arduino, and the blueprints for these products are shared openly and improved collectively.

5. If needed, the government and corporations can employ soft loans or a profit-sharing model, privately or through a rural development bank, to help establish these factories. Once this model of manufacturing is proven in one district, it will serve as an example for the rest.

4

COMPETITIVE MANUFACTURING AS THE NEXT ENGINE OF INDIA'S ECONOMIC GROWTH AND PROSPERITY: OPPORTUNITIES, CHALLENGES AND POLICIES

Prof. Nagesh Kumar

Director, Institute for Studies in Industrial Development (ISID)

As it celebrates 75 years as an independent nation, India can be proud of its many achievements in socio-economic development. These include its ability to sustain a rising trend of economic growth (which has helped India become the sixth-largest economy in the world); to lift over 500 million people out of poverty; and its ability to improve in different indicators of socio-economic progress. India has emerged as one of the largest producers in the world of many products including vaccines and generic pharmaceuticals; compact cars; two-wheelers; milk; and as the most preferred destination for IT services and business process outsourcing.[1]

Another transformation in the past 75 years has been from an agriculture-dominated Indian economy into a services-dominated one. While the service sector has delivered robust growth rates,

[1]Kumar, Nagesh, 'Indian Economy @75: Achievements, Gaps, and Aspirations for the Indian Centenary', *Indian Economic Journal*, Vol. 70, No. 3, 2022.

it has not been able to absorb workers, especially the unskilled and semi-skilled ones, in a proportionate manner. As a result, agriculture continues to sustain as much as 46 per cent of India's workforce with barely a 16.6 per cent share of GDP.[2] Therefore, the structural transformation, attributed to economist Arthur Lewis—where workers move from low productivity sectors (such as agriculture) to higher productivity sectors (such as industry and services) over time—has failed to take place in India.

The inability to tap the full potential of industrialization, especially in the manufacturing sector, is the key difference between the Indian growth trajectory and that of East Asian economies (including Japan, the Republic of Korea [ROK], Thailand, Malaysia, Vietnam and China). The share of the manufacturing industry in the country's GDP has stagnated at around 16 per cent, compared to 30–35 per cent in the East Asian countries. Neglect of manufacturing has cost the country in terms of the creation of productive jobs for workers that join the workforce every year. The manufacturing sector has the highest backward and forward linkages of any productive sector. Hence, its potential of creating direct and indirect jobs remain underexploited. Far from industrializing, there is evidence that India has witnessed a pre-mature de-industrialization with rising dependence on imports in final consumption.[3]

History corroborates that few countries, if any, have attained prosperity without industrialization. Economist Nicholas Kaldor has argued persuasively that growth of manufacturing will not only drive economic growth, but will also enhance the productivity of the overall economy with increasing returns-

---

[2]'Agriculture, Forestry, and Fishing, Value Added (% of GDP)', *The World Bank*, https://tinyurl.com/bdhvxd2w. Accessed on 19 July 2023.

[3]Amirapu, Amrit, and Arvind Subramanian, 'Manufacturing or Services? An Indian Illustration of a Development Dilemma', *Washington DC: Centre for Global Development*, 2015.

to-scale that could be dynamic in nature.[4] In both industrialized and newly-industrialized countries, the State has intervened extensively to build competitive industrial capacities in their earlier stages of development. The developmental role of the State in these countries and the aspects of strategic interventions deployed, that are collectively called the industrial policy, has been well documented in the works of Amsden, Bairoch, Nayyar and many more. The Agenda 2030 on Sustainable Development adopted at the United Nations Summit in September 2015 (comprising 17 Sustainable Development Goals [SDG]) also recognizes the transformative potential of industry, and seeks to enhance the share of the sector in employment and GDP. Industrialization through manufacturing is also critical for SDG-8 on accelerating growth and productive jobs creation. Therefore, faster jobs creation for rapid economic growth and industry-oriented structural transformation is the key to inclusive and sustainable prosperity of India in the run up to the celebration of the Indian centenary of independence in 2047 with a greater sense of national pride.

Against that backdrop, the 'Make in India' programme announced by Prime Minister (PM) Modi in 2014, that seeks to exploit the potential of manufacturing for India's development, was timely. It was further reinforced by AatmaNirbhar Bharat Abhiyan in 2020 as a strategy to pull the economy out of the Covid-19 pandemic, comprising production linked incentives (PLI) scheme to boost local production in 14 sectors. In implementing Make in India, we could learn from the experiences of the East Asian countries—fostering competitive manufacturing capacities through extensive strategic interventions.

---

[4]Kaldor, N., *Strategic Factors in Economic Development,* New York State School of Industrial and Labour Relations, Cornell University, 1967.

This chapter is organized as follows:

1. The first section provides an overview of the key opportunities that India could tap in the pursuit of its industrialization.
2. The second summarizes a few lessons from the experiences of the East Asian countries on strategic interventions that may be relevant in India's context.
3. The third section contains a few concluding remarks.

OPPORTUNITIES FOR INDUSTRIALIZATION IN INDIA

As India strives for building competitive manufacturing capabilities, an important question would be: what opportunities are available to India in terms of feeding the domestic demand in comparison to external markets and emerging opportunities? Given below are a few pointers for these opportunities.

Making for India

Clearly the biggest opportunity for expanding the manufacturing base of the country is by substituting imports with domestic consumption. One should start by reversing the trend of the rising share of imports in final consumption. This was happening as Indian companies outsourced production offshore to save costs in the decade following 2004 with an appreciation of the rupee.[5] Outsourcing has been practised widely by several well-known Indian companies by getting their products manufactured in other countries, mainly China, and then continuing to sell them under their brand names. Outsourcing of production was practised

[5]Kumar, Nagesh, 'Reversing the Pre-Mature De-industrialization for Job-Creation: Lessons for "Make-in-India" from Experiences of Industrialized and East Asian Countries', *Economic Theory and Policy amidst Global Discontent: Essays in Honour of Deepak Nayyar,* A. Ghosh Dastidar (ed.), Routledge, 2018.

even for several price-sensitive home electrical and electronic appliances (electric fans, toasters, mixer-grinders, juicers, wall clocks, televisions, refrigerators, air-conditioners etc.) that used to be manufactured in the country for many decades. Reversing this trend of hollowing out of the Indian industry is clearly the first step towards industrialization.

Then there are other industries with significant import dependence such as power equipment, electronics, a variety of organic and inorganic chemicals and active pharmaceutical ingredients (APIs), that can be manufactured within the country as adequate domestic demand exists. The PLI schemes announced by the PM as part of the AatmaNirbhar Bharat package in 2020 are addressing some of these sectors. Considering that India's manufactured imports add up to $300 billion per annum (out of the total imports of $610 billion in 2021–22), substitution of even 50 per cent of the manufactured imports in a gradual manner could enhance the current scale of manufacturing value-added by 33 per cent.[6] Therefore, there is considerable potential for strategic import substitution. Growing demand for consumer and capital goods and defence equipment would continue to provide additional opportunities for the local manufacturing base with scale economies. So, making for India is the biggest opportunity. It goes without saying that the competitive manufacturing plants, exploiting scale economies, would also be able to tap opportunities that may arise in the international markets.

Making for the World or Export-Oriented Manufacturing

A strategy of export-oriented industrialization, of the type pursued by the Southeast Asian countries in the past, may be

---

[6] 'Table 119 : Imports of Principal Commodities-US Dollar', *Handbook of Statistics on Indian Economy, Reserve Bank of India*, 15 September 2022, https://tinyurl.com/3c87uhk4. Accessed on 11 July 2023.

challenging in the current context of global economic slowdown and rising protectionist trends. However, given India's rather marginal 1.7 per cent share of global merchandise exports, even a very small rise of 0.5 per cent over the next 2–3 years will add US$ 100 billion to India's exports and possibly US$150 billion to manufacturing value-added (MVA). Strengthening India's presence in traditional areas such as textiles and clothing; leather goods; gems and jewellery; processed foods; vaccines and generic pharmaceuticals; automobiles and components; refined petroleum products; steel and non-ferrous metals; and some types of machinery and electrical equipment is vital, besides making inroads in new areas and markets. The strategy adopted by global corporations to diversify their supply chains using a 'China Plus One' strategy should help India integrate with global value chains.

Sun-Rise Industries: Digital and Green Industrialization

The digital revolution and green industrialization also provide fruitful opportunities for fostering manufacturing in India. India can leverage its unique strengths such as its pool of technical manpower, software and chip design capability and large domestic market for exploiting these opportunities. Annual imports of electronics are of the order of $50 billion, and are growing rapidly with projections of $400 billion of imports by 2025. The recent government initiatives to develop, design, manufacture and export semiconductor chips in the country are promising. They could transform the whole electronics ecosystem while reducing import dependence. The government has announced a Semiconductor Policy with an investment of US$10 billion. A number of investment proposals have already been lined up. Manufacture of semiconductors in the country will help to catalyse the electronics ecosystem, comprising a whole range of downstream products. The government has come out with a US$1 trillion digital economy vision. The manufacture of green hydrogen, solar panels, wind turbines, electric vehicles

(EVs), batteries and other storage solutions offer very promising industrialization avenues while also advancing the sustainability agenda. India should aim to become a global hub of compact EVs (including two and three-wheelers) and batteries.

Translating these opportunities for strategic import substitution; export promotion; and digital and green industrialization has the potential to lift India's MVA from the current $450 billion to $1 trillion by 2026–27. This will advance the government's $5 trillion economy target and create millions of decent jobs in the process.

STRATEGIC INTERVENTIONS FOR BUILDING COMPETITIVE MANUFACTURING SECTOR: LESSONS FROM EXPERIENCES OF EAST ASIAN COUNTRIES

The experiences of industrialized, as well as newly industrializing countries corroborate that the manufacturing sector generally requires considerable handholding and interventions by the government playing the role of a development state. Collectively these interventions are called industrial policy, a term which has become fashionable again across the world, including in the industrialized world, after falling out of favour for a while. Robert Wade in his essay, 'The Paradox of US Industrial Policy: The Development State in Disguise', highlights how industrial policy has been revived in the US (which was otherwise a strong proponent of trade liberalization in multilateral trade negotiations).[7] The Biden Administration has defined its industrial policy recently with the $280 billion CHIPS and Science Act; the $737 billion Inflation Reduction Act; and the $550 billion Infrastructure Investment and Jobs Act. This was done to foster local manufacturing and

[7]Wade, Robert, 'The Paradox of US Industrial Policy: The Development State in Disguise', *Transforming Economies: Making Industrial Policy Work for Growth, Jobs and Development, Geneva*, J.M. Salazar-Xirinachs, I. Nübler and R. Kozul-Wright (eds.), International Labour Office, 2014.

innovation of semiconductors chips; electric mobility; and other new technology products through hundreds of billions of dollars in subsidies and tax breaks.[8]

Firms may under-invest in the training of their workers because of fears of high labour turnover. History is rich in lessons of strategic interventions employed by industrialized and newly industrializing countries, as documented extensively in the works of Alice Amsden and Sanjaya Lall.[9] The strategic interventions that may be relevant in India's case are mentioned below.

Strategic Approach towards Trade and Exchange Rate Management

The East Asian countries have pursued a calibrated and strategic integration with the world economy in conjunction with industrial policy, rather than passively opening up to world trade.[10] The trade policy followed has been characterized by dualism—open for the exporting sector, but restrictive for importing sectors. East Asian countries have widely used Managed Exchange Rates as a tool for fostering industrialization. Japan extensively used the depreciated exchange rate of yen to boost competitiveness of its exports until the Plaza Accord of 1985. In the early years of industrialization, ROK rationed foreign exchange and gave priority to importers of

---

[8]Kumar, Nagesh, 'New Industrial Policy for New India', *The Hindu Business Line*, 26 January 2023, https://tinyurl.com/3un7v99f. Accessed on 12 July 2023.

[9]Amsden, Alice, *The Rise of 'the Rest': Challenges to the West from Late Industrializing Countries*, Oxford University Press, 2001; Lall, Sanjaya, 'Rethinking Industrial Strategy: The Role of the State in the Face of Globalization', *Putting Development First: The Importance of Policy Space in the WTO and IFIs*, Kevin P. Gallagher (ed.), Zed Books, 2005.

[10]Kozul-Wright, Richard, and Daniel Poon, 'Economic Openness and Development', *Asian Transformations: An Inquiry into the Development of Nations*, Deepak Nayyar (ed.), Oxford University Press, 2019.

capital goods and intermediate inputs.[11] The Chinese government initially adopted a dual-track exchange rate system, allowing the market-determined exchange rate to operate parallel with the over-valued official exchange rate. The dual-track system converged to a managed floating system in 1994.[12] This was followed by a hard peg during 1995–2005, allowing the exchange rate of yuan to move within a narrow band since 2005 as international pressure mounted with growing trade surpluses.

Achieving Scale Economies through Combination of Import Substitution and Export Promotion

Import substitution and export orientation are posited as two alternative industrialization strategies. The East Asian countries have generally combined the elements of both import substitution and export orientation to exploit the economies of scale, although the emphasis has changed with needs. Before embarking on the export-oriented manufacturing focussed on electronics and textiles in 1970s, Malaysia focussed on import substitution during 1957–67. In 1981, it launched another import-substitution focussing on heavier industries, followed by an export-oriented phase from the mid-1980s with greater emphasis on fostering domestic technologies.[13] The ROK government embarked on the Heavy and Chemical Industrialization (HCI) programme in 1973, when the country was at a relatively low level of development. This was done by protecting domestic 'infant industries' through quantitative

---

[11]Chang, Ha-Joon, and Kiryl Zach, 'Industrialization and Development', *Asian Transformations: An Inquiry into the Development of Nations*, Deepak Nayyar (ed.), Oxford University Press, 2019.

[12]Lin, Justin Yifu, 'China', *Asian Transformations: An Inquiry into the Development of Nations*, Deepak Nayyar (ed.), Oxford University Press, 2019.

[13]Kozul-Wright, Richard, and Daniel Poon, 'Economic Openness and Development', *Asian Transformations: An Inquiry into the Development of Nations*, Deepak Nayyar (ed.), Oxford University Press, 2019.

restrictions that were prevalent until 1980. Performance based subsidies were provided based on export performance or for development of research and development (R&D) capabilities.[14]

Selective approach towards Foreign Direct Investment (FDI)

The East Asian countries adopted a selective approach to FDI to improve its quality. ROK and Taiwan, following Japan, relied on non-equity modes to tap the resources of multinational enterprises (MNEs) such as technology licensing, managerial and technical assistance from Japanese companies (such as Nippon Steel and Kawasaki Shipbuilding) to build world class industries. They also used the special economic zones (SEZs) or export processing zones (EPZs) in a strategic manner to leverage FDI for building export capabilities, but also ensured domestic linkages by imposing local content requirements.[15] China engaged MNEs into strategic bargaining, leveraging the high-quality infrastructure of its SEZs, disciplined skilled workers; and large domestic market to impose informal conditions on local sourcing, export commitments or technology-transfer. The governments, at all levels, proactively approached prospective foreign investors to relocate their production to China with incentives such as tax holidays in SEZs and industrial parks.[16]

As a result, the share of FDI in China reached 17 per cent of gross fixed capital formation by 1994.[17] The preferential tax

---

[14]Chang, Ha-Joon, and Kiryl Zach, 'Industrialization and Development', *Asian Transformations: An Inquiry into the Development of Nations*, Deepak Nayyar (ed.), Oxford University Press, 2019.

[15]Kozul-Wright, Richard, and Daniel Poon, 'Economic Openness and Development', *Asian Transformations: An Inquiry into the Development of Nations*, Deepak Nayyar (ed.), Oxford University Press, 2019.

[16]Lin, Justin Yifu, 'China', *Asian Transformations: An Inquiry into the Development of Nations*, Deepak Nayyar (ed.), Oxford University Press, 2019.

[17]Kozul-Wright, Richard, and Daniel Poon, 'Economic Openness and

treatment of FDI in China was such that some of the domestic investment was round tripped to China via Hong Kong, to take advantage of the incentives. East Asian countries have also used performance requirements extensively to make FDI meet their objectives—deepening their integration with the local economy or export promotion, among others. Thailand, for instance, has emerged as the third-largest exporter of automobiles in Asia. This was done through performance requirements imposed on Toyota and Honda by initially insisting on local content requirements (to deepen production linkages). Then, once integrated production bases developed, they imposed the export performance requirements (to virtually turn these facilities into global sourcing hubs for certain models). Through these strategic interventions, East Asian countries were able to get FDI inflows to crowd-in domestic investments rather than crowding out.

Enterprise Development and National Champions

East Asian countries provided support to selected firms to nurture their managerial or technological capabilities or to encourage their horizontal and vertical expansion. This was done so that they were able to realize scale economies, not only in production but also in marketing, to develop global brand names and operations (as ROK and Taiwan did to create national champions like Samsung, LG and Foxconn). ROK promoted the chaebols (large and highly diversified industrial conglomerates) in an effort to harness scale economies. However, ROK also promoted fierce rivalry between the chaebols in order to enhance their manufacturing. China has facilitated mergers in an effort to create large-scale national champions besides extensively using state-owned enterprise (SOEs), subsidized credit, public procurement and public investments.

Development', *Asian Transformations: An Inquiry into the Development of Nations*, Deepak Nayyar (ed.), Oxford University Press, 2019.

Directed Credit Through National Development Banks and Investment Incentives

East Asian countries also intervened to develop sunrise industries through the use of subsidized credit in ROK, and by tax credits in Taiwan. National development banks (NDBs) have been employed extensively by East Asian countries to foster industrialization. In conjunction with the HCI programme that the ROK government created in 1973, the National Investment Fund accounted for 70 per cent of total manufacturing investment lending by institutions in the late 1970s. China established the China Development Bank, to finance large-scale infrastructure and industrial projects by providing long-term financing. Richard Kozul-Wright and Daniel Poon in their essay 'Economic Openness and Development', have shown how the outstanding loans extended by NDBs (as a proportion of GDP) has grown consistently since 1994—from under 2 per cent to over 13 per cent in China in 2016 and from 4 per cent to over 11 per cent in Malaysia.[18] Starting with the Malaysian Industrial Development Finance established in 1960, Malaysia has created 13 NDBs over time. Malaysia has also instituted pioneer industry programmes to provide investment incentives to new industries.

Domestic Technological Capability Building through Public Funding and Soft Intellectual Property Regimes

Building domestic technological and innovative capability has been an important objective of industrial policy. ROK created a powerful S&T (science and technology) Agency in the Prime Minister's Office in 1967, besides creating a network of government research institutes such as Korea Institute for S&T and the Korea Advanced Institute of Science in the late

---

[18]Ibid.

1960s.[19] Taiwan established the Industrial Technology Research Institute (ITRI) in 1973 to support strategic industries with key technology projects, and had 10,000 employees by early 1980s.[20] After building domestic production capabilities, China focussed on development of local R&D capacity, expansion of domestic linkages and vertical diversification especially in strategic sectors. The 'Made in China 2025' initiative was launched in 2015 to upgrade Chinese industries, and to enhance local content of core components to 40 per cent by 2020 and 70 per cent by 2025 (especially in priority sectors such as aerospace, robotics, IT, energy and pharmaceuticals).[21]

The East Asian countries have also used weak patent regimes extensively to facilitate the absorption of foreign inventions. Japan did not recognize product patents to facilitate absorption of others' innovations until the mid-1970s; ROK, till the mid-1980s; and China till 2002. Japan, ROK, Taiwan, China, Thailand, among others, have also used petty patents to promote incremental innovations by domestic enterprises, including the SMEs, that would not stand rigorous scrutiny in patent examinations.

Physical and Social Infrastructure and Investment Facilitation

The East Asian countries paid attention to human resource development through a heavy emphasis on education and health,

---

[19]Wade, Robert, 'The Paradox of US Industrial Policy: The Development State in Disguise', *Transforming Economies: Making Industrial Policy Work for Growth, Jobs and Development, Geneva*, J.M. Salazar-Xirinachs, I. Nübler and R. Kozul-Wright (eds.), International Labour Office, 2014.

[20]Kozul-Wright, Richard, and Daniel Poon, 'Economic Openness and Development', *Asian Transformations: An Inquiry into the Development of Nations*, Deepak Nayyar (ed.), Oxford University Press, 2019.

[21]Chang, Ha-Joon, and Kiryl Zach, 'Industrialization and Development', *Asian Transformations: An Inquiry into the Development of Nations*, Deepak Nayyar (ed.), Oxford University Press, 2019.

besides the development of physical infrastructure and SEZs. Some of the East Asian countries also had a strong culture of target setting and monitoring. In ROK, for instance, the President's Office monitored the targets set for exports by enterprises, followed by rewards and penalties.

A Coordinated and Dynamic Approach to Industrial Policy

The most important lesson from the East Asian countries is that different elements of industrial policy, such as trade and exchange rate management, FDI policy, technology development and enterprise development, need to be pursued in a coordinated manner to be effective. The industrial policy was also adapted over time to the changing requirements. ROK initially focussed on labour-intensive products (toys, textiles and garments, shoes) in the 1960s. They started heavy and chemical industries in the early 1970s, as wage costs started to rise, to stay competitive and focus on emerging industries such as automobiles and electronics. China upgraded its export structure from simple toys, textiles and other cheap products in the 1980s and 1990s to high-value, technologically advanced machinery and ICT (information and communication technology) products in the 2000s.[22]

CONCLUDING REMARKS

A manufacturing-oriented transformation is imperative for India to address the challenges of employment creation, reviving growth and sustainable management of balance of payments. In that context, Make in India and AatmaNirbhar Bharat are timely initiatives. The manufacturing sector can be boosted by tapping into opportunities to make for India and global markets, and

[22]Lin, Justin Yifu, 'China', *Asian Transformations: An Inquiry into the Development of Nations*, Deepak Nayyar (ed.), Oxford University Press, 2019.

exploiting the potential of new digital and green industries. India's talent pool and rising domestic demand provide opportunities for us to emerge as a manufacturing hub.

The experiences of East Asian countries in building competitive manufacturing capacities, using strategic interventions, have rich lessons for India as it tries to embark on its industrialization. These lessons can be suitably adapted for India and include: a coordinated implementation of strategic approach to trade and exchange rate management; achieving scale economies through privileged access to the domestic market and manufacturers; adopting a selective and proactive approach to FDI; focussing on enterprise-development and building domestic technological capability; and directed credit and development of physical and social infrastructure.

The Indian government has taken a number of steps in recent times, including: infrastructure support and help with land acquisition; facilitation of approvals through single-window clearances and ease-of-doing-business; infant industry protection; and PLIs within the framework of Make in India and AatmaNirbhar Bharat, Stand-Up India and MUDRA schemes. Maintaining a competitive exchange rate is perhaps most critical in an open-economy environment of low tariff barriers for the development of manufacturing, as demonstrated by the experiences of the East Asian countries. Domestic competition should be fostered to prevent the rent-seeking behaviour of domestic enterprises and to provide protection from external competition. In any case, the protection from external competition should be for a limited period and phased out gradually as the domestic capacities get entrenched.

One may wonder whether India's current manufacturing thrust will have the same fate as the import-substituting industrialization policy in the early post-Independence period. However, there are key differences between India's industrial policy of early post-Independence period and now that will ensure greater success. Today's policy is more strategically focussed on tapping opportunities of import-substitution or exports in specific sectors, especially sunrise and green industrial sectors. It is being implemented in an open economy context with a clear focus on competitiveness, including through scale economies.[23] This time around, India will be helped by its position as a 'geopolitical sweet spot' having friendly relations with key industrial countries in the West and East. This will allow India to benefit from global companies friend-shoring supply chains to diversify them away from China. India is also enjoying a 'demographic sweet spot' with a relatively young population, while populations are ageing in most industrialized and newly-industrializing countries. India is also attracting a lot of investment from global companies seeking to build global capability centres or offshore R&D centres. These centres aim to tap into India's abundant pool of skills; ICT software and chip design expertise; and national innovation system famed for its frugal engineering capabilities.[24]

The early results have been encouraging. India has turned into a net exporter of mobile handsets after being a net importer. Monthly exports of India-assembled mobile handsets crossed US$1 billion in September 2022. There are indications that Apple could be sourcing 25 per cent of its handsets from India by 2025, up from under 5 per cent at present. Leading Indian energy companies have also committed large investments in the manufacture of green hydrogen. There are also some credible proposals for the manufacture of semiconductor chips and display devices, including by Foxconn. The manufacturing momentum is therefore building up gradually.[25]

---

[23]Kumar, Nagesh, 'India's Evolving Industrial Policy Is Critical for Realizing Its Development Vision', *Promarket*, 21 March 2023, https://tinyurl.com/2p8m2dpz. Accessed on 30 June 2023.

[24]Ibid.

[25]Ibid.

To conclude, the manufacturing-led transformation would be the key engine of India's growth over the next quarter of the century. But one should be captivated by the jobs this new manufacturing activity will create, fostering inclusive and sustainable transformation of the Indian economy. This is critical for realizing India's 2047 developed economy vision.

5

MAKING INDIA SELF-RELIANT IN FOOD, ENERGY AND DEFENCE SECTORS

Prof. Shamika Ravi

Non-resident senior fellow, Governance Studies Program, Brookings Institution, Washington DC

Among the many casualties of the Covid-19 pandemic was the accelerated decline of the global rules-based order. This was most evident in the context of access to vaccines. The rich liberal democracies put national interest above global humanitarian needs. They stockpiled more vaccines than was warranted, while the developing countries were left to fend for themselves. There have been repeated pleas from World Health Organization (WHO) and representatives of poorer nations to improve vaccine access for vulnerable populations universally. However, global inequity remains significant even today. Vaccine nationalism revealed that in desperate and extreme circumstances, when global rules-based order conflicts with national interests, the latter will trump global humanitarian needs. In these dark circumstances, India was fortunate to vaccinate more than a billion people. This was primarily on account of its self-reliance in the production and research of Covid-19 vaccines. Had India not been self-reliant, we would have braced ourselves for a catastrophe of untold magnitude. The pandemic has compelled us to rethink national issues related to self-reliance, globalization and trade. The war in Ukraine has further escalated these concerns, as countries explore ways to reduce strategic dependence on others. In this essay, I explore three key sectors of India—food, energy and defence—which demand self-reliance and reduced dependence on external vicissitudes. In the final section of this paper, I highlight the underlying guiding principles to balance policies of trade liberalization and strengthening domestic social security nets.

SELF-RELIANCE NOT AUTARKY

It is important to state upfront that self-reliance does not imply autarky. Inspired by the 'infant industry' argument from trade theory, India experimented with decades of protectionism. The opportunity costs of this were in the form of decades of low economic growth, and high levels of poverty even 50 years after independence. However, a fundamental job of the administration is to protect the lives and safeguard its citizens' interests and take all necessary steps such that these are not in jeopardy. Having suffered for decades under inward-looking protectionist regimes, India must find the appropriate balance between gaining self-reliance in strategic sectors and avoiding the pitfalls of protectionism. Therefore, from the perspective of national interest, I identify three critical sectors to focus in the overall strategy of aatmanirbharta—food, energy and security.

Food Security

India's Green Revolution in the 1960s played an instrumental role in achieving food security. It is important to remind ourselves that India had food shortage in the mid-1960s, with a growing population and low productivity in the agriculture sector. Leading newspapers in India had reported that 'Millions of people in India were facing dire distress' in accessing food.[1] Under these

[1]Kugler, Maurice, and Shakti Sinha, 'The Impact of COVID-19 and the Policy

circumstances, the then government was compelled to seek food aid from the US (United States), under the PL–480 programme. It was evident to the leadership that external reliance on food—with the survival of millions of Indians dependent on 'ship to mouth'—was unsustainable socially, economically and politically. To achieve food security, India had to enhance farm productivity. This required adopting a high-yield variety of wheat, rice and other grains that were developed in Mexico and the Philippines (which the US-based Rockefeller Foundation facilitated). However, all this would not have been possible if the farmers had not cooperated with the government in adopting the high-yield variety of grains. One could argue that the success of the Green Revolution in making India self-reliant on food was an outcome of the availability and adoption of the best available global technology; farm-centric policies by the government; and the cooperation of the farmers in bringing a transformational change.

The data shows a dramatic increase in food production since 1966. The food production index rose from 23 in 1966 to 112 in 2019, where 2014–16 was the base at 100. These trends in the food production index over 50 years is presented in Figure 1a below. Food production index measures the changes in the production of food crops that are considered edible, and that contain nutrients in a given year relative to the base years. In the latest global ranking available (2020) of 188 countries, India was ranked 35.[2]

We also note a significant decline in food imports as a per cent of merchandise imports—a drop from 34 per cent in 1966 to less than 4 per cent in 2019 (as shown in Figure 1b). These measures indicate a robust improvement in food security for India and strengthening self-reliance, over the last few decades.

Response in India', *Brookings*, 13 July 2020, https://tinyurl.com/38pmwvrb. Accesssed on 20 June 2023.

[2]'Food Production Index-Country Rankings', *TheGlobalEconomy.com*, 2020, https://tinyurl.com/3b735vw9. Accessed on 19 July 2023.

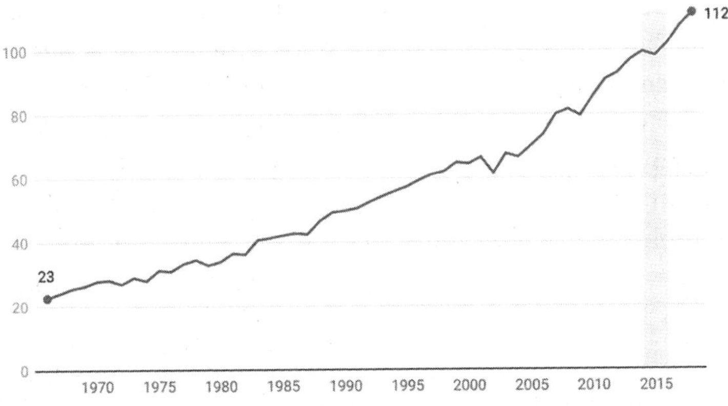

Figure 1a: Food Production Index

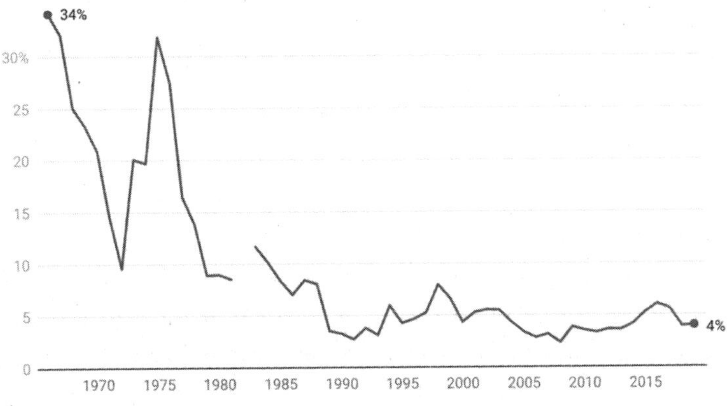

Figure 1b: Food Imports

Energy Security

From 2000 to 2019, the Indian per capita gross domestic product (GDP) has grown at an annual rate of 5.2 per cent, while per capita energy use in terms of oil consumption has increased at an annual rate of 3.04 per cent.[3] In terms of per capita oil consumption in kilograms (kg), it has grown from 417 in 2000 to 637 in 2014 (as shown in Figure 2a). As a result of increased per capita energy use, India's reliance on imports to meet its growing needs has increased significantly, from 20 per cent in 2000 to 34 per cent in 2014.

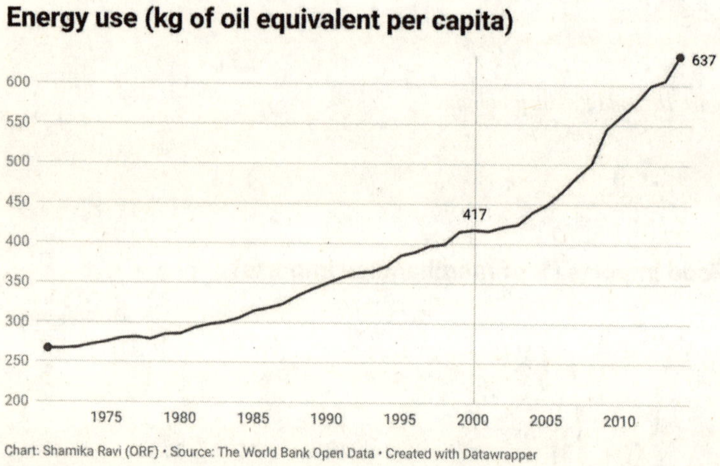

Figure 2a: Energy Use in India (Kg of oil equivalent per capita)

With the energy use of 6,961 kg and 2,237 kg of per capita oil consumption in 2014, we find that India has a much higher reliance on imports for its energy use as compared to the US and China (as reported in Figure 2b). Interestingly, the US has reduced its dependence on oil imports from approximately 24

---

[3]This is based on data from 2000 to 2014, data post 2014 is not available.

per cent in 2000 to 9 per cent in 2014. This reliance on imports implies that the future growth and development of the Indian economy would be subjected to global geopolitical events that influence the availability of oil. Such external dependence might not be desirable from an energy security perspective.

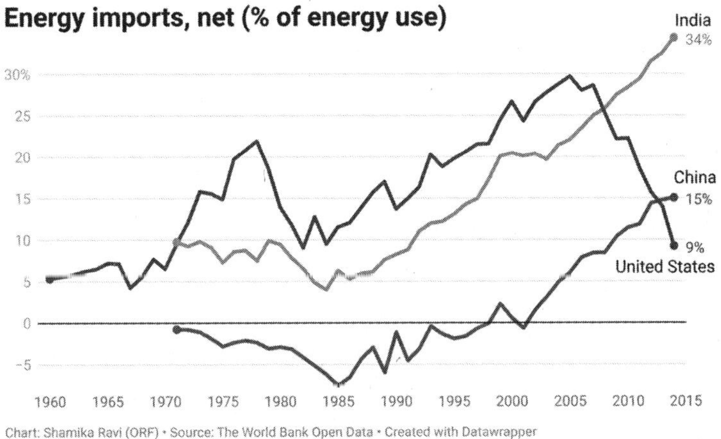

Figure 2b: Energy Imports (as percentage of energy use)

Given that domestic oil production might not be sufficient to meet our growing energy needs, we would have to redouble our efforts towards renewable energy which can be domestically sourced. Unfortunately, the data suggests that India's renewable energy consumption as a per cent of total energy consumption has reduced from 59 per cent in 1990 to 32 per cent in 2018 (as shown in Figure 2c). The data means that if India has to achieve energy security for sustained growth and development, and safeguard our interests from global geopolitical events that could influence the price and availability of oil, we would need an Energy Revolution (something similar to the Green Revolution). We would need a dramatic shift towards renewable sources, which would require government support and encouragement.

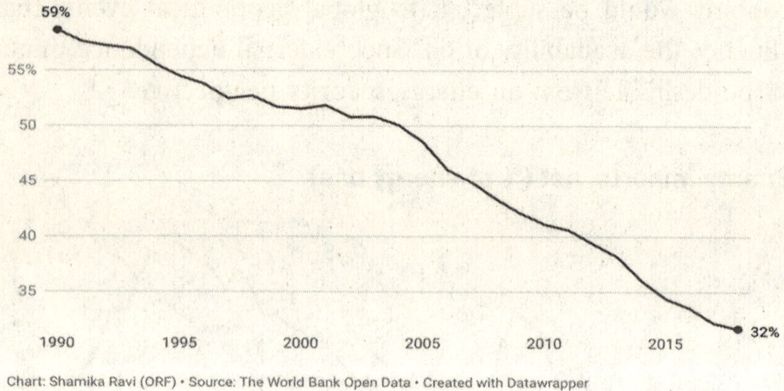

Figure 2c: Renewable Energy Consumption (as % of total energy consumption)

The present government has committed a change towards renewables, but it would need an equivalent commitment from the state and the local governments. In short, a shift towards renewables has to become a mass movement. However, unlike the Green Revolution—which was limited to a few states of Punjab, Haryana and western Uttar Pradesh—the Energy revolution has to become a pan India mass movement. An added benefit of moving towards renewables would be the positive impact on climate change, and towards achieving long-term sustainable growth targets for the global economy. The world cannot meet its climate targets without India's support and contribution. India must, therefore, be ready to seize this leadership opportunity.

Defence and National Security

The emergence of China as an economic and political power in the last two decades has disrupted the global political order. It is hard to predict the long-term global consequences of this phenomenon. There is a growing Chinese influence in the South

Asian region, regarding financial support and infrastructure. If India has to play an important role to provide a balance of power in the region, then it will have to pursue a twin strategy of economic development and growth. At the same time, India will also have to strengthen its national security. As far as national security is concerned, India must become self-reliant in the Arms Industrial complex with China's economic and political rise. India is currently dependent on other countries for the latest technology in aircraft, artillery, radar systems, missile and drone technology. For example, in 2020, it imported more than US$3 billion worth of arms (as shown in Figure 3a).

Arms imports (SIPRI* trend indicator values)

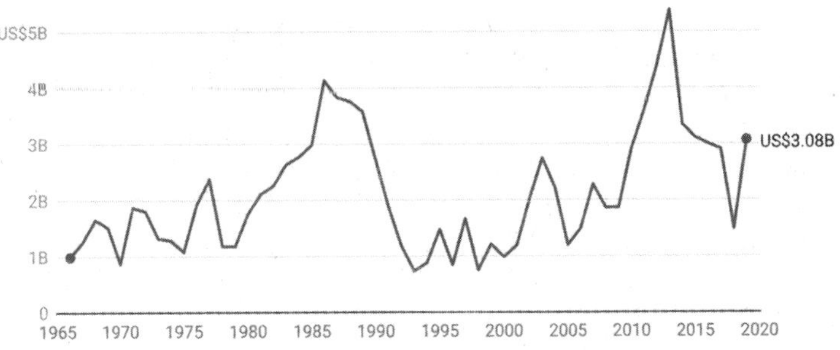

Arms transfers cover the supply of military weapons through sales, aid, gifts, and those made through manufacturing licenses. Data cover major conventional weapons such as aircraft, armored vehicles, artillery, radar systems, missiles, and ships designed for military use.
**Stockholm International Peace Research Institute (SIPRI), Arms Transfers Programme (http://portal.sipri.org/publications/pages/transfer/splash)*

Chart: Shamika Ravi (ORF) • Source: The World Bank Open Data • Created with Datawrapper

Figure 3a: Arms Imports of India

One major way for India to become self-reliant in the arms industry is to encourage public–private partnerships. In these partnerships, the private sector works with government grants to develop the latest technology. An explicit strategy to engage with the private sector should also involve the start-ups actively participating in the sector. The recent push for Make in India in the defence sector is a significant step in the right direction. A major development took place a few days back when India got its first ever export order for BrahMos missiles from the Philippines' Defence Ministry. They signed a contract worth US$ 374 million with the BrahMos Aerospace Pvt Ltd (BAPL) to supply an undisclosed number of missiles.[4] This is a very significant step towards bolstering India's young but robust defence industry.

Arms exports (SIPRI trend indicator values)

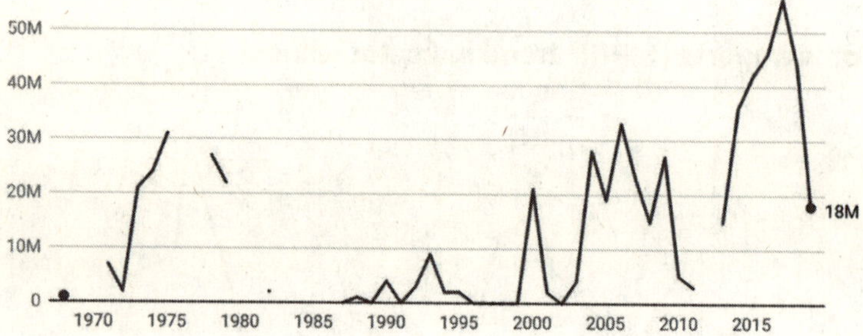

Arms transfers cover the supply of military weapons through sales, aid, gifts, and those made through manufacturing licenses. Data cover major conventional weapons such as aircraft, armored vehicles, artillery, radar systems, missiles, and ships designed for military use.
**Stockholm International Peace Research Institute (SIPRI), Arms Transfers Programme (http://portal.sipri.org/publications/pages/transfer/splash)*

Chart: Shamika Ravi (ORF) • Source: The World Bank Open Data • Created with Datawrapper

Figure 3b: Arms Exports by India

GLOBALIZATION AND TRADE

The early 1970s witnessed a unique phenomenon of stagflation—stagnant output, and inflation or rise in prices. Till then, the

[4]Saha, Premesha, 'How India's Brahmos Deal Is Not Just about Philippines but Gives a Stronger Message to the Region', *Observer Research Foundation*, 12 February 2022, https://tinyurl.com/bdd88954. Accessed on 11 July 2023.

economic policy of the governments across the world was primarily driven by an empirical regularity of a negative relationship between inflation and unemployment. Keynesianism, in the form of fiscal policy of the government, was used as an instrument to maintain a desired level of unemployment. However, stagflation compelled a rethink of economic policy. It led to a rise of an intellectual movement—neoliberal economics.

In contrast to Keynesian economics, where government was the solution to the problem of unemployment, neoliberal economics argued that government was the problem itself. An increase in public spending does not affect unemployment while leading to an acceleration in undesirable social inflation. The primary tenets of neoliberal economics are reduction in public expenditure, reduction in corporate taxes, deregulation of industry, increased emphasis on markets and free trade. These were not mere intellectual ideas and in the mid-1980s, neoliberal economics became a political movement in the world's leading economies—the US and the UK (United Kingdom). Neoliberal economics also influenced multilateral institutions such as the World Bank and the International Monetary Fund.

In the Indian context, neoliberal economic ideas came on the back of the economic crisis in the early 1990s. The Indian economic crisis of the 1990s had its roots in draconian government policies towards business in the 1960s. It was primarily an outcome of complete mistrust by politicians, bureaucrats and the intellectual elites of the business class. This led to bureaucratic strangulation of the economy via licence raj, protectionism and nationalization. Economic activity (except for the agriculture sector) was generally subjected to tyranny without a tyrant. In the guise of poverty reduction (or '*Garibi hatao*') and national interest, Indian industry was protected from competition from the outside world. Though there is evidence from other countries that, in the early stages of their development resorted to the protectionism of industry—the US in mid nineteenth century, Germany in the late nineteenth century, South Korea in the 1950s—this was primarily to help the domestic industry develop and reach the level of standards needed to compete globally. However, once the industry achieved global standards, protectionism was discarded in favour of free trade, to gain access to the international markets for its industry. Unfortunately, the Indian experience with protectionism was very different. It deprived Indians of global products. At the same time, the local industry did not develop to compete at the global level or take advantage of the global markets.

Even though neoliberal ideas (of deregulation, liberalization, free trade and markets) are an appealing alternative to draconian government policies of the 1960s, one must be cautious in blind adoption of these ideas. The global financial crisis in 2008 exposed the dark side of neoliberal economic ideas. One of the perilous effects of neoliberal economic ideas has been regarding the widening gap between the rich and the poor. For example, research on world inequality has shown that the bottom 50 per cent of the global population owns just 2 per cent of the global wealth, while the top 10 per cent own more than 80 per cent of the total global wealth. It has been argued that, 'contemporary global inequalities are close to their early 20th-century level, at the peak of Western imperialism'.

The other challenge to neoliberal economic ideas is concerning trade liberalization. A textbook analysis of free trade reveals its overall benefits. In reality, trade liberalization, even though beneficial to most people, could displace many people causing political and social disruption (as witnessed in some of the world's leading economies). The disgruntlement of those whose livelihood are disrupted due to trade liberalization would need to be addressed upfront. Paradoxically, this implies that trade liberalization would need to be simultaneously accompanied by government expansion of social safety nets.

Therefore, India needs an alternative and self-reliant development model with Indian characteristics. The Indian model of growth and development should encourage trade liberalization, but safety nets should be in place to address displacement issues. Market efficiency and privatization should be encouraged, but with sufficient safeguard that economic power is not concentrated in the hands of a few. Unfortunately, the neoliberal economic models that focus exclusively on efficiency do not address political and social issues arising from the concentration of wealth. Most of the Western democracies today are reeling under anti-globalization pressures from within. Over the last three decades India has been a net gainer from globalization, but moving forward will require a fine balance between trade liberalization and strengthening of domestic safety nets across the country. We must learn from the experiences of Western democracies and avoid their pitfalls.

Given the rise of China as an economic and global political power, India has to provide a balance of power for peace and stability in the region. For that to happen, India must address domestic development issues via growth and technological advancement. This requires significant investments in hard infrastructure and, more importantly, major investments in human capital by raising the quantity (and quality) of education and health available to our citizens. The recent evacuation exercises of nearly 20,000 Indian students from conflict-ridden Ukraine are a sharp reminder for the need to strengthen our higher education sector to accommodate the aspirations of our youth. People build nations. And to build a strong and self-reliant India, we must invest greatly in our people.

6

INDIAN ECONOMY: PROSPECTS AND POSSIBILITIES

Dr V. Anantha Nageswaran

Chief economic advisor to the Government of India

POLICYMAKING AMIDST GLOBAL UNCERTAINTY

The last few years have exposed the global economy to unprecedented challenges. While the global economic sentiment was still recovering from the setback of the pandemic, the emergence of geopolitical tensions, persistent inflation, rising sovereign debts and magnifying financial instabilities have added new dimensions to the overall recovery challenge. The tightening of monetary policy by the Central banks around the globe in response to inflation has, besides fostering a sense of uncertainty, triggered exchange rate fluctuations and capital outflows from emerging markets (including India). There have been few parallels to shocks like these, leaving policymakers with no fixed template to follow. This simultaneous interplay of various headwinds has prepared the global economy for slower growth, and a likely recession in the coming years.

In its latest update on World Economic Outlook (WEO), the International Monetary Fund (IMF) forecasted global GDP (gross domestic product) growth to fall from 3.4 per cent in 2022 to 2.8 per cent in 2023. Though inflationary pressures have begun to ease, the impact of monetary tightening is starting to show in slowing economic activity (especially in advanced economies). Advanced economies are expected to witness a significant growth slowdown from 2.7 per cent in 2022 to 1.3 per cent in 2023. Emerging Market and Developing Economies (EMDEs) are expected to be less impacted, with overall growth projected to decline from 4 per cent in 2022 to 3.9 per cent in 2023.

Global developments have also affected India's economic growth momentum, as seen in the downward revisions of growth estimates. Nonetheless, in the changing world order, India is projected to be the fastest-growing major economy in the world. Hence, it is relatively better placed than most other nations to weather the storm.

The resilience in the Indian economy is evident from the swift and sustained recovery observed from the pandemic-induced contraction in 2020–21. It is a testament to the economy's preparedness to handle unforeseen challenges through self-reliance, innovation and transformative reforms. Even during the global disturbances of 2022–23, the strong macroeconomic fundamentals and agile stabilization policies helped India brace the risks effectively. Continuing the policy strategy of sustained focus on structural reforms, and maintaining a guarded and strategic integration with the global economy will pave the way for India's growth prospects in this decade up to 2030. It will lay the foundation for building a more robust economy during the *Amritkaal.*

INDIAN RESILIENCE ANCHORED ON STRUCTURAL REFORMS, SELF-RELIANCE AND CALIBRATED POLICY RESPONSE

Sound macroeconomic fundamentals are always a blessing for policymakers. They provide a unique opportunity to strive for rapid and inclusive development, besides helping create buffers for unwarranted future downside risks. However, they are neither gifted nor can be taken for granted. The challenge is even more significant when we operate in an economically intertwined world. Hence, it is essential to appreciate that under such daunting circumstances, India has pursued and pushed critical structural reforms and focussed on innovation. This is while also balancing the macro-fundamentals of the economy.

Before the pandemic, India's growth trajectory from 2014–15 to 2019–20 was stable, with real GDP growth averaging 6.8 per cent—significantly higher than any comparable peer (both among advanced and emerging market economies). During 2020, the Covid-19 pandemic pushed economies across the globe (including India) into deep contraction. Faced with unprecedented uncertainty, the distinguishing feature of India's response to the pandemic centred around AatmaNirbhar Bharat. This was along with supply-side reforms rather than a total reliance on demand management.

Since the first wave of the pandemic, the government focussed on saving lives through emergency policy actions. Important initiatives included the world's largest free food programme under the Pradhan Mantri Garib Kalyan Anna Yojana; direct cash transfers under the Pradhan Mantri Jan Dhan Yojana; and relief measures for small businesses, including Emergency Credit Line Guarantee Scheme (ECLGS) for MSMEs (micro, small and medium enterprises). The government's fiscal, monetary and health policy responses were measured and calibrated to address the needs of the evolving situation without losing control over the fiscal space.

Once safety nets for society's vulnerable sections were put in place, the government's policy emphasis shifted to demand management. Investment boosting measures such as increasing the government's capital expenditure and introducing production-linked incentives (PLIs) for the manufacturing sector proved critical in bringing back the spirit of the economy. The structural reforms undertaken in the past few years have also propelled the economy towards a steady recovery from the pandemic. India's ambitious vaccination programme—with its mammoth scale, pace and coverage—played an important role in the smooth and gradual reopening of the economy. The coordinated policy actions taken by the central and state governments enabled the Indian economy to recover completely from the pandemic in 2021–22, with real GDP showing a full recovery over 2019–20.

While the Indian economy was progressing to resume the pre-pandemic growth trajectory, 2022–23 exposed it to new global challenges and uncertainties. The inflationary pressures emanating from the overheating of the global economy, resulting from ultra-loose fiscal and monetary policies adopted by economies during the pandemic, were further aggravated by geopolitical disturbances. The Central banks worldwide took up aggressive monetary tightening, to control the rising inflation. The Government of India and the RBI also coordinated their efforts to maintain a relatively controlled inflation, while ensuring a sustained growth momentum. When inflation reached a multi-decade high for several countries worldwide in 2022, India exceeded its inflation target range of 2 to 6 per cent by a maximum of 1.8 percentage points. The consumer price index inflation has since gradually moderated from a peak of 7.8 per cent in April 2022 to an 18-month low of 4.7 per cent in April 2023.[1]

Similar to the experiences of other economies, the adverse global economic situation also put India's balance of payments under pressure in the first half of 2022–23. The sharp rise in commodity and oil prices, policy tightening by the US (United States) Federal Reserve and the strengthening of the US dollar led to the widening of the current account deficit (CAD) and FPI (foreign portfolio investment) outflows during 2022–23. However, the resultant depreciation of the Indian rupee was more on account of the appreciation of the US dollar rather

[1]'Table 38 : Consumer Price Index-Annual Average', *Handbook of Statistics on Indian Economy, Reserve Bank of India*, 15 September 2022, https://tinyurl.com/3d8khdxw. Accessed on 11 July 2023.

than the weakness in the macroeconomic fundamentals of the Indian economy. Sufficient buffers in foreign exchange reserves (equivalent to nearly 10 months of imports), foreign investment flows, stable external debt and surplus on 'invisible' accounts (services, transfer and income) imparted resilience to India's external sector. With the easing of commodity prices and the decline in the trade deficit, India's current account might narrow in Q3 (third quarter) of FY(financial year) 2023.

As we have seen above, the resilience in India's growth draws upon its underlying fundamentals and inbuilt buffers in the economy. India's fiscal policy strategy has also reflected a similar approach over the last three budgets. During the pandemic, when consumption and investment demand were subdued, it was paramount for the government to expand its budget. However, the increase in government expenditure was accompanied by a change in mix towards higher productive capital expenditure (CapEx), highlighting a long-term strategy for sustained growth and fiscal sustainability. The proportion of the Centre's CapEx in total spending increased from 12 per cent in FY2018 to 22 per cent in FY2024 budget estimates. The state governments were also incentivized to enhance their CapEx by availing of interest-free CapEx loans and Capex-linked additional borrowing limits. With a larger multiplier effect and higher employment elasticity, CapEx spending will generate more productive economic growth and employment in the medium term.

The continued momentum in revenue buoyancy is an essential pillar of the economy's recovery. A series of tax reforms, such as adopting a unified goods and services tax (GST), reducing corporate and income tax rates, implementing faceless tax assessment and appeal systems and digitizing the return filing systems, have enhanced tax compliance and enabled the mobilization of a larger amount of resources. In particular, the vision of 'one nation, one tax' embodied in the introduction of the landmark GST Bill is now maturing, reaffirming the true spirit of cooperative federalism. The record GST collections supported by the increased tax base, various rate rationalization measures and systemic changes in the GST return filing system have improved the buoyancy of GST revenues over the pre-GST regime. The average monthly gross collection has consistently increased from ₹0.9 lakh crore in FY2018 to ₹1.5 lakh crore in FY2023. The GST collection for April 2023 of ₹1.87 lakh crore is the highest-ever monthly collection. Apart from supporting the revenue buoyancy, GST has also played a significant role in the ongoing formalization of the economy—as seen by an increasing number of firms entering the GST net (₹66 lakhs in 2017 to ₹1.4 crores in 2022).

Several other structural reforms in the past years have prepared the Indian economy to face various external and domestic challenges. Following the credit boom in the millennium's first decade, the Indian economy faced a severe financial system crisis up to 2020. The private non-financial sector's credit to GDP ratio, which had risen from 58.8 per cent in March 2000 to 113.6 per cent by December 2010, came down to 83.8 per cent in December 2018. The government undertook several reforms to strengthen the financial sector as the banking, non-banking and non-financial sector de-leveraged their balance sheet. From the recapitalization and merger of Public Sector Banks (PSB) and amendment of the SARFAESI Act 2002 to enacting the Insolvency and Bankruptcy Code 2016, these reforms have helped clean up the balance sheets of banks and corporates. The Insolvency and Bankruptcy Code has improved the business environment by nudging thousands of debtors to resolve distress in the early stages. Until December 2022, 24,222 applications for initiating the Corporate Insolvency Resolution Process (CIRP) of corporate debtors with an underlying default of ₹7.7 lakh crore were resolved.

As a result of these reforms, today's banking sector remains adequately capitalized and comparable to developed economies. The asset quality of banks are improving, as both the stressed asset ratio and the ratio of the non-performing assets to overall bank assets are declining. The overall non-performing asset ratio for banks dropped to a decade low of 4.5 per cent in December 2022. Moreover, the robust double-digit growth in non-food bank credit since April 2022 indicates the strength in bank balance sheets. Much of this increase is attributable to the industry offtake, particularly the MSMEs.

Along with credit availability in the economy, the overall business environment has transformed in the last few years. There have been reforms such as simplification of regulatory frameworks; setting up of the Centre for Processing Accelerated Corporate Exit; decriminalizing minor economic offences under the Companies Act of 2013; and removing the retrospective taxation. These reforms have removed policy uncertainty, reduced compliances, created a business-friendly environment and have improved investor sentiment. Initiatives for revamping the privatization and disinvestment policy; opening up strategic sectors such as defence, mining and space to the private sector; extending production-linked incentives (PLIs) to businesses; and further liberalizing the FDI policy have attracted fresh investments in the business ecosystem. They have created an environment for start-ups to nurture. The number of recognized start-ups has increased from 452 in 2016 to more than 92,000 in 2023.[2]

It is well established that structural reforms with this scale of potential impact have long gestation periods. However, due to the one-off external shocks over the past years, there has been little time for these reforms to bear fruit in terms of improved and sustained economic growth. There is a need for an uninterrupted period of stable global and regional economic environment, for these reforms to manifest themselves in the economic output and employment generation.

---

[2] 'More than 92,000 Entities Recognized as Startups since Launch of Startup India', *PIBDelhi*, 5 April 2023, https://tinyurl.com/nnm3j3k5. Accessed on 11 July 2023.

FROM INDIA TO THE WORLD: THE DIGITAL PUBLIC GOODS STORY

While international discourses cite that there are many global practices that India should follow, it is also pertinent to state that many Indian practices and systems offer policy learnings for other countries. For instance, India's Covid-19 vaccination drive; the best practices adopted by the Securities and Exchange Board of India (SEBI) in the capital markets; and the development of digital infrastructure including India Stack, Open Network for Digital Commerce (ONDC), Open Credit Enablement Network (OCEN) and GST Sahay. These stand out as policy models which can be replicated in other countries.

The performance of Digital Public Goods (DPG) in India has been an enormous success. Today, we have a powerful story on DPG to tell and sell. The economy is seeing an increase in new-age FinTech firms and start-ups. India has the highest FinTech adoption rate of 87 per cent compared to the global average of 64 per cent.[3] Digital payment modes have grown exponentially in India over the last few years, with 40 per cent of all payments being done digitally. Digital payments are being made for even the smallest of transactions, with nearly 50 per cent classified as small or micropayments. As small businesses can now plug in through digital platforms, it will be exciting to estimate what percentage of DPG contributes to India's GDP growth.

Low-cost accessibility (Aadhaar), simple and interoperable designs (Co-Win) and large-scale adoption and reach (DigiLocker, MyGov) add feathers to India's digital success story. Open digital ecosystems have the potential to unlock various opportunities and can be used for further innovation

[3] '"At 87%, India Has the Highest Fintech Adoption Rate in the World against the Global Average of 64%": Shri Piyush Goyal', *PIB Delhi*, 30 September 2021, https://tinyurl.com/4cmbraan. Accessed on 11 July 2023.

at a low cost. With the increasing need for digital infrastructure solutions, especially in emerging nations, the India Stack model can easily be scaled up to meet other countries' demands. These demands could be enabling financial inclusion, addressing small businesses' marketing and credit needs, streamlining government operations, and encouraging entrepreneurship. With the untapped potential in the DPG space, this could be a defining aspect of India's growth story for the world to embrace. It needs to be nurtured effectively with facilitative and agile regulatory, and policy support.

THE WAY FORWARD

Formulating and implementing economic policy in a globally intertwined world comes with its share of costs and benefits. There are gains to be made from being integrated in the form of large foreign investments, knowledge and research and development (R&D) exchange and efficiency gains via comparative trade advantages. At the same time, a high degree of integration also has costs that are amplified in times of crises. Countries are exposed to volatilities of trade and foreign capital outflow shocks, besides episodes of unwarranted imported inflation.

Given this reality, it must be appreciated that integration vis-à-vis self-reliance need not be an either–or choice. Being self-reliant has merits, but that does not necessarily imply that open trade and integration reflect an adverse policy choice. The design and effective implementation of self-reliance measures are key determinants of sustainable growth in the medium term, and also act as a buffer against any unforeseen global shocks. However, the strength and stability of macro fundamentals and the sustainability of economic growth depend on the overall impact of multiple policy levers (both external and domestic). Some of these will work to their potential only when the channels of operation are integrated with the global economy.

At present, the Indian economy has a balanced emphasis on domestic and external linkages. Over the last 20 years, there has been a significant increase in India's trade openness—with trade to GDP increasing from around 30 per cent of GDP in 2002 to 45 per cent in 2022. India intends to capitalize on evolving trade and diplomatic relations by strengthening its exports and diversifying its export partners. This will be done from a medium- to long-term perspective through liberalized free trade agreements (FTAs), rupee settlement, PLI, etc. The new Foreign Trade Policy aims to increase the country's exports to US$ 2 trillion by 2030. It is an ambitious target, but the performance of Indian exports over two years (2021–22 and 2022–23) is a good start in this direction. Structural reforms, such as simplification of compliances and strengthening of physical infrastructure, are beginning to enhance the competitiveness of India's merchandise exports. Healthy balance sheets of the banking, non-banking financial and non-financial sectors have enabled the exporting firms to ramp up their investments. The service sector has recovered from the pandemic and contributes robustly to India's exports. India is today the most favoured investment destination globally. Moreover, multinational companies' diversification of supply chains in recent years has opened a window of opportunity for new destinations to emerge as manufacturing hubs. China was the world's manufacturing centre for the longest time, and as it vacates that space an opportunity opens up for India (even though countries like Vietnam have made a headstart).

The strength of the domestic economy is visible in the healthy growth shown by India's manufacturing and service sectors. India is outperforming the other countries on the manufacturing PMI (purchasing managers' index), and its services PMI has reached its highest in over a decade. The increasing capacity utilization in the manufacturing sector highlights the scope for higher capital investments by the firms to increase. The pandemic and geopolitical uncertainties had temporarily delayed the arrival of a full-blown CapEx cycle in the country. However, the private sector capital expenditure is prepared to emerge as a source of economic strength. The domestic environment is conducive to a virtuous private investment cycle, and early green shoots of private sector investment spending are visible.

The government's economic policy focus has been to restore India's growth potential. This is done by getting the financial sector back on track, facilitating economic activity by easing business conditions and massively augmenting physical and digital infrastructure to enhance India's connectivity. These inturn, help increase the competitiveness of India's manufacturing. India is enjoying macroeconomic momentum and has emerged as a bright spot among its peers. However, it must stand guard against global headwinds. In the shifting sands of geopolitical alliances, India must remain watchful and not take its relatively better position for granted. Fiscal and monetary policies are alive to the situation, and must remain so for some more time. The multiple structural changes in the past and reform push towards trust-based governance will pave the way for a sustained medium-term growth of 6–7 per cent, strengthening the foundation of Vision India@2047.

7

INTERPRETING 'AATMANIRBHAR'

Prof. Ashima Goyal

Emeritus professor,

Indira Gandhi Institute of Development Research, Mumbai

The term 'aatmanirbhar' has generated much discussion. There are varied interpretations, which tend to be dominated by the literal translation of the word—self-reliant. In the context of Indias post-Independence experience, there is fear that self-reliance means a reversal of liberalization and a closing of the economy again.

This paper, however, argues that the key aspect of AatmaNirbhar Bharat is strengthening domestic capacity. Achieving this requires pragmatism and diversity. Both of these entail more, not less, openness while staying away from policy extremes of a fully-open or fully-closed market. It also requires coordination between governments and producers, that involves reliance on others. This paper illustrates these principles with India's recent export drive.

EXPORT COMPETITION

Pre-reform import substitution protected and prolonged weakness. The new export competition is about creating and using strength in a virtuous cycle.

During the post-Independence import-substituting

regime, Indian manufacturing settled into a comfortable high-cost—low-quality outcome in a protected market. However, liberalization was an import competition regime. In that regime, manufacturing found it difficult to survive given its high costs and unfair government subsidized competition from China. After experimenting with these unproductive extremes, the more sustainable current regime can be called 'export competition'. [1]

Manufacturing has to compete internationally and therefore, has to become efficient in order to export. But it will be protected from unfair competition, and helped to develop economies of scale under a broad set of policies that lower costs of doing business.

Without such support, India's past free trade agreements (FTAs) with various East Asian economies only resulted in large net imports into India. They are being retooled for easier exports of goods and services in which India has a comparative advantage, even as the general costs of production are brought down.

COSTS OF DOING BUSINESS

There is systematic work in reducing the cost of all factors of production for industry. GST-led domestic integration into one market and government-led infrastructure investment lowers transport costs. The World Bank logistics index 2018 shows that Indian logistics were at 14 per cent of GDP against a global average of 8 per cent. India's rank was 44 compared to China's 26. PM (Prime Minister) Gati Shakti led interventions aim to lower logistics costs by 3–5 per cent of GDP. They specifically target better coordination across departments and states in order to do so.

---

[1]This paper draws on and further develops some of the author's earlier articles. The term 'export competition' was first used in one of the author's 2020 *Hindu Business Line* articles. Some of the literature mentioned can be found in the introduction of the author's Oxford University Press edited handbook on the Indian economy.

Labour law reform gives more freedom in decision-making. It simplifies compliance by reducing an unwieldy set of laws into four codes. Efforts towards reducing the cost of capital have been continuing over the last decade. The financial sector has reached a level of reform and diversification where multiple sources of funding are available and interest costs are coming down. Improvements in corporate governance and disclosure, which are in the industry's hands, are necessary for robust corporate bond markets.

The compliance burden remains very high for Indian industry partly due to multiple regulators. But there are moves to create automatically populated central repositories of information that all regulators can access, facilitating one-window compliance. India's advantages in technology can be leveraged for improved e-governance.

Cross subsidization is a major source of high costs for industry, whether in rail freight or in electricity and water charges. Reforms that would replace this and many other price distorting interventions are in progress, with direct benefit transfers and income support for the poor. As lower costs allow industry to expand employment, the need for income support should fall.

Supply-side measures that reduce the cost of producing and living in India, and smart-green infrastructure investment also help contain inflation. Supporting renewable energy in a well-sequenced manner, is essential to tackle climate change as well as reduce dependence on imported oil.

INDUSTRIAL POLICY

One of the tenets of liberalization is that governments rarely get industrial policy right. So it is best to cut tariffs, giving consumers the advantage of low prices. The industrial structure should be left to evolve according to a country's comparative advantage. However, it takes time to build scale that gives the advantage of low costs. Modern industry is often subject to network effects and to lock-ins. Demand migrates to the corporate that grows enough to reduce costs and improve quality. Others then find it difficult to compete.

The Spence Commission set up by the World Bank examined 13 economies that, after 1950, grew at over 7 per cent for more than 25 years.[2] They found that they embraced openness but did not blindly apply reform orthodoxies. Governments were pragmatic and flexible, rather than ideological. Nine of these countries were from Asia. They were willing to intervene in markets to promote exports through industrial policies and to manage exchange rates (with the use of select capital controls and reserve accumulation). They were also flexible enough to not get locked into distorting policies, and to anticipate and change as required for sustained growth. Their other common characteristics included openness, macroeconomic stability, high savings and investment rates and market allocation of resources. Resource mobility and urbanization were supported. Public investment in infrastructure accounted for 5 to 7 per cent of GDP or more. Specific contextual interventions and the microeconomic incentives created were important. Thus, external drivers and opening out alone did not create growth. The report supports intelligent use of industrial policy.

The production linked incentives (PLI) scheme, announced in March 2020 by the Government of India, is an attempt at this. It provides eligible manufacturing companies incentives largely ranging between 4–6 per cent on incremental sales over the base year of 2019–20 for a four- to six-year period. The direct payment subsidy has expanded to cover 15 mostly high tech or critical sectors. Committed payments have touched ₹2 lakh

---

[2]Spence, Michael, and Dannt Liepziger (ed.), 'Globalization and Growth: Implications for a Post-crisis World', *Commission on Growth and Development*, 2010, https://tinyurl.com/4mvecuax. Accessed on 11 July 2023.

crores.[3] Deliverables include exports, employment and quality improvement to be evaluated and standardized across sectors under NITI Aayog.

It is an example of pragmatic industrial policy. It differs from the past blanket protection by being temporary and well-targeted, with clear deliverables. It will encourage investment and help industries reach economies of scale, after which they have to survive on their own. If time bars are credible, only inherently competitive industries will enter. It is also timely, as it may help attract firms that want to shift away from China. Careful selection, credibility of exit, data-based implementation and monitoring of deliverables across industries will be critical. However, an escape clause for external disruptions is also required. For example, in the Covid-19 period supply chain disruption meant only 3–4 out of 14 companies approved were able to meet their committed sales targets to qualify for the incentives.

PUBLIC–PRIVATE PARTNERSHIP (PPP)

Public–private partnerships (PPP), with an appropriate allocation of risk across the public and private is critical for infrastructure expansion. However, here we discuss a different kind of PPP. The non-performing asset cycle that followed the global financial crisis (GFC) together with suspicions of public funds and resources being siphoned off by private promoters lead to sustained investigations over the last decade, and that vitiated the atmosphere for industry. But today, while the Indian bankruptcy code has improved the credit culture, the distinction between

---

[3] Analysts expect it to create as much and more in investment and in annual export increments, while adding ₹30–35 lakh crores to revenue over the next few years; "'PLI to Account For 13-15% Capex in Key Sectors in 3-4 Years'", *The Indian Express*, 24 March 2022, https://tinyurl.com/ycxt3txf. Accessed on 30 June 2023.

commercial and criminal losses is increasingly being understood and enshrined in law. For example, the Prevention of Corruption Act (1988) put many bankers under investigation. This Act defined criminal misconduct by a public servant, to include obtaining a pecuniary advantage for anyone where no public interest is involved. But it was modified in 2018, so that a case is only possible if assets are disproportionate to income. The 2013 Company Act has also been amended in 2020 to replace criminal offences with civil ones that can be settled with a fine. The aim is for policy certainty, without flip-flops such as retrospective taxation.

More stability and diversity in the financial sector with stronger institutions is necessary for finance growth. A key objective should be to build up the diversity of the financial sector so that it can meet public and private funding needs, and serve India's diverse population. A major strength is that the share of household savings in financial assets is increasing. This will reduce over-dependence on foreign savings. Diversity also makes for resilience, since exposures vary across entities. That the financial sector has done well despite the stresses of Covid-19 points to progress in these objectives, as well as some resolution of past issues. Current initiatives towards building a Development Finance Institute and setting up a bad bank are in the right direction.

The government is committed to providing a broad and smooth road for industry to run on. Moreover, the Covid-19 shock has shifted policymakers' perspectives. Coordination with the private sector improved in this period. For example, in the domestic production of vaccines and other medical equipment. This helped the country pull through the crisis.

Governments are ready to work with industry now to revive the economy. But it will be a combination of discipline and support, not the old-style lobbying and special favours. Industry has to act responsibly to build a vibrant ecosystem. It has to invest in labour skills and well-being in local communities through its CSR (Corporate social responsibility) obligations, build supplier clusters with upfront payments to smaller firms and develop environmentally sustainable practices with zero waste. When *jugaad* (inventive short-term fixes) is no longer just against obstacles, but part of growth, it can release a burst of productive innovation.

DIVERSIFICATION

Covid-19 has led to a faster adoption of digital processes. Indian tech services exports, where it has a comparative advantage, are booming. The world has realized that dependence on one country is dangerous. Diversification of supply chains from China is an opportunity for India to expand labour-intensive and new tech manufacturing exports. This will help create a range of jobs that have eluded its youth so far.

Diversification requires increase in home production of defence equipment, while spreading necessary imports over more countries. Multiplying US sanctions are also emphasizing the importance of aatmanirbharta. Critical weaknesses and dependencies on any one country can be exploited at any point. Diversification across countries and within a country itself, is the way to reduce these risks. In the future, the world will move away from extreme dependence on China for its imports and on the US for its payments and financial systems. India's innovations in payment systems, united payments interface (UPI) and the Aadhar Stack, can be leveraged. India can remedy its under-representation in global trade and financial systems as part of a diversifying and strengthening strategy.

Given India's one billion plus population, with a large share of youth, multiple specializations are both possible and necessary. In its pre-British rule golden age, India was a major exporter.

ECONOMIC INCLUSION

A major puzzle is why, despite being a vibrant democracy, India has been unable to create full economic inclusion. Poverty persists and equality of opportunity is still lacking. Inadequate public services—such as healthcare, education, air quality—hit the poor more since the well-off are able to afford private substitutes. Why didn't voters demand and succeed in getting these services? The characteristics of inclusive economic institutions are competitive entry, low broad-based taxes, absence of arbitrariness in policy and public services that enhance human capital equitably.

Countries without broadly inclusive political and economic institutions often fail in the long run despite openness. India had universal democratic franchise, but its economic institutions remained extractive due to the British colonial legacy. However, the British also left India with effective legal and democratic institutions and 75 years is long enough for political equality to change economic institutions. Why did dysfunctional institutions persist in a broad, inclusive democracy like India?

Democracy was inclusive but divisions of caste, religion and region could be exploited to maintain a stagnant equilibrium that delivered neither growth nor equity. At the time of Independence, the dominant development ideas favoured a closed economy with government led growth and redistribution. Economic controls gave additional power to elites to enrich themselves, with minimal doles for groups that kept them in power. Continuing poverty created dependence through a need for further doles. Thus, dominant development ideas imposed on inherited heterogeneous structure and colonial institutions created stagnancy.

A change in ideas favouring openness, the government's emphasis on empowerment as well as a rise in the proportion that benefits from growth are pushing for 'active inclusion'. This inclusion will allow more and more to participate in opportunities, while creating jobs for the lower skill segment as well. Technological change, such as in telecommunications, is also available for the less well-off. The demand for better public service in health, education and infrastructure is rising. These enable more to make use of new opportunities that growth creates. But will governments deliver?

TRANSFORMING GOVERNMENT

For this public service delivery, the government has to transform into a facilitator and a builder of capacity. Government assets can be restructured towards providing public services that have major externalities and are therefore, underprovided by the private sector. This restructuring of the public sector can partly be financed by privatizing state business activities. More than the financing, this asset monetization will create many opportunities and improve efficiencies. Both public and private sectors have to be strengthened to contribute in line with their comparative advantage.

Political capital should not be wasted on reforms that impact large groups, encounter resistance and create shocks for the system. It would be better to focus on feasible reforms and critical bottlenecks in infrastructure. An example of such reform is improved data privacy, which can enhance favourable technology trends to increase India's advantage in digital initiatives. The most significant of India's unique opportunities is the advantage of skilled youth, together with technological changes that give them the opportunity for entrepreneurship and innovation. The path for this change has to be made smooth.

For better health and education outcomes, as well as for a rise in public investment, states have to be on board. The most critical policy initiatives at the present juncture, require the Centre and the states to coordinate well. The states have exclusive jurisdiction in agriculture, public health, sanitation, water and a large share in infrastructure investment. Aspects of education, policing and commerce, come under the concurrent list of the constitution.

Excessive centralization under the British was initially encouraged due to concerns regarding national integration. The constitution mandated an inter-state council but a strong central government in the early years and the emphasis on planning, denied it the weight it required. Plan schemes, on which the first Finance Commission had focussed, took attention away from general public services for the average citizen. In particular, public services under state jurisdiction were neglected. The states reduced investment to fund populist freebies while staying within their budget constraints, thus reducing productivity growth. Punjab is a tragic example of this. It has fallen from the top to the bottom rank among states due to excessive use of such policies.

A state fiscal council could help states converge on best accounting and payment practices, along with taxing and spending effectively with delegation to the third tier. The formal responsibilities of the council could be to improve data, accounting systems and incentive mechanisms. Better technology, transparency and predictability could enable timely payments. Introducing norms such as ensuring funding before announcing schemes, and pre-announced expenditure totals from finance ministries could reduce competitive bidding-up of expenditures. As rationalization of centrally sponsored schemes (CSS) gets underway, discussion with and rationalization of state-level schemes could also be a game changer. Multiple state-level schemes create duplication and waste, but are rarely shut since each gives rise to some interest groups that want continuity.

Such a council could help put peer pressure on the laggards, raise awareness and convergence to best practices. Crucial reforms that encounter resistance at the central level may be feasible if one state starts and others follow, as evidence of better outcomes accumulate.

States have to be weaned off from policies such as providing free electricity that cause large distortions. India is facing multiple cases, as in 2017 our per capita income crossed the level after which the World Trade Organization (WTO) rules disallow support through price intervention (that distort resource allocation). Improving conditions for all industry is WTO compatible, but industry-specific support is not. Despite many schemes announced by the central government pending payments from state discoms to producer, companies continue to increase. External pressures could be used to modify state policies. Income transfers are WTO compatible but given India's narrow tax base and large population, they must be targeted and restricted to the really vulnerable. This was done in order to release funds for capacity building.

Evidence of very low conditional tax convergence across Indian states, suggests better incentives are required to improve tax effort. Since a gap-filling approach can motivate states to remain weak, recent Finance Commissions have given states incentives to improve their finances. This was done with some grants, conditional to better types of expenditure. Since transfers are their rights, conditionalities can only apply to grants. A viable fiscal union needs transfers plus some discipline. Transfers are necessary for equity and because central taxes are more elastic. But fiscal unions with unconditional central bailouts tend to have very poor macroeconomic outcomes.

For example, in Argentina and Brazil sub-national debt got added on to the national debt. Without adequate tax revenue, it was serviced by printing money and this led to hyperinflation. Foreign debt ended in default. The US changed after a similar experience. Since the centre bailed out states from their war of independence debt, the states overspent. After bailouts were refused and states began to balance their budgets, the centre did mandate transfers for state health and education programmes. In Canada, bailouts were available only under severe conditionality so provinces preferred to default. Market discipline worked to improve finances as risk rose in high debt periods. Since they first have to get the Centre's permission, scope for market borrowings by Indian states is limited. But so is market discipline, since the Centre absorbs the risk. Gradually this should change. Those with higher debt should pay higher rates with the threat of possible bankruptcy.

Many CSS schemes are designed to fill gaps in state public services. Tight restrictions on end use and delays in sanctioning, however, reduce their utility for state governments. But the latter are guilty of the same treatment of lower-level bodies such as municipalities and panchayats. Decentralization needed to be strengthened in the constitution, and this was attempted with the 73rd and 74th Amendments on direct local level democracy. However, implementation remains uneven with some states able to use clauses to resist effective devolution. They fear it as a way for the Centre to bypass them. Making transfers largely non-discretionary and more time-bound as they are in the Finance Commission awards may help. Incentives from non-discretionary mechanisms work best when they are immune to political re-negotiation. More transfers could be made conditional upon improved public services, to help convergence among states.

User charges retained by local governments would force more accountability in public service delivery. Incentives to increase prosperity and the tax base rise if incremental tax is retained. The most common 'fiscal contract' Chinese provinces had with the Centre, allowed them to retain revenues they raised after the first 50 per cent (which was shared). This gave them a strong marginal incentive for reform. In a federal system, such non-linear transfer schemes improve incentives even while delivering vertical and horizontal equity.

But dialogue must also complement incentives. States do want to be part of and contribute to the Indian growth story. Leadership from the Centre can help get them on-board. India over-achieving its $400 billion export target in 2022, suggests that coordination across government departments, states and industry has improved.

CONCLUSION

Emerging markets (EMs) had weathered the GFC itself well because of a shift from foreign short-term debt financing to risk-sharing equity, a lesson learned from the East Asian crisis. But in the 2010–20 decade EMs growth fell. This was partly due to repeated surges and stops in foreign portfolio flows, caused by the quantitative easing advanced economies (AEs) undertook. For example, 10 major EMs had a mean IIP (India Industrial Production) growth rate of 4.3 pre-GFC (2000–08) and just 1.3 post-GFC (2009–17). The AEs share of global income is lower, as it had fallen to 42.18 per cent in April 2021 from 54 per cent in 2004 in purchasing power parity (PPP) exchange rates. This makes it worth their while to protect EM growth, since the latter can pull up global growth. But AEs cannot be relied upon to do so. During the Covid-19 period as well, they looked after themselves first. They stocked up on vaccines rather than sharing them with EMs, even though this inequity increased the chances of a deadlier virus mutation. Therefore, aatmanirbharta requires greater diversification and resilience to smooth global shocks (while reaping the benefits of globalization).

But *aatma* (soul), in the sense of a higher spiritual and moral purpose, is thought to be the same in everyone. Therefore, aatmanirbharta is consistent also with principled policies that enhance coordination between trading partners. This makes trade the non-zero-sum game that it is meant to be.

8

AATMANIRBHAR BHARAT: HOW DOES IT FIT INTO INDIA'S ECONOMIC STRATEGY FOR THE 21ST CENTURY?

Sanjeev Sanyal

Member, Prime Minister's Economic Advisory Council

In recent years, the term 'aatmanirbhar Bharat' has been mentioned frequently by senior officials as a key tenet of PM (Prime Minister) Narendra Modi's economic strategy. The term is usually translated as 'self-reliant India' but what does it mean in theory and in practice? Is it a return to the pre-1991 idea of import-substitution as some of its critics allege, or an entirely new idea? Is it a sign of a withdrawal of India from global trade towards a more autarchic economic model? This brief paper will attempt to clarify this idea and its practical application in policy.

WHAT AATMANIRBHAR BHARAT IS NOT

It is important to be clear that AatmaNirbhar Bharat is not a return to socialist-era import substitution and the licence permit raj that accompanied it. It is also not an attempt to close off India from global supply chains, foreign technologies or international investment. That approach was clearly a failure during the pre-liberalization era. It led India into a minefield of inefficiency, bureaucratic hurdles, rent-seeking and low economic performance.

Indeed, India still suffers many of the after-effects of that short-sighted approach. No serious economist or policymaker would wish for a return to the shoddy products and chronic shortages that marked that era.

The reluctance to join a particular trade bloc, the Regional Comprehensive Economic Partnership (RCEP), is not an ideological mind-block against free trade agreements (FTAs) in general. It is a practical assessment that a particular trade deal was not in national interest. Just like one should not be blind to the advantages of certain trade deals, one should also not be accepting of any and every FTA. What matters is that policymakers do a realistic assessment of the advantages and disadvantages of each deal. Even as the Government of India decided against RCEP, it has continued to pursue FTAs with other countries such as Australia, the UK (United Kingdom) and the UAE (United Arab Emirates).

LEVERAGING INDIGENOUS STRENGTHS

At its simplest, the idea of AatmaNirbhar Bharat is about leveraging India's internal strengths. These strengths involve encouraging indigenous entrepreneurship, innovation and risk-taking to compete in an evolving competitive world. Thus, it is about participating in global supply chains from a position of strength. This is not mere sloganeering but derives from a particular worldview that the future trajectory of the global economy is inherently unpredictable, and open to random shocks from all manner of sources. Anyone who has lived through the Covid-19 pandemic and geopolitical events of 2020–22 will know what that means. Readers will note that this is a clear detour from the deterministic idea of static efficiency that underpins the old Washington Consensus. In a dynamic and unpredictable world, there is no 'optimal equilibrium' to aspire to. The game is about how to best deal with a succession of unpredictable shocks from technology, consumer behaviour, geopolitical events, pandemics, climate change and so on. Thus, the AatmaNirbhar Bharat strategy includes two elements—flexibility and resilience.

Flexibility entails that policymakers create a framework that is able to adapt to various changes as quickly as possible, in order to take advantages of new opportunities. This is why old-style import-substitution driven by issuance of permits, by a slow bureaucratic machinery, is untenable in this model. Instead every effort is made to improve ease of doing business, factor market flexibility and remove bureaucratic hurdles. This is done so that Indian entrepreneurs can quickly respond to the evolving situation. Start-ups in emerging sectors are especially welcome. This is how even in the midst of a global pandemic, the Indian government continued to open out sectors such as drones, space, trade finance factoring and geospatial mapping. This is also the reason why the government has placed such a lot of emphasis on infrastructure investment. Improvements in infrastructure such as highways, airports, railways and sea ports provide the physical landscape that allow Indian businesses to adapt and compete.

Although the general idea behind economic flexibility is sector agnostic, policymakers recognize that scale matters in some sectors. Therefore, a targeted production linked incentive (PLI) scheme was devised to help some sectors scale up. The PLI scheme is time bound and meant as a one-time support for scaling up. Over time, depending on its success, the scheme can revolve across different sectors as per the circumstances.

Foreign direct investment (FDI) is encouraged in this model as it creates domestic production, brings in technology, provides capital and builds international linkages. Again, note that AatmaNirbhar Bharat is not about being closed to foreigners (although some areas may continue to be restricted for strategic and security considerations).

THE IMPORTANCE OF RESILIENCE

The emphasis on flexibility, the few industrial policy interventions notwithstanding, is still within the realm of the Washington Consensus model. What makes the AatmaNirbhar Bharat model different is the extra dimension of resilience. A fully globalized world, optimized for short-term efficiency may be very attractive in theory but is prone to catastrophic breakdowns in supply chains. This issue came to the fore repeatedly in the 2020–22 period.

A few illustrations will make the point clear. As is well known, India has a large and globally competitive pharmaceuticals industry. However, early in the Covid-19 pandemic cycle in March 2020, the government woke up to the fact that many critical ingredients came from a single foreign source—China. As supply chains got disrupted, it put a lot of pressure on business continuity at a critical juncture of a health crisis. The same can be said of the automobiles industry where a global shortage of semiconductor chips from early 2021 caused severe problems. A large and competitive industry was again forced to operate well below the installed capacity, because of the breakdown in the supply chain of a single input.

Given the above experience, it would be rational for the Indian government to provide incentives and support for some domestic manufacturing of key pharmaceutical inputs and chips. This can hardly be called protectionism or isolationism. It is a sensible investment in the resilience of a large and globally competitive industry. This is not just good for India but also for the world, as its supplies of pharmaceuticals and other Indian products will become more resilient. The need to invest in key defence industry capabilities should also be obvious.

The same approach is also true of global energy supplies. As Europe has discovered, its single-minded pursuit of 'green' renewable energy sources led to a growing reliance on Russian energy. Other domestic options, including nuclear energy, were ignored or phased out. This is now being reviewed by the Europeans but an unpredictable shock has exposed the risk of a unidimensional optimization strategy. As a country that is not rich in hydrocarbons, India has good reason to invest in renewable energy capacity (quite apart from its climate-related obligations under the Paris Agreement). Large amounts of public and private resources have been put into creating solar energy capacity. Nonetheless, the Indian government continues to maintain a commitment to a bouquet of energy sources including nuclear options. This is not due to some misplaced love for old carbon technologies, but due to a recognition of the resilience and transition issues.

Of course, not all countries can invest in an aatmanirbhar strategy. A small country like Singapore or Sri Lanka simply cannot be self-reliant in most areas, and must find other ways to build resilience. However, India is a large and diverse economy that is capable of an aatmanirbhar strategy, as its internal market can provide a large enough scale for viable operations in many sectors (albeit not all). This is the crux of the aatmanirbhar strategy.

CONCLUSION

The AatmaNirbhar Bharat approach is a key ingredient of the overall economic thinking of the Indian government. It is designed for an uncertain and unpredictable world. By investing in an economic framework that is both flexible and resilient, Indian policymakers are simply being pragmatic. This is not ideologically blinkered isolationism or protectionism. Moreover, the strategy is open to evolution. What may make sense at one point of time, may not work at another point.

The Covid-19 pandemic as well as geopolitical developments mean that there is a much greater appreciation today of the risks of an over-optimized, and over-integrated global system. This does not mean that we should plan for a de-globalized world. Far from it, rapid adoption of real-time communications technology during the pandemic (such as Zoom) have made us even more interconnected in some ways. The pandemic itself forced more global policy coordination in terms of travel protocols, vaccine distribution and so on. However, there is now greater acceptance of the basic idea of a more decentralized and distributed global system. This comes with greater national level capacity, at least within larger countries, where it is possible. In other words, we may be headed not just for an aatmanirbhar Bharat but for a more aatmanirbhar world.

9

AATMANIRBHARTA: THEN AND NOW

Dr Sanjaya Baru
Distinguished fellow, United Service Institution of India;
Former media advisor and chief spokesperson PMO
(under former Prime Minister Dr Manmohan Singh)

The concept of aatmanirbharta, that best translates in the English language as 'self-reliance', is not new to India or to the discipline of economics. Indeed, it lies deeply rooted in the ideas that shaped late industrialization in many countries.[1] India's struggle for freedom from colonial rule defined Indian thinking on the necessity not just of 'self-rule' but also of 'self-reliance'. Dadabhai Naoroji's classic treatise that linked India's mass poverty to colonial rule became the manifesto that defined the foundations of post-colonial economic policy.[2]

Inspired by the development experience of another Asian nation, Japan, nationalists like Swami Vivekananda and Mokshagundam Viswesvaraya gave a call for the spread of scientific education and modern industrialization. Among the prominent Indians who had visited Japan and were impressed by its scientific and technological prowess, combined with

---

[1]Gerschenkron, Alexander, *Economic Backwardness in Historical Perspective: A Book of Essays,* Belknap Press of Harvard University Press, Cambridge, Massachusetts, 1962.

[2]Naoroji, Dadabhai, *Poverty and Un-British Rule in India,* Swan Sonnenschein & Co., 1901.

deep patriotism and a distinct Japanese way of life, was none other than Swami Vivekananda. On his sea voyage to Chicago in 1893, where he addressed the World Congress of Religions, Swami Vivekananda met industrialist Jamsetji Tata. The two had stopped over in Japan and had long conversations about Japan's modernization and its lessons for India. On his return to India, Tata sought and secured Swamiji's blessings for setting up the Indian Institute of Science. The engineer Mokshagundam Visvesvaraya, founder of the Institution of Engineers and the Mysore Chamber of Commerce, returned home from a visit to Japan in 1898. He was hugely impressed by its economic development and industrial prowess and gave India the slogan, 'Industrialise or Perish!'[3]

THE INTELLECTUAL ROOTS OF AATMANIRBHARTA

Several developments around the beginning of the twentieth century shaped Indian thinking about the importance of industrialization and modernization. The communist revolution in Russia in 1917; the weakening of European power as a consequence of the First World War; and the rise of Asian nationalism (first in Japan, then in India and subsequently across Asia) contributed to new thinking in Asia on development policy. Indian economists also understood that if industrialization had to take root in the subcontinent, then local enterprise would require protection from external competition. This was a lesson learnt from the experience of all late industrializers like Russia, Germany, Japan and even the United States (US). It was during the inter-War period that the government of British India began to take policy steps aimed at promoting industrial development.

[3]'How Swami Vivekananda's Meeting With Jamsetji Tata Changed India's Scientific Vision', *GetBengal*, 3 March 2021, https://tinyurl.com/4ekvf624. Accessed on 21 June 2023.

There was considerable awareness among educated Indians, especially trained economists, about the extent of and the limits to development in colonial India. The economist, J. Krishnamurty, of the Delhi School of Economics, has put together some of the more important essays written by Indian economists through the first half of the twentieth century. These essays analyse the state of the economy and point to the kind of policy intervention required to promote economic and human development. The key propositions of most of these studies, as summed up by Krishnamurty, were as follows[4]:

- That the Indian economy was in a poor state of health marked by widespread poverty, lack of access to basic education and training in skills, a shortage of capital and a consequent low rate of investment;
- That Indian society was characterized by a variety of social practices that were seen as being inimical to economic development and the betterment of a wide cross section of people;
- That while the potential for development existed its realization would depend upon state support. The state would have to invest in education, agriculture, infrastructure and in ways through which productivity of the factors of production (land, labour and capital) could be enhanced.

Specific policy interventions were identified in every sector of the economy, ranging from sanitation and public health to banking and finance; and from land tenure systems and rural credit to deficit financing and public investment. The distinguished economist, Vaman Govind Kale (who was later elected president of the Indian Economic Conference), presented an essay at the Indian Industrial Conference at Lahore in 1909. In his essay,

[4]J. Krishnamurthy (ed.), *Towards Development Economics: Indian Contributions 1900-1945*, Oxford University Press, New Delhi, 2009.

'The Present Economic Condition of India', he summed up the situation in these words: 'An economic revolution is in progress in the land. The old national industries are dead and dying. New ones have not yet taken their place. The competition around us is keen and killing. We lack enterprise, capital, experience, scientific knowledge and sufficient State protection. Agriculture is in the most backward condition. Poverty and ignorance stalk over the land.'[5] Kale, like many in his generation, was deeply influenced by Japan's rise as a modern industrial nation.

In his submissions to the Indian Fiscal Commission (1921) Jehangir C. Coyajee, advocated a policy of 'discriminating protection' through supportive tariff rates.[6] The Fiscal Commission accepted this suggestion and laid down the criterion for such protection. That the industry securing tariff protection: (a) should have 'natural advantage' such as abundant supply of raw material, labour, adequate power and demand; (b) would require such protection for its development; and (c) would be able to face international competition once such protection is withdrawn.

The Indian National Congress, under the presidentship of Subhas Chandra Bose, constituted a National Planning Committee (NPC) in 1938 to prepare a policy framework for India's development. They recognized the importance of State support for economic development and eradication of poverty. The composition of the NPC is interesting and shows how the leadership of the national movement viewed the priorities for planned development in a free India. It included four industrialists (Purshottamdas Thakurdas [one of the principal authors of the so-called 'Bombay Plan'], Walchand Hirachand, A.D. Shroff and

[5]Kale, V.G., 'The Present Economic Condition of India', *Towards Development Economics: Indian Contributions 1900–1945,* J. Krishnamurthy (ed.), Oxford University Press, New Delhi, 2009, p. 16.

[6]Coyajee, Jehangir C., *Towards Development Economics: Indian Contributions 1900–1945,* J. Krishnamurthy (ed.), Oxford University Press, New Delhi, 2009, pp. 63–84.

Ambalal Sarabhai); five scientists (Meghnad Saha, A.K. Saha, Nazir Ahmed, V.S. Dubey and J.C. Ghosh); two economists (K.T. Shah and Radha Kamal Mukherjee); an engineer (M. Visvesvaraya); a labour leader (N.M. Joshi); and, a Gandhian (J.C. Kumarappa).[7]

The composition reflected the fact that there were several strands of thinking on the direction of the economic policy. Mahatma Gandhi was known for his views about safeguarding cottage industries and the village economy. Indian business leaders sought rapid industrialization. The rising labour movement sought a socialist economy. Nehru himself was deeply committed to promoting the role of modern science and technology in economic development.

While developments around the world (especially in Europe, Russia and Japan) greatly influenced Indian thinking on economic policy, there was a vibrant debate among Indian political and intellectual leaders about the direction economic policy should take. Adherents of Mahatma Gandhi's views promoted the concept of Gandhian economics, giving primacy to the village economy and to the protection of traditional crafts. Influenced by the impressive achievements of the then Soviet Union, the socialists advocated nationalization of private property, land reforms and public investment. The emerging Indian business leadership wanted a mixed economy in which state support would be available for private enterprise, and the government would undertake land reforms and invest in education and basic services.

The first and most promising effort at shaping economic policy was made by a group of business leaders led by Purushottamdas Thakurdas. He was a member of the NPC and may have been familiar with its initial work. He brought together India's top business leaders—J.R.D. Tata, G.D. Birla, Lala Shri Ram—as well as economists and administrators like Ardeshir Dalal and John

---

[7]Chakravarty, Bidyut, 'Jawaharlal Nehru and Planning, 1938–41: India at the Crossroads', *Modern Asian Studies*, Vol. 26, No. 2, May 1992, p. 282.

Mathai (later a minister of finance in Nehru's first cabinet) to put together a document that became famous as the Bombay Plan. Published in 1944, the document was titled *A Plan of Economic Development for India*. In many ways, the Bombay Plan reflected many of the views expressed by the NPC. These views included the emphasis on the role of government in promoting industrial and agricultural development; investing in education; housing and health; and in infrastructure development.

The principal objective of the Bombay Plan was 'to bring about a doubling of the present per capita income within a period of fifteen years from the time the plan comes into operation'.[8] It emphasized the need for public investment in capital goods industry and power generation, reduced dependence on foreign capital and imported consumer goods. The Plan did explicitly state that once domestic private sector had come into its own and had adequate capital and capability, the government should vacate the industrial sector and allow the private sector to grow. The authors of the Plan undertook detailed statistical analyses of the needs of the economy and tried to arrive at the best estimates possible. These estimates were of the actual cash required for investment in various sectors; the actual food production required for the country to offer all its citizens a minimum healthy diet; the output of cement, steel and other materials required to provide housing for all; the total textile production required to provide clothing for all and so on.

The Bombay Plan was quite obviously influenced by the thinking within the NPC. However, it sought to distinguish itself by emphasizing the role of private enterprise and viewing the public sector as a 'transitional' necessity rather than as a permanent feature of post-colonial development. Congress leaders like Subhas Chandra Bose and Jawaharlal Nehru (who played

---

[8]Mariwala, Vibhav, 'Don't Blame Nehru's Socialism for Air India Fate. Read the 1944 Bombay Plan First', *The Print*, 26 October 2021, https://tinyurl.com/3ee5hrez. Accessed on 30 June 2023.

an important role in the NPC) placed greater emphasis on the role of the State, influenced by the successful experience of industrialization in the then Soviet Union. However, the authors of the Bombay Plan were prominent Indian industrialists who saw domestic business as capable of playing a larger role in economic development over time.

The Bombay Plan was a unique document in terms of its detailed specifics. Giving a 15-year macroeconomic objective, it outlined the steps needed to get there. Nowhere in the developing world had such a document been written before.[9] The plan was based on the assumption that the government could 'create' money to finance development, through deficit financing, and need not feel constrained by its current revenue generating capacity. The Plan also recognized the need for land reforms aimed at giving the direct producer, the tiller, a stake in land improvement. This was needed to boost productivity of both land and labour. The interesting thing about the Bombay Plan was its focus on public investment—not just in industrial development, but also in education and health. The document explicitly stated: 'The real capital of a country consists of its resources in materials and manpower, and money is simply a means of mobilising these resources and canalising them into specific forms of activity.'[10]

PLANNING AND SELF-RELIANCE

It is these ideas that shaped India's First and Second Five Year Plan (1952–62). They helped ensure that India became one of the fastest growing post-colonial developing countries during

---

[9]Baru, Sanjaya, and Meghnad Desai (eds.), *The Bombay Plan: Blueprint for Economic Resurgence,* Rupa Publications, New Delhi, 2018.

[10]Jayadev, Arjun, 'Emergent Nation State and the Class of Capitalists through the Lens of the Bombay Plan', *Economic and Political Weekly,* Vol. LIV, No. 43, October 2019, https://tinyurl.com/5n7hrfxb. Accessed on 21 June 2023.

the 1950s. However, Indian policymakers made three mistakes during this decade. First, there was inadequate appreciation of the importance of investing in universal basic education and skill development. Second, there was inadequate appreciation of the role of foreign trade in building a competitive industrial economy. Third, there was inadequate attention paid to regional and rural development. As a consequence, several constraints began to impinge on India's growth process in the 1960s and '70s.

In managing these challenges, the state became increasingly intrusive. Private enterprise was curtailed and inward-orientation of industrial and trade policy took root. The Union government created several institutions of excellence but paid inadequate attention to school, college and technical education. The so-called 'licence permit control raj' came to be established and high tariff walls encouraged the growth of inefficient industrialization. The neglect of agrarian reform and agricultural development resulted in a food crisis in the mid-1960s, spurring the government to promote the Green Revolution.

In East Asia, on the other hand, we see developing economies invest in human capital. This enabled them to promote labour productivity and globally competitive firms.[11] While most East Asian economies pursued labour-intensive industrialization, Indian industrialization was excessively capital- and import-intensive. Consequently, by the 1980s, many East Asian economies had become more industrially developed than India. China too began to catch up as it liberalized its trade and industrial policies.

LOOKING AND LEARNING FROM THE EAST

It was only in 1991 that India woke up to the 'Asian economic miracle', and began to encourage private enterprise and foreign

[11]Amsden, Alice, *The Rise of 'The Rest': Challenges to the West from Late-Industrializing Economies*, Oxford University Press, 2001.

trade. Thanks to the new economic thinking unleashed by the then Prime Minister (PM) P.V. Narasimha Rao and his Finance Minister Dr Manmohan Singh, India's economic growth accelerated after the mid-1990s. India's share of world trade also more than doubled from around 0.5 per cent to over 1.5 per cent. While average annual rate of growth of national income was 3.5 per cent in the period 1950–80, it increased to 5.5 per cent in 1980–2000 and to over 7.5 per cent in 2000–18 (as shown in Table 1).

Table 1

India's Economic Growth: 1950–2018

Sectors	**Growth (in per cent) from 1950–2018**						
	1950s	**1960s**	**1970s**	**1980s**	**1991–2003**	**2003–08**	**2012–18**
Industry	5.8	6.2	4.4	6.4	6.0	8.5	7.2
Services	4.2	5.2	4.0	6.3	7.0	10.5	7.9
Real GDP	3.6	4.0	2.9	5.6	5.5	8.7	6.9

Source: Annual Economic Survey, different years, author's calculations

Narasimha Rao's, 'Look East Policy' was not merely a foreign policy initiative. It was also an economic lesson for India. The Indian leadership told the country to 'look East' and learn from its experience. It was no longer the nineteenth-century experience of a Japan that so inspired Swami Vivekananda and Visvesvaraya. East Asia was full of 'miracle' and 'tiger' economies that were emerging as the new engines of global growth. India looked East and altered its growth model.

While the economy did perform better during the post-liberalization era, a large part of the growth was due to the impressive performance of the services sector. This sector had benefitted from the investment made in higher education, especially in engineering, electronics, medicine, biotechnology and pharmacology. The share of the manufacturing sector increased from around 9 per cent in 1950 to 15 per cent by 1990 and to a further 16 per cent by 1995. However, it remained stuck at that level for an entire decade there after.

THE MANUFACTURING PLAN

To examine and address the challenge of stagnation in manufacturing growth, former PM Manmohan Singh constituted the National Manufacturing Competitiveness Council (NMCC) in 2005. The NMCC produced a National Strategy on Manufacturing (2006) that set a target of raising this share to 20 per cent by 2020. The first variant of a 'Make in India' programme was launched. The Planning Commission then produced a document titled, *The Manufacturing Plan* which blandly stated:

> Currently, India's manufacturing sector contributes about 16 per cent to the GDP, and India's share in world manufacturing is only 1.8 per cent. This is in stark contrast to China; where manufacturing contributes 34 per cent to the GDP and is 13.7 per cent of world manufacturing—up from 2.9 per cent in 1991. India's growth has been on the back of a booming services sector which contributes 62.5 per cent of the GDP. These statistics clearly indicate that while manufacturing has not been the engine of growth for the Indian economy, it now needs to grow at a much faster rate.[12]

The Planning Commission's *The Manufacturing Plan* is probably the most comprehensive assessment and strategy for accelerating the pace of growth of Indian manufacturing. It was comprehensive because it did not look at the manufacturing sector in isolation from the rest of the economy. It underscored the importance

---

[12]*The Manufacturing Plan: Strategies for Accelerating Growth of Manufacturing in India in the 12th Five Year Plan and Beyond*, Planning Commission, Government of India, 2012.

of investment in education and skill development; increasing labour and capital productivity; investing in research and development; and enhancing the technological foundations of Indian manufacturing. The Plan defined five specific objectives[13]:

1. Increase manufacturing sector growth to about 2–4 per cent more than GDP growth to make it the engine of growth for the economy, and increase share to about 25 per cent of overall GDP by 2025.
2. Increase the rate of job creation in manufacturing to create about 100 million additional jobs by 2025.
3. Increase 'depth' in manufacturing, with focus on the level of domestic value addition.
4. Enhance global competitiveness of Indian manufacturing through appropriate policy support.
5. Ensure sustainability of growth, particularly with regard to the environment.

The 'Make in India' programme launched by PM Narendra Modi was nothing more than a recasting of the Manmohan Singh government's 'Manufacturing Plan'. The Modi government's programme included additional sectors like tourism within the plan. Despite the best of intentions, the share of manufacturing in GDP has remained stuck at around 16 per cent of GDP over the past decade. It is also not likely to rise to the target of 25 per cent by 2025.

Concerned about the stubborn stagnation of this ratio, the Modi government initially tried to use trade policy as an instrument to promote manufacturing. It alleged that India's liberal trade policy and the large number of free trade agreements (FTAs) signed with trading partners had contributed to a process of stunted industrialization, if not de-industrialization. In response to an inward-oriented trade policy, with hikes in tariffs, India

---

[13]Ibid.

experienced a slowing down of its export growth.

It took some time for the government's policymakers to understand that given global supply chains and global value-chain linkages, export growth is linked to import growth. One feeds the other. China emerged as a manufacturing and trading superpower by promoting both export and import growth simultaneously.

MAKE IN INDIA, MAKE FOR THE WORLD

Recognizing this link between export and import growth, the government has more recently changed its trade policy by redefining the 'Make in India' policy as 'Make in India and Make for the World'. This helped re-establish the link between manufacturing and trade policy. The government has also redeployed industrial policy by introducing the production linked incentive (PLI) scheme, and a range of other fiscal incentives. It has also undertaken financial and structural reform, aimed at facilitating new investment.

Yet, there is little evidence of any significant increase in the share of manufacturing in the GDP (gross domestic product). The one sector in which Make in India could have progressed rapidly was the defence manufacturing sector. The government took several decisions to encourage localization of manufacturing defence equipment. However, the progress so far has been very limited.

This draws attention to several underlying factors contributing to stunted industrial development in India. First and foremost, the size of India's industrial sector remains constrained by the extent of the home market. The expansion of the home market based on the income growth generated by the Green Revolution (and the emergence of a larger middle class that found employment within the services economy), fuelled the industrial demand of the post-1991 period. However, this home market growth seems to have tapered off since the mid-2010s.

While export demand sustained economic growth in the

period 2005–15, there has since been a slowdown in export demand as well. This was partly on account of global factors, including the slowdown in global trade after 2009–10; and partly on account of domestic policies, including trade, tariff and exchange rate policies. No rapidly industrializing economy has grown on the basis of the home market alone. All newly industrializing economies, including continental economies like China, have seen the share of manufacturing in their respective national income rise. This was both on account of an expansion of the home market and on the basis of an increase in their share of global trade. Reviving export growth is, therefore, critical to the success of the new AatmaNirbhar Bharat Abhiyan.

This draws attention to a fundamental change in outlook in the Indian policymaker's attitude to foreign trade that was the basis of the policy reset of 1991 and requires reiteration once again. Many post-colonial societies had been ravaged by colonial trade policy and persistent neocolonialism of the post-War period. In India too, foreign trade was viewed as a dependency creating process that would undermine national economic development. Andre Gunder Frank's classic treatise on dependence and development pointed to the in-equalizing impact of trade between developing and developed economies, and shaped much of the inward-orientation of many developing economies.[14]

It was, however, the East and Southeast Asian experience of trade-based development that changed development thinking on trade policy. Rather than viewing trade as creating 'dependence', the 'miracle' economies of Asia pointed to the virtuous cycle of 'inter-dependence' created by trade between developed and developing economies.[15] That India could push both import and export growth

---

[14]Gunder Frank, Andre, 'Capitalism and Underdevelopment in Latin America', *Monthly Review Press*, New York, 1967.

[15]Baru, Sanjaya, 'The Economic Imperative to Indian Foreign Policy', *India and the World: Essays on Geoeconomics and Foreign Policy*, Sanjaya Baru (ed.),

simultaneously after 1991 lent credence to this view in India.

India's slower economic development compared to the economies of East and Southeast Asia also draws attention to the inadequate investment in human capital. Economist Surjit Bhalla (presently India's executive director on the board of the International Monetary Fund and an economic advisor to PM Modi's government) has convincingly argued in his book, *The New Wealth of Nations*, that investment in the education of the populace created the firm foundation on which Asia's rapidly growing economies grew.[16] This is where India has lagged behind and this is where we must focus our energies. Investing in education and creating human capital to turn a large population from being viewed as a social liability is key to aatmanirbharta.

An improvement in capital and labour productivity, however, requires an all-of-the-economy approach to reform. It has to begin with investment in good quality basic and technical education; healthcare and livelihood security; adequate social and economic infrastructure that contribute to the exploitation of scale economies; and reduced transaction and transport costs. While policy has sought to address these challenges over time, much remains to be done. A focus on these institutional aspects of development, and on improving the quality and productivity of human capital, is key to building an aatmanirbhar Bharat.

NEW CHALLENGES

The experience of the past seven years suggests that the stagnation in the share of manufacturing in GDP is not linked mainly to external trade policy. Rather, the causes of a slowdown in manufacturing growth seem to lie elsewhere. Several factors may have contributed to the slow progress of the 'Make in India' and

---

Academic Foundation, Delhi, 2016.

[16]Bhalla, Surjit, *The New Wealth of Nations*, Simon & Schuster, New York, 2017.

AatmaNirbhar Bharat policy. Principle among these would be: (a) sub-optimal scale economies in Indian manufacturing; and (b) persistently low capital and labour productivity. During the decade 1998–2008, Chinese manufacturing recorded significantly higher total factor productivity across several industries compared to India.[17] This draws attention to the need for institutional reform aimed at enhancing total factor productivity. This will have to be the cornerstone of any strategy of AatmaNirbhar Bharat.

More recently, new challenges have presented themselves. Responding to the rise of Asian economies and the relative decline of the trans-Atlantic economies, many developed economies have become increasingly protectionist. Even when they do wish to negotiate FTAs with India, they continue to insist on the inclusion of what India has long regarded as 'non-trade' issues. From labour standards to environment standards, what were once called the 'Singapore Issues' in multilateral trade negotiations and trade policy is getting linked to matters of domestic, economic and social policy. Even in the case of the recently launched Indo–Pacific Economic Framework (IPEF) there has been a flagging of these issues, in the name of 'fair trade'.

The case for 'fair trade', rather than 'free trade', has been made by developed economies. This is because they are facing an anti-globalization tirade at home from those who have not relatively benefitted from globalization. All this contributes to an increasingly challenging global trade environment, and this reinforces the relevance of AatmaNirbhar Bharat in economic development.

Attention must also be drawn to the more recent challenge posed by the imposition of economic and financial sanctions by the US (United States) and the EU (European Union), in response to the Russian invasion of Ukraine. These sanctions are targeted against Russia but have impacted other countries,

[17]Dong, Xiao-yuan, 'Manufacturing productivity in China and India: The Role of Institutional Changes', *China Economic Review*, 2009, pp. 754–66.

including India, in a variety of ways including through a spike in energy and commodity prices. In an assessment of the economic consequences of the Ukraine war, the World Bank identified trade and investment channels through which countries would be affected. These included disruption of commodity markets (especially food and energy), logistic networks, supply chains, foreign direct investment flows and specific sectoral shortages. The World Bank report estimated that world trade could drop by 1 per cent, with global real GDP growth reduced by 1.2 per cent. Beyond these direct effects, the World Bank concluded saying:

> The war's long-term implications for global trade and investment will largely depend on how governments respond to the changing geopolitical environment. Russia and Ukraine rank among the top seven global producers and exporters of wheat, corn, barley, sunflower seeds, and sunflower oil. Russia is also a major supplier of fossil fuels, such as crude oil and natural gas, in addition to fertilizer and agricultural commodities. Disruptions of these supplies are fuelling a surge in prices, with negative consequences for global trade and welfare and asymmetric effects on exporting and importing countries.[18]

In a candid assessment of the impact of the Russia–Ukraine war and Western economic sanctions, Dr Michael Debabrata Patra (a deputy governor of the Reserve Bank of India [RBI]) recently observed:

> The escalation of geopolitical tensions into war from late February 2022 delivered a brutal blow to the global economy, battered as it had been through 2021 by the pandemic, supply chain and logistics disruptions, elevated inflation and bouts of financial market turbulence triggered by diverging

[18]'The Impact of the War in Ukraine on Global Trade and Investment', *elibrary, World Bank Group*, https://tinyurl.com/2a6x8e9p. Accessed on 19 July 2023.

> paths of monetary policy normalisation. Since then, the global macroeconomic outlook has become suddenly overcast with the economic costs of the war and retaliatory sanctions. Emerging market and developing economies (EMDEs) are bearing the brunt of these geopolitical spill overs as I speak, despite being bystanders. Capital outflows and currency depreciations have tightened external funding conditions, and along with elevated debt levels, put their hesitant and incomplete recoveries in danger. Heightened volatility in financial markets and surges in prices of commodities—especially of energy, metals, grain futures and fertilizers—have accentuated risks to growth, inflation and financial stability.[19]

The reason why these sanctions can be more worrisome for the world economy, especially emerging markets, is because they hit at the very roots of globalization. These are the roots that have underpinned global income and trade growth, and have reduced world poverty over the past quarter century. Former RBI governor, Raghuram Rajan has dubbed them as weapons of mass destruction. He said:

> When fully unleashed, sanctions, too, are weapons of mass destruction. They may not topple buildings or collapse bridges, but they destroy firms, financial institutions, livelihoods, and even lives. Like military WMDs, they inflict pain indiscriminately, striking both the culpable and the innocent. And if they are used too widely, they could reverse the process of globalization that has allowed the modern world to prosper.[20]

---

[19]Debabrata Patra, Michael, 'Geopolitical Spillovers and the Indian Economy', *BIS*, 24 June 2022, https://tinyurl.com/ycp2tntz. Accessed on 30 June 2023.

[20]Rajan, Raghuram G., 'Economic Weapons of Mass Destruction', *Project Syndicate*, 17 March 2022, https://tinyurl.com/34ax6fcc. Accessed on 21 June 2023.

Two days after the Russian invasion of Ukraine, the US, the EU, the UK, Canada, France, Germany and Italy announced a joint action to remove some Russian banks from the SWIFT (Society for Worldwide Interbank Financial Telecommunications) system. They effectively prevented the Russian central bank from using its foreign exchange reserves to undermine the enforcement of sanctions in any way. Shutting Russia out of the SWIFT payments system and freezing Russia's foreign exchange denominated accounts is a warning to Russia today. But they also constitute a warning to all countries for the future. India will have to re-examine its foreign exchange management policy, consider in what form to maintain its forex reserves and in what currencies to conduct trade in years to come. Trust is key to the power of currencies, and the post-Ukraine war sanctions have diluted global trust in major western currencies (including the USD, GBP and EUR).

It has been reported that India's biggest cement producer, UltraTech Cement has recently paid for coal imports from Russia in Chinese Yuan.[21] While the Rupee–Rouble arrangement of the Cold War era has not been resumed, it may well be at some point. India also has a domestic option of further promoting its own payment platform, the Unified Payments Interface (UPI). The UPI system is far more advanced than any other system, apart from SWIFT, and can easily find users in countries like Nepal, the UAE (United Arab Emirates), Singapore, the UK and so on.

The US–EU decision to freeze Russian financial assets raises larger questions about the security offered by large foreign exchange reserves. After the balance of payments crisis of 1991, when India's forex reserves dipped below US$1 billion, and after the experience with the post-Pokhran II sanctions imposed by the US, Japan and some other OECD economies in 1998, India chose

[21]'India's Top Cement Maker Paying for Russian Coal in Chinese Yuan', *The Times of India*, 29 June 2022, https://tinyurl.com/52x4wkw2. Accessed on 21 June 2023.

to build its forex reserves as a security against future challenges. This approach was adopted by several developing countries after the Asian financial crisis of 1998, and further continued after the trans-Atlantic financial crisis of 2008. The Western decision to freeze Russia's Dollar, Euro and Yen assets, and shutting it out of the SWIFT system presents a serious cautionary message to India about the limits to its own strategic autonomy presented by large forex reserves.

Going beyond the purely economic and financial consequences of the sanctions, there is the larger issue of adherence to principles of law and trust. Many of the financial sanctions imposed by the US and its allies amount to a breach of trust, and non-adherence to legal commitments. It is worth noting that despite a series of wars with Pakistan and the challenge of cross-border terrorism emanating from within its territory, India never reneged on its commitments under the Indus Water Treaty.

The weaponization of economic and financial links and the reneging of contracts that have economic consequences hurt the entire populace of target countries. They amount to the targeting of innocent civilians, in a battle between armed forces. Clearly, the Ukraine war sanctions have raised larger issues of global governance and globalization that will remain for a long time and require closer study by India's policymakers.

In this emerging context, the importance of greater self-reliance in economic development, as well as in defence preparedness, cannot be underestimated. India's 'Make in India' programme for defence equipment manufacturing gains greater urgency given these new global developments. Equally, a more cautious approach towards global finance, global financial integration and the management of balance of payments is warranted. The external economic environment has become uncertain, and has been destabilized by recent events and actions. All this only reinforces the relevance of the AatmaNirbhar Bharat Abhiyan.

10

AATMANIRBHAR BHARAT: THE VISION AND ITS CHALLENGES

[*]Dr Rajiv Kumar and [**]Dr Shashank Shah

[*]Former vice chairman, NITI Aayog
[**]Senior specialist, NITI Aayog

AATMANIRBHAR BHARAT IN THE GLOBAL CONTEXT

According to Angus Maddison, in his seminal article in the *The World Economy*, India's share of worldwide gross domestic product (GDP) in the first century AD was 32.9 per cent. A millennium later, in eleventh century AD, India continued to be the largest contributor to global GDP at 28.9 per cent. In 1700, when the Mughals had ruled India for nearly 200 years, India's share was still a very formidable 24.4 per cent. It's no wonder that Columbus and other buccaneers set out in search of India, the proverbial 'bird of gold', to try and establish trading relations between a relatively poor Europe and a prosperous India (Bharat). Over the next 120 years (prior to the beginning of British colonial rule), which saw perpetual conflict among different ruling groups, India's share in global GDP declined to 16 per cent.[1]

With the onset of the colonial rule and its concomitant wealth

[1]Maddison, Angus, *The World Economy: A Millennial Perspective*, Organisation for Economic Co-operation and Development, 2001, https://tinyurl.com/bdhpcsy4. Accessed on 21 June 2023.

drain, India's share in world GDP was reduced to a mere 4 per cent by 1950. Today, in the second decade of the twenty-first century, India's share in world output remains at about 4 per cent in nominal terms and about 8 per cent when estimated in PPP (Purchasing Power Parities) terms. Our share in global manufacturing was also more than 20 per cent prior to the deindustrialization proactively goaded by our colonial masters. It plummeted to a mere 2 per cent by 1947. We managed to increase this only to 3.1 per cent by 2019. In comparison, China, which also suffered from colonial exploitation and deindustrialization, has been able to raise its share in global GDP from 4.5 per cent in 1950 to more than 15 per cent in 2020. Its share in global manufacturing, which was significantly lower than India's in the seventeenth and eighteenth centuries, was more than 28 per cent in 2019. This was a clear 10 per cent higher than the share of the US, which was for long the largest manufacturing economy in the world.

Given the above context, aatmanirbharta means restoring India's share in world GDP and in global manufacturing to at least the same level as it was prior to the beginning of colonial rule. Therefore, we have to set ourselves the target of achieving at least a 16 per cent share in global GDP, and a 20 per cent share in global manufacturing for true aatmanirbharta.

Increasing our share in global manufacturing is critical for two fundamental reasons. First, that despite all the chatter about robotization and AI-driven machines, manufacturing will continue to be the largest generator of good quality jobs for the next few decades. Secondly, for a continental-sized economy like ours, we cannot indefinitely afford to depend upon imports of manufactured products (especially those having strategic importance). The present government has clearly recognized that continuing to import more than 70 per cent of our strategic equipment requirements is simply untenable, and leaves us very vulnerable to geopolitical pressures. Global quality defence production, both for meeting domestic needs and for exports, can become a major employment generator.

Dramatically reducing our dependence on energy imports is another critical aspect of building an aatmanirbhar Bharat. Our current near-complete dependence on imported energy can become a significant security problem as a large proportion is sourced through the Persian Gulf, where our logistics can be easily put under pressure by unfriendly powers. This vulnerability could constrain us from playing our due role on the global stage.

Production or generation of sufficient volumes of non-fossil energy is surely another critical aspect of becoming aatmanirbhar. India imports 85 per cent of its crude oil requirement (5 million barrels a day).[2] Even for our renewable energy generation, there is fairly high level of import dependence. This must be reduced. India is the second largest producer of coal, with nearly 400 years' worth of domestic coal reserves. Yet, it is the second largest importer of coal. Despite a declining trend over the last 3 years, India imported 209 million tons of coal in the financial year (FY) 2022 worth $30.62 billon. We need to undertake R&D (research and development) projects to use our vast coal reserves such that the carbon emitted can be safely sequestered, and clean coal technologies can be put to use to reduce our dependence on imported energy. [3]

Thus, to achieve aatmanirbharta, over the next 25 years (the Amritkaal) we must strive to attain four objectives. One, increase our share in global GDP to at least 16 per cent. Two, increase the share of the Indian manufacturing sector in global manufacturing to 20 per cent. Three, reduce our dependence on imported energy to a bare minimum. Four, successfully expand

[2]'India imports 85% of its Crude Oil: Sources', *The Economic Times*, 18 March 2022, https://tinyurl.com/4ttymnts. Accessed on 21 June 2023.

[3]'Coal Import Declines to 209 Million Ton in 2021-22 against 248 MT in 2019–20', *PIB Delhi*, 2 June 2022, https://tinyurl.com/yv657849. Accessed on 21 June 2023.

our share in world trade from the present level of less than 3 per cent (taking merchandise and services trade together) to at least 12 per cent.

In our understanding, it is vital to view AatmaNirbhar Bharat in the global context. Without this vision of restoring India's position in the world economy, we face the strong downside risk of equating aatmanirbharta with self-sufficiency to be achieved in a closed economy. This has been tried in the past—in the 1960s, '70s and '80s—and has proven to be disastrous. The current evolving context of increasing fragmentation of global markets in the aftermath of the Ukrainian conflict, and consequent fears of rising protectionism in a few countries, should not result in another bout of export pessimism. India's economic growth has suffered in the past due to this sentiment, which should not be allowed to take roots again. India cannot achieve its goals of raising per capita incomes to a middle-income economy status without recourse to external demand, and better access to global markets.

India is a country with a very large population. However, that does not directly translate into being a large economy with high levels of purchasing power. Every country attempting to successfully make the transition from a low-income economy to a middle- or high-income economy has had to take recourse to external demand. We should not try and prove to be an exception. Ramping up our exports of both merchandise and services, and garnering a larger share in world flows of both goods and services, will keep us globally competitive. It will also push us to achieve the required scales of production; improve the quality of our services to world standards; generate increased quantum of quality employment opportunities; and promote goal-oriented R&D.

All these efforts, taken in the global context, will yield the desired goal of a higher share in global trade and manufacturing. Along with this we will also have minimal import dependence for energy and a consequent higher share in global output. We discuss the challenges in achieving these goals in the following sections.

RAISING INDIA'S SHARE IN WORLD TRADE

India was traditionally a trading nation, with our globally-renowned traders travelling to nearly all parts of the Old World. Indian traders travelled with their much demanded goods to Europe; to Indonesia (the Prambanan Temples in Yogyakarta built by the Hindu Sanjay Dynasty in 850 AD reflect the majesty of Indian traders who established a kingdom through peaceful means, not by conquest); to Cambodia (as testified by the Angkor Wat Temple complex built in the twelfth century AD); to Myanmar (then Burma, where the hundreds of Bangan Temples in Mandalay are testament to the thriving trade between Indian and Chinese traders); and to West Asia and Eastern Africa (where Indian presence is historically recognized since the second century BC).

India prospered when it was a leader in global trade. Colonial rule forcibly brought a stop to that prosperity with a clear objective of destroying the much-vaunted Indian handicrafts and incipient manufacturing. India was reduced to being a supplier of raw materials and indentured labour for its colonial masters. Consequently, our share in world exports declined to a mere 2.53 per cent in 1947. This showed up dramatically in rising levels of poverty, frequent famines and a population that was merely at survival levels with a per capita annual income of ₹11,570 in 1950. It further declined to only 0.4 per cent in 1980. Thankfully, trade started expanding again after reforms in 1991.[4]

The share of trade in global trade flows went up to 2.1 per cent by 1990 and further to 2.7 per cent by 2010, as a result of the liberalization of the '90s. Since then, India's share in global merchandise trade has stagnated at less than 2 per cent. But its share in services, buoyed by IT-enabled software services, increased

[4]'India: April 1998', *World Trade Organization*, 1 April 1998, https://tinyurl.com/ycy49t23. Accessed on 21 June 2023.

from 0.5 per cent in 1995 to 3.5 per cent in 2019. To achieve the goal of raising the share of trade to pre-colonial levels will require a concerted and converged effort from all relevant stakeholders. The following suggestions may merit policy attention.

First, instead of preparing a pan-India export promotion policy—which is akin to Brussels producing an export policy for all EU countries combined—each state should be encouraged to design and implement its own Exim policy with clearly-stated timebound goals, and selection of priority export sectors. This will bring about a much-needed focus on exports in every state, and help generate quality employment.

Second, export industries should get their energy and other inputs at global-comparable prices. They should not be expected to subsidize household consumption by being charged higher tariffs for their energy, logistics and raw-material inputs. This again should be done by taking the states on board.

Third, the RBI (Reserve Bank of India) must ensure that the exchange rate remains neutral between exports and imports. It should not penalize exports by keeping the rupee exchange rate over-valued, when measured in terms of the real effective exchange rate. This will also encourage domestic generation of energy rather than just encouraging imports by keeping them cheaper.

Finally, export policy in each state should be sector agnostic. As many countries have demonstrated, exports of minerals, agro-products, low-tech manufactured products or services (such as medical, education and mass tourism) are as valuable in generating employment and foreign exchange earnings as high-tech exports.

RAISING THE SHARE OF INDIAN MANUFACTURING IN WORLD MARKETS

Over the last 30 years, successive Central governments have declared their goal of achieving a 25 per cent share of manufacturing in the country's GDP. This has not been achieved because of the present and evolving structure of the economy, and currently stands at 17 per cent. To achieve this ambitious target, we should focus on raising the share of Indian manufacturing in specific sectors in world markets. If successful, the share of manufacturing in domestic GDP will also rise simultaneously.

This is a propitious time, both externally and domestically, for India to achieve this objective. Global companies are now trying to diversify away from China, the global leader, and reducing country risk. With the sharp rise in domestic wages in China in recent years Chinese companies are themselves under pressure to relocate capacities overseas. They are vacating low technology sectors, as they seek to raise productivity levels in line with rising wages. Domestically, it is evident that governance capability in India has significantly improved over the last eight years. India improved its position in global ranking for ease of doing business from 142 to 63, and finally tackled the problems of too much regulatory cholesterol in the system (that particularly stymies manufacturing).

The most significant reflection of this change is the implementation of the production linked incentive (PLI) schemes across 13, mostly sunrise, sectors of the economy. The government has committed ₹2 trillion ($27 billion) to be given out as direct cash incentives to firms which are selected for these schemes, after they achieve the stipulated targets. It is estimated by NITI Aayog that, if successful, PLIs will generate $500 billion of new manufacturing sector output and 200,000 quality jobs. To ensure the success of PLIs, its implementation should be monitored regularly and rigorously. Coordination with state governments is instrumental in getting the capacities up and running, will be critical. Therefore, it is advisable that an independent agency be given the authority and responsibility to ensure its successful implementation.

It is also important that the tariff structures be constantly monitored and changed to reflect changing global price and supply conditions. The time lag between changes in global markets and domestic regime has to be minimized, to provide a necessary competitive edge to Indian companies. But at the same time, all tariff protection has to come with a clearly defined sunset clause. Otherwise, we could quickly slip into the earlier paradigm of Indian companies being indefinitely protected while becoming globally uncompetitive. They will then be unable to increase their share in global markets. PLIs, if successful, can be a huge step in raising India's manufacturing sector's presence globally.

Along with the PLIs, states can be urged to come up with their own version of industrial policies. This can take the shape of 'one district, one product', a scheme launched by Government of India with an objective of balanced reginal development. This scheme would be implemented across all the district of the country for enabling holistic social economic growth across all regions, or putting in place industrial clusters that benefit from synergies generated within the cluster. The focus has to be on creating globally competitive capacities, and not repeat the earlier practice of geographic and sector specific fiscal incentives. These incentives create distortions and are seen to be unsustainable.

To achieve a higher share in global markets for our manufacturing, Indians have to completely give up their 'fear of the ghost of the East India Company'. This has been overcome to a large extent as reflected in the Central government's policy of liberalizing nearly all sectors, including defence production for entry of foreign investors. This is bound to show positive results in due course. However, the Central government's initiatives must be reinforced with similar positive response from the state governments. We can and should prefer export-oriented foreign direct investment (FDI) which creates new capacities and generates additional employment. The present practice of combining the direct investment flows with private equity flows, that take over existing capacities and even take finance capital in the same category, has to be stopped. Such clearly segregated data should be made publicly available to assure the people that

FDI is generating both employment and foreign exchange. Finally, it will be useful to annually compare India's performance with other recipient countries. Even intra-state comparisons can be made to encourage them to focus their efforts on such positive FDI inflows.

ACHIEVING AATMANIRBHARTA IN ENERGY

By declaring that India should be self-sufficient for its energy requirements by 2047, Prime Minister (PM) Narendra Modi has emphatically pointed to the need for and the measures of achieving energy independence. Despite some scepticism, this is an eminently achievable goal. Many steps have already been taken in pursuit of this target. First, ethanol mixing with petrol has already crossed 10 per cent from a mere 1.8 per cent just seven years ago. This can and will increase to 20 per cent in the coming years, thereby reducing dependence on imported fossil fuel. Second, renewable energy targets have been ramped up to 450 gigawatt (GW) by 2030 and the good news is that about 150 GW was already installed by December 2021. Third, the electric mobility policy is being vigorously pursued by the Centre and 22 States having already announced their own policies. This will definitely reduce imported fossil fuel demand. Fourth, Indian Railways have announced ambitious investment plans to try and recover some of the share that was lost to road transport over the decades. Moreover, the target of 100 per cent electrification of railways is now well in sight. Fifth, with the promotion of projects under the PM Gati Shakti programme, seamless multi-modal transit will be encouraged. This will shift some of the freight traffic to less energy intensive modes like waterways and ropeways.

As is often remarked, Mother Nature did not provide India with abundant reserves of mineral oil and natural gas. But it has been endowed with infinite supplies of solar energy that can be used to produce 'green hydrogen'. With shore-based green hydrogen plants, the sea water can be desalinated using solar power and then converted to green ammonia for further conversion. Solar power plus hydrogen can be the cleanest aatmanirbhar energy solution for India. Already, commercial production of green hydrogen has commenced in relatively small plants which are now sought to be quickly upscaled. The vision of producing green hydrogen, at costs comparable to fossil fuel in energy equivalent terms, looks easily achievable within this decade. That will be the transformative breakthrough in reducing energy import dependence that policy must now push, with focus and convergence.

In the meantime, some challenges also need to be addressed. First, India remains one of the least explored geologies. This can change with the entry of private venture capital, for which the reforms have already been suggested by NITI Aayog. Second, domestic production of both oil and gas can be ramped up significantly by reducing the regulatory flab in the sector. The process has already started, but needs to be accelerated and concluded in a timebound manner. Third, the complex administrative pricing mechanism—which has been in place for decades—discourages investment in domestic gas production capacities. These should be replaced at the earliest with a rational, simple and transparent pricing system. Fourth, R&D activities in clean coal technologies should be taken up on a mission mode. This should be done with the same zeal and focus as has been done in our space and atomic energy programmes. Finally—though there are reservations about storage of nuclear waste—new advances in small modular nuclear reactors along with waste disposal technologies may be pursued within a timebound programme. Increasing the share of nuclear and hydro energy, both of which have significant untapped potential, can safely and certainly contribute towards minimizing our energy dependence on imports.

CONCLUSION

Aatmanirbharta should not be seen as a goal in itself, but as a means to regain India's share in the global economy and trade. This must be done while simultaneously improving the quality of life for the common Indian. India will achieve true aatmanirbharta when the world becomes dependent on us for its growth, and critical supplies. This was a reality in the pre-colonial period. Seen in this context, aatmanirbharta will become a driving principle for sustainable and inclusive growth that will help India achieve its ambitious yet desirable goals. Globally competitive manufacturing and trade flows will lead the way in achieving this goal. It will also imply that India will use the latest frontline technological breakthroughs, to achieve its energy independence through the vast expansion of green energies. Such a vision of AatmaNirbhar Bharat will inspire our young population to give their best to serve this national cause. AatmaNirbhar Bharat will thus become a *Jan Aandolan* (People's Movement), to support India's inexorable rise on the global stage.

11

AATMANIRBHAR BHARAT THROUGH INTERNATIONAL TRADE: OPPORTUNITIES AND THREATS

Prof. Abhijit Das

Former head and professor,

Centre for WTO Studies, Indian Institute of Foreign Trade

The AatmaNirbhar Bharat initiative, announced by Prime Minister (PM) Narendra Modi in 2020, has become the keystone of India's economic policymaking. Although the objectives and elements of this initiative have not been specifically articulated in any policy document, it is generally understood to include boosting the production of goods and services for domestic consumption and exports. It also envisages enhancing technological capabilities and encouraging investment, including from foreign sources, to propel Indian economy to a higher growth trajectory. However, AatmaNirbhar Bharat must not be misunderstood as restricting imports and seeking to produce most of the goods domestically. Instead, this initiative must be viewed from the perspective of using international trade strategically for securing the country's objectives.

Given the growing salience of international trade (for both goods and services) to the Indian economy, it is important to ask the following question: What role can international trade agreements play in fulfilling the aspirations underlying

AatmaNirbhar Bharat? This paper addresses this fundamental question in the background of India presently being engaged in negotiating free trade agreements (FTAs) with three trading partners that comprise developed countries—Canada, the European Union (EU) and the United Kingdom (UK).

Specifically, this paper examines the opportunities and challenges to the objectives of AatmaNirbhar Bharat that might arise from the FTAs. These challenges might be on the issues related to manufacturing, agriculture, government procurement, intellectual property rights, environment, digital trade and gender. It is relevant to note that as the outcomes of the FTA negotiations are likely to impose restrictions on the policy flexibilities (available to the government for taking initiatives to boost domestic production), these would have crucial implications for AatmaNirbhar Bharat.

No doubt, the final text which emerges from the FTA negotiations is what will be relevant for assessing the impact of the outcome of the negotiations on AatmaNirbhar Bharat. It is likely that some of the provisions in the past FTAs of Canada, EU and the UK would also be included in their FTAs with India. In order to assess the impact of India's FTAs with these three trading partners, it may be appropriate to use some of the provisions existing in their FTAs.

MANUFACTURING SECTOR

International trade agreements, particularly FTAs, provide an opportunity for India to enhance its exports of merchandise by seeking reduction in import tariffs by the partner country. As Canada, EU and the UK are characterized by large gross domestic product (GDP) and high per capita GDP (as shown in Table 1), FTAs with these trading partners offer exciting prospects for Indian exporters. The increased market size that may arise from an FTA may enable firms from India to exploit economies of scale, resulting in lower prices. It also helps them gain a relative advantage over excluded competing firms from other countries that do not enjoy preferential market access. FTA negotiations provide an opportunity for finalizing mutual recognition agreements, in respect of standards and conformity assessment procedures for goods having India's export interest. This can also play a crucial role in boosting India's exports, and contributing to AatmaNirbhar Bharat.

Table 1
Comparison of GDP and Per Capita GDP of India, Canada, the EU and the UK

Country/ Territory Name	**GDP (current US$ trillion) in 2021**	**GDP per capita (current US$) in 2021**
India	3.17	2,277
Canada	1.99	52,051
European Union (Excluding UK)	17.09	38,234
United Kingdom	3.19	47,334

Source: Data from database of World Development Indicators, Last Updated: 20 July 2022

It needs to be noted that import tariffs in the developed countries with whom India is in the process of negotiating FTAs—be it the EU, the UK or Canada—are already quite low in most sectors (Table 2). Thus, the boost that India's exports might enjoy from duty-free access into these countries under an FTA might be rather limited. In the EU and the UK, in the textiles and clothing sector, the FTA can, at best, help create a level playing field in import tariffs between Indian exporters and those from least-developed countries.

Table 2

Comparison of Average Bound Rates and MFN (Most Favoured Nation) Applied Duties in India, Canada, the EU and the UK

Product Groups	**Average Bound Duties**				**Average MFN Applied Duties (2021)**			
	India	**Canada**	**EU**	**UK**	**India**	**Canada**	**EU**	**UK**
Fish & fish products	135.7	1	12	12	30	0.9	11.5	10.8
Minerals & metals	38.3	2.7	1.9	1.9	11.8	1	2	0.8
Petroleum		6.4	3.2	3.2	9.2	0.9	2.5	1.6
Chemicals	39.6	4.4	4.6	4.5	10.3	0.7	4.5	3
Wood, paper, tec.	36.6	1.5	0.7	1	10.5	1	0.9	0.6
Textiles	27.3	10.6	6.5	6.5	25.5	2.3	6.5	5.1
Clothing	37.7	17.3	11.5	11.5	24.1	16.6	11.5	11.4
Leather, footwear, etc.	34.6	7.2	4.1	4.1	14.6	3.8	4.1	3.1
Non-electrical machinery	28.6	3.2	1.7	1.7	8.2	0.4	1.8	0.6
Electrical machinery	27.8	3.7	1.9	1.9	10.3	0.8	2.1	0.8
Transport equipment	35.7	5.6	4.5	4.5	31.1	5.5	4.7	3.2
Manufactures, NES	33.5	3.9	2	2	11.9	2.4	2.1	0.8

Source: Tariff Profiles 2022, WTO (World Trade Organization)

Can there be adverse consequences of FTAs with these three trading partners on AatmaNirbhar Bharat? While no two FTAs have identical provisions, it is also a reality that the developed countries follow a similar template in their FTAs. So if some of the provisions in the past FTAs of Canada, EU and the UK are also included in their FTA with India, then India would be required to comply with certain onerous obligations. A few of these obligations are as follows: prohibition on imposing export duties and taxes[1]; according to less favourable treatment of remanufactured goods than that accorded to equivalent goods in new condition[2]; and facilitating trade or removing barriers to trade of environmental/climate-friendly goods[3]. As discussed below, these obligations could have a crippling impact on some sectors of manufacturing in India, thereby undermining AatmaNirbhar Bharat.

India has, in the past, resorted to export duties for enhancing domestic availability of raw materials for giving a fillip to downstream processing industry. For example, India had been imposing an export tax of 40 per cent on exports of raw hides and skin which was reduced to 30 per cent in 2022.[4] India also imposes export duty on certain inputs of the steel industry. If a similar provision of prohibition on imposing export duties is included in

---

[1]See, for example: 'Article 2.12 Export Duties, Taxes or Other Charges', *Australia-UK FTA Official Text, Australian Government, Department of Foreign Affairs and Trade*, https://tinyurl.com/yed4zrr2. Accessed on 12 July 2023.

[2]See, for example: 'Article 2.15 Remanufactured Goods', *Australia-UK FTA Official Text, Australian Government, Department of Foreign Affairs and Trade*, https://tinyurl.com/yed4zrr2. Accessed on 12 July 2023.

[3]See, for example Article 12.11.2 of EU Singapore FTA, which requires parties to pay special attention to facilitating the removal of obstacles to trade and investment concerning climate-friendly goods and services.

'Article 12.11: Trade and Investment Promoting Sustainable Development', *Free Trade Agreement between the European Union and the Republic of Singapore, European Commission*, https://tinyurl.com/mr2efbvx. Accessed on 12 July 2023.

[4]'CUSTOMS Notification No 10 of 2022 dated 1st February, 2022', Government of India, Ministry of Finance (Department of Revenue), 1 February 2022.

the FTA with India, then it will adversely affect the ability of the government to create a thriving downstream industry of value-added goods (based on raw materials available in the country).

Prohibition on imposing additional restrictions on imports of remanufactured goods, over and above those applied to new goods, could inject substantial challenges for the domestic industry. This is because it would have to compete with similar low-priced imports. This could undermine the efforts of enhancing value-addition in many manufacturing sectors.

India may be required to join the initiative on environmental goods, and facilitate trade of climate-friendly products. Without tariff protection, India may not be able to create a vibrant domestic manufacturing industry of environmental goods. In the transition to a low-carbon economy, India would become overwhelmingly dependent on imports of these products.

AGRICULTURE

While FTAs require the trading partners to eliminate import tariffs on substantially all trade, they can negotiate to exclude a narrow category of products from the zero-duty regime. The obligation to eliminate tariffs could have a devastating impact on India's agriculture. It is well known that the developed countries provide tens of billions of dollars as direct subsidy to their farmers. As FTAs generally do not contain any rules on reducing the domestic farm subsidies, India's farmers would be under perpetual threat of being inundated by heavily subsidized exports from some of the developed countries. If India were required to eliminate tariffs on substantially all trade, the government would have no policy instrument to protect the livelihood of farmers. They would have to face challenges posed by the likely surge in subsidized imports from some of the developed countries. It is, therefore, essential that the list of products to be excluded from tariff reduction/elimination be carefully negotiated to protect the interests of Indian farmers. Otherwise, it is apprehended that tariff concessions on agricultural products could result in a surge in imports of subsidized products (from Canada, EU and the UK). These would considerably undermine the objectives of AatmaNirbhar Bharat.

GOVERNMENT PROCUREMENT

Under the rules of GATT (General Agreement on Tariffs and Trade)/World Trade Organization (WTO) in non-commercial governmental purchases, the government is allowed to grant preferential treatment to its domestic manufacturers and service suppliers. This is an effective policy instrument available in the hands of the government, to give a fillip to domestic manufacturing in the country. Historically, even developed countries have made effective use of government procurement to support their local industry. However, provisions in FTAs of Canada[5], EU[6] and the UK[7] prohibit the FTA partner from discriminating against the suppliers of the other.

It could be argued by some that market access commitments in government procurement would provide an opportunity for India's exporters to access the market of the partner country. But the reality is that in most developed countries, particularly the EU, procurement from foreign sources is extremely low. A

---

[5]See, for example: 'Chapter Nineteen: Government Procurement', *Comprehensive Economic and Trade Agreement (CETA) Between Canada, of the One Part, and the European Union and Its Member States, of the Other Part, European Commission,* https://tinyurl.com/fr8x6ub5. Accessed on 12 July 2023.

[6]See, for example: 'Chapter Nine: Government Procurement', *Free Trade Agreemeent between the European Union and the Republic of Singapore, European Commission,* https://tinyurl.com/mr2efbvx. Accessed on 12 July 2023.

[7]See, for example: 'Chapter 16: Government Procurement', *Australia-UK FTA Official Text, Australian Government, Department of Foreign Affairs and Trade,* https://tinyurl.com/vybh3uwk. Accessed on 12 July 2023.

study by the UNCTAD (United Nations Conference on Trade and Development) India programme had calculated that the EU sourced less than 0.3 per cent of government procurement from non-EU sources. In other words, if the EU procures €100 under government procurement, less than €1 is procured from non-EU sources. The export opportunities available for Indian exporters in government procurement markets of the EU, and other developed countries, is likely to be almost veering towards zero. On the other hand, the FTA provisions are likely to require India to provide non-discriminatory market access to its FTA partners. Overall, market access commitments on government procurement would not be aligned with the objectives of AatmaNirbhar Bharat.

INTELLECTUAL PROPERTY RIGHTS

It is hidden from no one that one of the main drivers of the agenda for negotiating stringent rules for protecting intellectual property rights (IPRs) is the pharmaceutical sector in the developed countries. Provisions in FTAs have now become the vehicle for taking forward this agenda. At the core of the IPR provisions in FTAs of developed countries is the aim to create pathways for delaying the entry of generic medicines manufactured by India and other developing countries in their markets. This perpetuates the windfall profits of the multinational firms manufacturing patented medicines. A few illustrations are given below:

1. By mandating the grant of patents for even insignificant improvements or for new uses of a known product[8],

[8]See, for example Article 18.37.2 of the TPP which confirms that patents are available for new uses of a known product, new methods of using a known product or new processes of using a known product. It may be noted that the application of this provision has been suspended by the members of CPTPP (Comprehensive and Progressive Agreement for Trans-Pacific Partnership). Article 20.36 of the USMCA (United States–Mexico–Canada Agreement) lowers the bar on patentability by

evergreening of existing patents is likely to become more widespread especially for blockbuster medicines. Through this process of evergreening of patents, competition from generic pharmaceutical products would either be delayed or even blocked. This will require India to make changes in Section 3(d) of its Patent Act, thereby abandoning its sound policy that has helped curtail evergreening of patents.

2. Some provisions mandate countries to extend the patent term beyond 20 years to supposedly compensate for delays in patent offices.[9] This will delay the entry of generics in the market.
3. Certain provisions in the FTAs prohibit regulatory authorities from relying on the data concerning safety and efficacy of the product submitted by the patent applicant, while granting marketing approval to the second applicant (normally a generic medicine). Some FTAs provide an initial period of marketing exclusively for five years[10], which

---

requiring that the terms 'inventive step' and 'capable of industrial application' be synonymous with the terms 'non-obvious' and 'useful', respectively. These types of provisions will substantially facilitate evergreening of patents.

'Article 18.37: Patentable Subject Matter', *Trans-Pacific Partnership, USTR*, https://tinyurl.com/53bxrb9j. Accessed on 12 July 2023; 'Article 20.36: Patentable Subject Matter', *Agreement between the United States of America, the United Mexican States, and Canada, International Trade Administration*, https://tinyurl.com/32a7z47y. Accessed on 12 July 2023.

[9]See, for example, Article 20.46 of the USMCA, which requires the FTA partners to adjust the patent term in order to compensate for delays in marketing approvals. 'Article 20.46: Patent Term Adjustment for Unreasonable Curtailment', *Agreement between the United States of America, the United Mexican States, and Canada, International Trade Administration*, https://tinyurl.com/32a7z47y. Accessed on 12 July 2023.

[10]See, for example, Article 20.48 of the USMCA which provides for protection of undisclosed test data for at least five years. 'Article 20.48: Protection of Undisclosed Test or Other Data', *Agreement between the United States of America, the United Mexican States, and Canada, International Trade Administration*, https://tinyurl.com/32a7z47y. Accessed on 12 July 2023.

> can be enhanced by another three years for a new indication or a new dosage form of an existing medicine. Marketing exclusivity protection can exist even in the absence of patent protection. During the period of data exclusivity, generic medicines would not be able to secure marketing authorization. This is because the regulator would be unable to rely on the data, concerning safety and efficacy of the product, submitted by the originator. As medicines cannot be sold without marketing approval, generic versions of the originator drug cannot be approved by the regulator and cannot be sold for five years. This would provide a fresh lease of monopoly market protection to old molecules, some of which may no longer enjoy patent protection.

If the FTAs require India to implement some of the provisions mentioned above, then not only would it hit India's export prospects but also significantly hit sales of generic pharmaceuticals in the domestic market. This poses a devastating threat to AatmaNirbhar Bharat. Equally importantly, it will hamper access to affordable healthcare for millions of sick people in India.

TRADE AND ENVIRONMENT

While India may not be opposed to promoting sustainability, the underlying agenda in FTAs is very clear—erode the policy space available to India to develop its 'green' industry. This will facilitate unhindered market access for 'green' products of developed countries. It is apprehended that some of the provisions related to sustainability that could be pursued in FTA negotiations by the developed countries (particularly the EU and the UK) include the following: circular economy, disciplines on fossil fuels, eliminating tariffs for the so-called environmental products etc. Further, under the garb of promoting sustainability, it is also likely that the developed countries will seek legal protection. This protection would be for imposing restrictions on imports, which is likely to disproportionately hurt India's exports.

A superficial argument that some make is that if India accepts commitments on trade and environment, it would be able to attract foreign investment for green products and technologies. However, there is very little rational basis for this argument. Further, India's past experience has been that foreign investments get attracted to those manufacturing sectors where India has imposed high tariffs. The automobile sector in the 1990s and mobile phones industry in more recent years bear testament to this fact. On the other hand, reducing tariffs runs the risk of driving away foreign investment. This was evident in Australia, where the auto giants decided not to make fresh investments after it became clear that the country would eliminate tariffs on automobiles (under the TPP [Trans-Pacific Partnership] agreement). It is apprehended that if India eliminates tariffs on green products, then it may not be able to attract foreign investment in this sector. Overall, India does not appear to have any export-related interest on issues related to sustainability.

In the context of AatmaNirbhar Bharat, it is crucial that India's transition to a low-carbon economy is facilitated largely by domestic firms. However, this objective will be completely undermined if the FTA provisions compel India to rely on imports of 'green products'. That is for the following reasons:

1. Facilitating trade in climate-friendly goods[11], or

---

[11]See, for example, Article 22.6.2 of Australia–UK FTA which requires the parties to facilitate trade in environmental goods; Article 24.9 of Canada–EU CETA (Comprehensive Economic and Trade Agreement) which requires parties to make best efforts to promote trade in environmental goods; and Article 12.11.2 of EU–Singapore FTA which mandates parties to pay special attention to facilitating the removal of obstacles to trade and investment concerning climate-friendly goods and services.

'Article 22.6 Environmental Goods and Services', *Australia-UK FTA Official Text, Australian Government, Department of Foreign Affairs and Trade*, https://

eliminating tariffs on green products (the so-called environmental goods), will prevent India from using tariff as a policy instrument to nurture the development of a vibrant domestic industry.

2. Premature liberalization of services related to environment would prevent domestic players emerging in this sector.
3. Creating benchmarks for industrial products and common green product standards may be difficult for Indian domestic producers to comply with. In such a situation, they may not even be able to sell in the domestic market. This leaves the market almost open for exporters from developed countries.
4. It can be apprehended that commitments on circular economy would prevent India from imposing restrictions on imports of second-hand goods/remanufactured goods, particularly on automobiles. Consequently, second-hand imports would displace domestically manufactured goods. This would have adverse impact on employment and income generation in the manufacturing sector.

ELECTRONIC COMMERCE AND DIGITAL TRADE

With data access becoming a crucial determinant of commercial success, outcome of FTA negotiations should be examined. This should be done from the perspective of whether it will facilitate

---

tinyurl.com/3hjjhk5w. Accessed on 12 July 2023; 'Article 24.9: Trade Favouring Environmental Protection', *Comprehensive Economic and Trade Agreement (CETA) Between Canada, of the One Part, and the European Union and Its Member States, of the Other Part, European Commission,* https://tinyurl.com/fr8x6ub5. Accessed on 12 July 2023; 'Article 12.11: Trade and Investment Promoting Sustainable Development', *Free Trade Agreement between the European Union and the Republic of Singapore, European Commission,* https://tinyurl.com/mr2efbvx. Accessed on 12 July 2023.

India from leveraging its data advantage to create jobs, or whether it will pose roadblocks in this objective. It is extremely unlikely that India will have any substantial gains from provisions on electronic commerce in FTAs. Almost all the provisions in the FTAs of the developed countries are aimed at eliminating competition from firms based in developing countries, including India, and boosting the windfall profits of their firms in the digital sector.

Superficially, it can be argued that free flow of data will benefit India's Information Technology (IT) and Information Technology Enabled Services (ITES) exports, thereby promoting the objectives of AatmaNirbhar Bharat. This is based on the premise that if free flow of data is mandated, the developed countries will not be able to use privacy as the ground for putting restrictions on outflow of data to Indian BPOs (business process outsourcing). This premise is flawed, particularly in respect of the EU. Protecting privacy is a core value in the EU and the UK. Even if an agreement with the EU mandates free flow of data, it is quite likely that this will be accompanied with an exception for privacy. Further, outflow of personal data from the EU is governed by the GDPR (General Data Protection Regulation) framework. For Indian BPOs to secure personal data from the EU, India will need to obtain data secure status under the GDPR. It is, thus, extremely unlikely that provisions on free flow of data in FTAs will facilitate Indian IT and ITES exports. The right way for this would be to obtain data secure status for India, which can be sought even outside the FTA framework.

The provisions on digital trade are unlikely to promote export objective under AatmaNirbhar Bharat. However, it is also relevant to analyse whether these provisions can undermine India's ability to create a vibrant domestic digital economy. The provisions in the existing FTAs of Canada, EU and the UK are likely to have the following adverse implications for India:

1. Mandating cross-border data flows and prohibiting server localization will prevent India from leveraging its data advantage for nurturing domestic digital firms.
2. Many provisions will eliminate competition from Indian firms and perpetuate the monopoly-like stranglehold of first movers.
3. Move towards deregulation and light-touch regulation will prevent India from regulating market failures.
4. Likely to substantially constrain India from implementing catch-up policies in the digital arena.
5. Substantially reducing India's ability to impose direct and indirect tax (moratorium on customs duties on electronic transmissions) on digital products, and suppliers of digital services.
6. Some provisions could require India to divert financial resources towards initiatives aimed at benefiting e-commerce players of the developed countries.
7. Substantially expanding commitments in respect of digitally delivered services, beyond India's sector-specific commitments under the General Agreement on Trade in Services at the WTO.

Overall, it would be fair to conclude that provisions on digital trade are likely to prevent India from becoming a vibrant digital economy. The obligations under the FTAs are likely to result in India becoming overwhelmingly dependent on imports of digital products. This would strike at the objectives of AatmaNirbhar Bharat.

TRADE AND GENDER

Empirical evidence on the link between trade liberalization and gender is scant. Nevertheless, some research has emerged which suggests that inequality in wages between the genders may have contributed to the export success of developing countries in several cases.[12] The need to minimize the gender wage gap and blunt the competitive edge of some developing countries may be the main trigger for developed countries seeking provisions on trade and gender at the multilateral level, as well as in FTAs.

Canada is the main proponent of trade and gender linkage. Two FTAs of Canada have a dedicated chapter on Trade and Gender.[13] These bilateral cooperation activities are aimed at improving the capacity and conditions for women—including workers, businesswomen and entrepreneurs—to access and fully benefit from the opportunities created by trade and investment. A few specific areas of cooperation are noteworthy: conducting gender-based analysis and sharing methods for collection of gender-disaggregated data; monitoring and evaluation methodologies; and the analysis of gender-focussed statistics related to trade.

It is apprehended that the latent objective of the provision on cooperation is to compel India to spend resources in collecting gender-based trade data and undertake gender-based analysis. Thereafter, the results are used to create pressure points for reducing the wage gap between men and women in India. While the gender wage gap cannot be justified, it is equally true that the wage gap must be reduced through domestic policies that take into account local realities and imperatives. Seeking to reduce the wage gap through the provisions in trade agreements can prove to be counterproductive for female employment, thereby adversely impacting AatmaNirbhar Bharat.

---

[12]See, for example: Seguino, Stephanie, 'Gender Wage Inequality and Export-led Growth in South Korea', *Journal of Development Studies*, Vol. 34, No. 2, 1997, pp. 102–37.

[13]See for example: 'Appendix II – Chapter N Bis–Trade and Gender', *Government of Canada*, https://tinyurl.com/mr2pk9x5. Accessed on 19 July 2023; 'Chapter Thirteen: Trade and Gender', *Canada-Israel Free Trade Agreement, Government of Canada*, https://tinyurl.com/mr4xhb9h. Accessed on 19 July 2023.

CONCLUSION

FTAs are no longer about imports and exports of goods and services. These agreements can also result in binding commitments in areas that have very little, or almost nothing, to do with international trade. If some of the provisions existing in the FTAs of Canada, EU and the UK are also included in their FTAs with India, then these could have a significant adverse impact on PM Modi's vision for AatmaNirbhar Bharat. The marginal gains from the FTAs cannot outweigh the damages that are likely to arise for India from many of the FTA provisions. Instead of hurtling ahead with negotiating FTAs with the developed countries, wisdom lies in undertaking a detailed assessment of the implications of provisions. As discussed in this chapter, the future course of action should be decided thereafter.

12

AUTARKY, SWADESHI AND AATMANIRBHAR BHARAT

Prof. Ashok Kumar Lahiri

Former chief economic advisor, Government of India

India has never been autarchic. In the ancient days, the rest of the world wanted to import goods from India but India demanded little from others. Even then, India engaged in trade with other countries and did not have a closed economy. In those days, traders from abroad carried bullion to settle the trade in India. In other words, for centuries, countries importing from India financed the external trade surplus of India by gold and silver specie flow. India has never been a major producer of gold, yet one conservative estimate puts India's private gold ownership at about 18,000 tonnes. This is a little less than 10 per cent of all the gold mined in history, and almost 2.5 times the United States (US) official gold reserves.[1] Much of this Indian horde of gold is the balance of trade surpluses settled in gold, and accumulated over centuries. Protectionist trends in India, for example, the Swadeshi Movement, started only in reaction to the colonial misrule under the British.

The Swadeshi Movement started in Bengal in 1905, when the colonial government wanted to divide Bengal along communal

---

[1]'India: Heart of Gold–Revival', *Goldhub*, 10 November 2010, https://tinyurl.com/y52vz9sn. Accessed on 21 June 2023.

lines. The movement advocated purchase of products produced in the country, and not only boycott of goods produced in foreign lands (particularly in the United Kingdom [UK]) but even burning and destroying of such foreign goods. Over and above its economic motivation, the Swadeshi Movement had a political agenda. It threatened the British imperial venture's commercial interests. The imperial government did little to develop India and its education, health and physical infrastructure. With extremely unequal development, under open-trade policy, it was unfair competition between the two. Domestic industry, for example textiles, were very adversely affected by the colonial open-trade policy (particularly vis-à-vis the UK). Even the Indian Fiscal Commission in 1922 had recommended 'discriminating protection'.[2] It is important to remember though that under Swadeshi, while imports were discouraged, exports were not discouraged. Swadeshi was not autarky.

INDIA'S JOURNEY WITH SELF-RELIANCE

Lala Harkishen Lal, an Indian businessman, was the author of the oft-quoted imperative, 'Nurse the baby, protect the child and free the adult.'[3] While there was general support for discriminating protection, there were economists like Jehangir Cooverjee Coyajee who cautioned against such policies becoming 'the breeding ground for fallacies like the home market argument, indiscriminate protection and autarky'. He wanted protective duties only 'when no other means [were] available to bring national resources to the aid of a particular backward industry'.[4] In the event, what we followed in the first three or four decades after Independence

[2]Lavington, F., 'The Indian Fiscal Commission, 1921-22', *The Economic Journal*, Vol. 33, No. 129, March 1923, pp. 51–59.

[3]Ibid.

[4]Coyajee, Jehangir Cooverjee, *The Indian Fiscal Problem*, Patna University, 1923.

was a policy of severe restrictions on imports. Apart from high import tariffs, there was indiscriminate protection through quantitative restrictions (QRs). Such a policy was rooted in the pre-Independence period's widespread belief that with severe British competition, industrialization in India could not be promoted under free trade.

Even after decades of protection, every industry in India continued to be looked at as an infant industry and there were no 'adults' among industries to be freed. The QRs, which were in forms such as non-automatic licences; imports through canalized agencies; special import licences; and actual users' criteria, could not be removed because of domestic vested interests. On 9 April 1999, the Dispute Settlement Panel of the WTO suggested that India remove its QRs within a period of 15 months. A mutual agreement was arrived at between India and the US (United States) for India to remove QRs on 1,429 items in two phases: 715 by end of March 2000 and 714 by end of March 2001.[5]

In the context of our interaction with the rest of the world, one thing needs to be kept firmly in mind. This is that because of limitations of our natural resource endowments, even if we tried to, we could not produce everything that we need. For example, we were and are seriously short in petroleum and petroleum products. Furthermore, trying to produce everything reduces the availability of resources; expertise to produce what we are good at, and what we have comparative advantage in producing. We should not be autarchic but, for what we import, we should be able to pay with our export and foreign exchange proceeds. In other words, we should be self-reliant.

Apart from foreign trade, another area where swadeshi arguments held sway was foreign investment. India had a very unfortunate experience with foreign investment. The East India

[5]Mehta, Rajesh, 'Removal of QRs and Impact on India's Import', *Economic and Political Weekly*, Vol. 35, No. 19, 2000.

Company, which was established in 1600 with a royal charter, got a monopoly on English trade with all countries east of the Cape of Good Hope and west of the Straits of Magellan. After its decisive victory in the Battle of Plassey on 23 June 1757, the Company rapidly transformed itself from a foreign investor to a ruler with effective control over much of the country. The Company and its successor, the imperial government, used this power of control to bestow commercial benefit to British companies. After independence, India naturally took a very cautious approach to foreign investment. Foreigners needed permission to invest in India, both through the foreign direct investment (FDI) or foreign portfolio investment (FPI) routes.

For developing itself and even running its economy, every country has to rely primarily on itself. India is no exception. The painful lessons of not being self-reliant have clearly come to the fore recently with the balance of payments crisis in neighbouring Sri Lanka. In May 2022, the island state officially defaulted on its foreign-currency denominated loans. It ran out of foreign currency, and no one would lend it to them. They could not pay for imports, most crucially fuel, food and medicines. With fuel shortage, doctors could not get to work; hospitals could not run ambulances; and food from the hinterland could not reach the cities. Sri Lanka ran out of paper and could not import them to even print question papers. School examinations had to be postponed. Angry people stormed the presidential palace in early July 2022. President Gotabaya Rajapaksa had to first hide, then in mid-July had to run away from the country and resign from his post.

India's leadership has advocated the principle of self-reliance for at least a century and a quarter under various names, such as swadeshi. In India, the principle of self-reliance has got highlighted in recent times as AatmaNirbhar Bharat. This initiative is the outcome of a long evolution of the idea of self-reliance.

The failure of the extremely protectionist policies of the first four decades after Independence was manifested in the country's recurrent balance of payments problems until the early-1990s. India had to go for stand-by arrangements with the International Monetary Fund (IMF) in March 1957, July 1962, July 1963, March 1965, January 1991 and October 1991. It also had to ask for an Extended Fund Facility in 1981. Stand-by arrangements with the IMF are devised to help member countries with exceptional balance of payments support.

Comparing India's economic performance in the first four post-Independence decades with that of some of our neighbours to the East—namely Hong Kong, Singapore, South Korea, Taiwan and China (after Mao and under Deng Xiao Ping)—clearly demonstrated that all was not well with our swadeshi policies, together with the restrictive industrial licensing regime. East Asian Tigers were racing ahead, and capturing increasing shares of the world export markets. They had comfortable foreign exchange reserves, and were growing at a much faster rate than India. India continued to grow at an extremely low rate of growth, of close to 3–3.5 per cent and suffered from periodic balance of payments crisis.

India faced a severe economic crisis around the Gulf War of 1991, when the world price of petroleum more than doubled; remittances from the Middle East dried up; and 180,000 Indian workers from the war-affected zones had to be repatriated and rehabilitated. Inflation (on an end-of-period basis) was already in double digits at 12.1 per cent in 1990–91. Foreign currency assets of the Reserve Bank of India (RBI) came down to $975 million on 12 July 1991, equivalent to less than a month's import cover. A part of the government's gold had to be transported and pledged to borrow abroad, and foreign loans had to be raised on a continuous (often an overnight) basis to avert a default on external debt. India went for a stand-by arrangement with the IMF in 1991. There was change of gears post that in Indian economic policy.

The 1991 IMF programme involved considerable internal and external liberalization of the economy. How much of the 1991 reforms reflected a genuine political resolve for change—and how much the compulsive necessity of observing IMF and World Bank conditionalities—continue to be debated. With the dismantling of much of the licence permit raj, 1991 also saw a change in the institutional design of the Indian state. It endured through changes in governments. It is possible that the conditionalities once observed were found to be beneficial and hence not reversed. If the reforms were only because of the conditionalities, then they would have been reversed once the crisis was over and they no longer operated. Such reversals were seen several times in the past, after various IMF programmes. But not in 1991.

From the mid-1990s, coalition governments replaced single party rule at the centre, and right at the outset the coalitions brought out documents committing themselves to specific policies. The United Front Government under Prime Minister (PM) Deve Gowda came out with its Common Minimum Programme in 1996. The National Development Alliance (NDA) under PM Atal Bihari Vajpayee, a day before assuming office in 1998, released its National Agenda for Governance (NAG).

The NAG highlighted the aim of achieving GDP growth of 7–8 per cent; controlling fiscal deficit; enhancing national savings to 30 per cent of GDP; promoting infrastructure, agriculture, rural development and irrigation; and removing bureaucratic control on industry. Along with this, encouraging FDI in core areas and discouraging it in others; comprehensively reforming the public sector enterprises owned and controlled by the Central government through restructuring, rehabilitation and divestment; and establishing an appropriate legal framework for the protection of the environment, and unveiling a National Environment Policy to balance development and ecology was also included. In the NAG, the NDA committed itself to not only continue with the reform process but also to give it a strong swadeshi or indigenous thrust. While it clarified that this was to ensure that the national economy grows on the principle that 'India shall be built by Indians', many worried whether it implied a move back to protectionism.[6] While there was some emphasis on a minimum level of customs tariff on imports, the main debate was in the realm of FDI. From the late 1970s, fully foreign-owned companies were allowed only in highly export-oriented sectors or sophisticated technology areas. Later in the early 1990s, this approach was memorably summarized by the then Bharatiya Janata Party (BJP) President Dr Murli Manohar Joshi, when he said: 'Computer chips YES, potato chips NO.'

The then Finance Minister Yashwant Sinha's Budget speech, on 1 June 1998, hinted at how swadeshi did not mean autarchic or isolationist but self-reliant. One leading magazine reported, 'The Union Budget for 1998–99 has stayed squarely within the framework of the post-1991 economic reform process and its tenets of privatisation, liberalisation and a significantly reduced economic role for the state.'[7] After coming to power in 2014, the NDA government under PM Narendra Modi announced the Make in India programme to boost the domestic manufacturing sector and augment investment into the country. After the Covid-19 outbreak, PM Modi, in his address to the nation (on 12 May 2020) announced an economic stimulus package for ₹20 lakh crore towards building an AatmaNirbhar Bharat. The package was to cater to various sections including cottage industry; medium, small and micro enterprises (MSMEs); labourers; middle class; and industries, among others.

Successive governments (post 1991) kept the need to avert balance of payments problems fairly high on its policy agenda. The current account balance—which is the difference between receipts from exports of goods and services, and their imports

[6]'Prime Minister Shri Atal Bihari Vajpayee at Conference of Chief Executives of Public Sector Enterprises', *Speeches, Government of India*, 1 April 2000, https://tinyurl.com/ycyw7msz. Accessed on 11 July 2023.

[7]'Let Them Eat the Bomb', *Frontline*, 6 June 1998, https://tinyurl.com/5n683uf4. Accessed on 21 June 2023.

together with unrequited transfers—was a deficit from 1978–79. Yet, with buoyant capital flows, foreign exchange reserves grew from $5.8 billion in 1990–91 to $42.3 billion in 2001–02, 141.5 billion in 2004–05, $279.1 billion in 2009–10 and $341.6 billion in 2014–15.[8] The reserves in 2014–15 was equivalent to almost nine months of imports, and created a comfortable position. Yet, the government also knew how easy it was to lose such reserves and face renewed foreign exchange crises.

LESSONS FROM OUR NEIGHBOURS

In the context given above, there are lessons to be learnt from our neighbours to the east—namely Hong Kong, Singapore, South Korea, Taiwan and China. In mid-2022, the foreign exchange reserves of China were $3.5 trillion; of Taiwan and Hong Kong over $500 billion each; and of Singapore and South Korea $449 billion and $365 billion, respectively, compared to India's $599 billion. In sharp contrast to India, these East Asian neighbours also generated current account surpluses—that is excess of export proceeds over import payments—that contributed significantly to their foreign exchange reserves. Given that only China had a population comparable to that of India and the others had 0.5–1.5 per cent of India's population, their foreign exchange reserves clearly demonstrate how far ahead they are in attaining self-reliance. Furthermore, these neighbours to our east have pursued a much more open policy than India's regarding foreign trade and investment.

The question is do you maximize exports and minimize imports by being open to foreign trade and investment or by being restrictive? China's accession to the World Trade Organization (WTO) at the end of 2001 provides a possible answer to this. It

[8]'Table 146: Foreign Exchange Reserves', *Reserve Bank of India*, 15 September 2022, https://tinyurl.com/5n7etnrc. Accessed on 21 June 2023.

took almost a decade-and-a-half for China to gain accession to WTO. In this long accession period, China was asked to take on a host of trade reforms and commitments as a precondition for admission to WTO. These included substantial tariff reductions, and dismantling of most non-tariff barriers. For example, import tariffs on pork had to come down from 20 per cent to 12 per cent; on barley from 114 per cent to just 3 per cent; and on automobiles from 100 per cent to 25 per cent.

There were apprehensions about the impact of WTO accession on the Chinese economy like how gains from such accession would accrue mostly to foreigners; Chinese workers would lose their jobs; and how angry mobs of displaced workers would destabilize the regime in Beijing. But defying all such doomsday predictions, China emerged stronger from the WTO accession. Trade as well as current account balances improved, and soon there were allegations of a mercantilist China snatching jobs from other countries, most notably the United States (US).

Our experience after the external liberalization in 1991—and the Chinese experience after its accession to WTO in 2001—have confirmed that after making suitable progress in education, health and physical infrastructure, these countries can not only compete with foreign goods in domestic markets but also compete in markets abroad. If what we produce and export can compete with foreign goods in markets abroad, it is difficult to see how in our own markets foreign goods can dominate what we produce.

THE WAY FORWARD

With global supply chains, a country can be both an exporter and importer of parts. Consider the complexity of the supply chain in the automotive industry. It involves approximately 20,000 components, with about 1,000 sub-assemblies or modules. The dependence of the country's automobile and auto-component industry on the rest of the world was painfully revealed when there was a shortage of semiconductor auto-chips in 2020, after the pandemic. The uncertainty continues with the Ukraine–Russia conflict. Ukraine supplies 25 to 35 per cent of the world's purified neon gas and Russia supplies 25–30 per cent of palladium, a rare metal used for semiconductors.[9] In an integrated world with so many trade linkages, a policy to limit imports may end up affecting exports.

A policy of not limiting imports does not mean that there is no need to monitor whether India is becoming too dependent on one country for keeping the domestic industry, including the export sector, running. The experience during the recent Covid-19 pandemic together with the US–China trade war has got lessons in this context. Producers of many commodities all over the world, including India, relied heavily on suppliers from China for some of the inputs (including specialized parts). Disruption of Chinese supplies because of the pandemic and geo-strategic reasons, affected economic activity in many countries. Such disruptions triggered a rise in economic nationalism and emphasis on self-reliance. Trying to produce everything within the country without imports is not the right lesson to derive from the Covid-19 pandemic and the US–China trade war. But it is important to be vigilant that India is not becoming too dependent on China, or any other country, for raw materials or processed inputs. AatmaNirbhar Bharat requires having a diversified industrial base and multiple countries for sourcing inputs through appropriate policy interventions.

Since the launch of economic reforms in 1991, India has chosen a path of gradual import liberalization by reducing import duties. Such duties have been reduced to a fraction, sometimes a fourth, of the WTO bound rates. Simultaneously,

---

[9]Burkacky, Ondrej, et al., 'Semiconductor Shortage: How the Automotive Industry Can Succeed', *McKinsey & Company*, 10 June 2022, https://tinyurl.com/mwuzb447. Accessed on 21 June 2023.

the manufacturing sector, particularly large firms in the organized sector, have not been able to rapidly increase their share in value-added or employment. Domestic manufacturers have not been able to compete with foreign goods, particularly those coming from China. With its developed infrastructure, scale economies and subsidies, China has flooded the domestic market with a variety of goods from toys and electrical goods to chemicals.

Competitiveness of Indian manufacturing is seriously constrained by the lack of infrastructure such as roads and ports; high cost of power for subsidizing agriculture and households; high railway freight cost to subsidize passenger traffic; absence of scale economies; problems in land acquisition; and inflexibilities in the labour market. These root causes of lack of competitiveness need to be removed to achieve the goals of AatmaNirbhar Bharat. Until these fundamental lacunae are removed or reduced substantially, there is a need to be vigilant on the duty-reductions front. Also, there may be a need to intervene selectively with WTO-approved anti-dumping measures.

Mercantilism was a school of thought that called for maximizing exports and minimizing imports. Before the early part of the last century, for a country with an adverse balance of payments, gold and silver were the main instruments of squaring off a deficit in receipts vis-à-vis payments. Between the sixteenth and the eighteenth centuries, the strength of a nation was often judged by the amount of gold and silver it possessed. Thus, the mercantilists encouraged policies to acquire gold and silver by maximizing their exports and minimizing the imports. Some argue that, unlike us, our East Asian neighbours followed a mercantilist policy. It is also argued that one instrument for pursuing such a policy was their competitive exchange rate policy.

Even when the nominal exchange rate of the currency is kept unchanged, the currency appreciates when domestic inflation is higher than inflation in partner countries. Higher inflation at home can always be compensated by nominally depreciating the currency. But such a depreciation is politically difficult owing to the negative public reaction. India's East Asian neighbours have successfully pursued prudent macroeconomic policies, and have had low inflation and competitive exchange rates. It is important to keep an eye on the real effective exchange rate of the rupee, and not allow it to appreciate.

Experience with foreign investment has been quite similar to the one with trade in goods. The fear that well-known foreign brands of pizza, hot-dogs and hamburgers, once allowed in would dominate the Indian market, has proved to be false. Domestic entrepreneurs have not only held their own, but also learnt from their foreign competitors and expanded their business. There are enough domestic entrepreneurs, even some unicorns, who are willing to try new ideas. The fear of a new East India Company taking charge of India appears like a figment of the imagination.

After 75 years of Independence, India has come a long way from the colonial days. Literacy has almost quadrupled from 16.7 per cent in 1951 to 64.3 per cent in 2011. By 2010, an average Indian's life expectancy was at around 67 years (twice that of 1951). The average Indian is not only more educated, well-informed and healthy, but also more prosperous. At constant 2004–05 prices, per capita income increased more than five-fold, from ₹7,114 in 1950–51 to ₹39,904 in 2013–14.[10] Furthermore, a lot of water has flown in the Ganges since the Battle of Plassey. India has become a nuclear power. The vulnerabilities that needed to be guarded against around the time of Independence, no longer exist.

[10]Lahiri, Ashok Kumar, *India in Search of Glory: Political Calculus and the Economy*, Penguin Random House, Delhi, 2022.

13

CAPITAL OF, FOR AND BY INDIANS: AATMANIRBHARTA IN DOMESTIC CAPITAL

Gopal Srinivasan

Chairman, TVS Capital Funds Limited

In January 2022, the Hon'ble Prime Minister (PM) Narendra Modi called 'start-up' the backbone of self-reliant, self-confident India. This underscored the importance of start-ups in India's growth. In this new era, the PM cited that start-ups are coming up in Tier II and Tier III towns and that the youth is required to be prepared for the massive opportunities that lie ahead. He cited that today's start-ups can become tomorrow's MNCs (Multinational Corporations) as India seeks to make its start-up system inclusive to ensure speedy development.

THE NEW START-UP ECONOMY

It is increasingly clear that the new start-up economy will be driven by the shift in disruptive technologies, manufacturing automation and internet-based technological solutions. This has not only propelled a start-up culture, but also generated vast opportunities for young Indians.

The Alternative Investment Funds (AIF) regime in 2012 also ushered in an unprecedented deployment of robust, patient and high-risk capital to Indian entrepreneurs. This lead India to become the third-largest start-up ecosystem in the world with over 90,000 registered start-ups, 100 unicorns and nearly $350 billion investments.[1] Start-ups have given a big hope to millions of engineers coming out of colleges every year by providing direct employment to 9 lakh people, and indirect employment to 34 lakh people in the last decade. Estimates suggest this number would grow to more than 100,000 start-ups by 2025 with more than $1 trillion in value.

FUNDING THE DIGITAL AGE

India is in the midst of a digital revolution-based growth in lending and payments enabled by the Jan Dhan Aadhaar Mobile (JAM) trinity, Unified Payment Interface (UPI), Open Credit Enablement Network (OCEN), etc. Digital infrastructure created in India, starting with UPI, is unparalleled in the world. Digital and app-based services primarily used to be popular among Gen-Z (generation born between 1997 and 2012) but the older generations found more takers as the pandemic pushed consumers online, broadening markets.

The invisible force behind all this, is start-up funding. Expansion of the private equity/venture capital (PE/VC) ecosystem has played an important role in promoting entrepreneurship. A report published in February 2022 estimates that there were 70,000 tech start-ups in India in 2021, and that this number is expected to grow to more than 100,000 by 2025. The report also estimates that the value of these start-ups is expected to grow to more than $1 trillion by 2025, establishing innovative and disruptive start-ups in India. Fuelled by the Information Technology (IT) revolution that started in the early 1990s, now India exports more software than Saudi Arabia does oil.

[1]'New Ecosystem Enabled Growth of Startups in India from 350 to 90000 in 9 Years: Jitendra Singh', *ETGovernment.com*, 10 April 2023, https://tinyurl.com/3jhewm7m. Accessed on 11 July 2023.

Since 1998, India invested ₹24 lakh crore in PE/VC, including AIFs. Excluding exits and divestments of ₹12 lakh crore, about ₹15 lakh crore remains as Assets Under Management (AUM). According to Indian Private Equity and Venture Capital Association (IVCA), PE/VC investments in India in 2021 were a record-breaking $77 billion (₹5.77 lakh crore) versus the $47.6 billion (₹3.57 lakh crore) in 2020.

THE CASE FOR MORE INVESTMENTS

An interesting study by McKinsey (2016 report) revealed that investments by PE/VC funds build better companies, create 1.3 times more jobs and pay 1.9 times more taxes than non-PE/VC-backed companies. Each billion dollars invested resulted in portfolio companies generating $200 million in direct tax, and $600 million in indirect taxes in the FY (financial year) 2018.

It is therefore necessary to create a robust enabling environment for the growth of the PE/VC ecosystem in India, to create skilled employment and generate more revenue. For example, the US has 20 per cent of Gross Domestic Product (GDP) as PE/VC pools versus less than 5 per cent in India. Indeed, India needs to develop funding scenarios tailored to its own growth requirements.

$10 TRILLION ECONOMY (INDIA@100): THE WAY FORWARD

In the midst of Azadi ka Amrit Mahotsav to take India to a $5-trillion economy, it's time we think of India@100 building a $10-trillion digital economy. To fuel this high growth target, a simple calculation reveals that India would require ₹100 lakh crore in PE/VC AUM, with ₹25–30 lakh crore of new investments annually in start-ups and private equity and credit. Such investments would truly change the economic landscape, and develop a start-up ecosystem that is at par with the world standards. Three strategies are suggested for the same: the long-term, medium-term and short-term strategies.

Long-term Reforms

Reforms (industrial, financial, tax, fiscal and external) boosted India's economy tenfold since the process began in 1991, catapulting India to the position of the sixth-largest economy. A Department for Promotion of Industry and Internal Trade (DPIIT) release shows the government has initiated more than 650 regulatory reforms (47 at the Central level, 610 at state levels). These reforms permit Employees Provident Fund Organization (EPFO) to invest 5 per cent of their investible surpluses in Category-I and -II AIFs. This is yet to become operational. But these were largely incremental, and the space has not been addressed holistically.

Harmonized Regulations

High growth at such a large scale requires the removal of friction. The entire end-to-end regulation of AIFs, which are primary vehicles for PE/VC investments, needs to be unified. Regulations across the Security and Exchange Board of India (SEBI), and direct and indirect taxes need to be harmonized. The PE/VC AIF industry is different from companies and partnerships. Hence, it needs its own framework.

Due to the excesses by a few aggressive entrepreneurs, regulations/laws have been brought in, that kill the enthusiasm in the entrepreneurial ecosystem. It is basically an overreaction to crisis situations without proactive thinking and approaches. The recent Customs Excise and Service Tax Appellate Tribunal (CESTAT) ruling on the application of Goods and Service Tax (GST) on share in capital gains is another classic example of a myopic view. Every circular or regulation by agencies has been post-facto.

The most recent example of an excellent unified and comprehensive framework is the Insolvency and Bankruptcy Code

(IBC) amending 11 Acts, suspending two and affecting 49 sections. The IBC puts in place the role of Resolution Professionals (RPs), the body of RPs codes, standards and the necessary legislative support to sanctify the process. This addresses the Insurance Regulatory and Development Authority of India (IRDAI), the Pension Fund Regulatory and Development Authority (PFRDA), the National Company Law Appellate Tribunal (NCLAT) and the National Company Law Tribunal (NCLT), besides regulatory changes in SEBI.

Given the scale of start-up funding and the PE/VC AIF category, the entire ecosystem and principal enablers, the Government of India constituted an expert committee under the Chairmanship of Shri S. Damodaran. The industry body representing interests of PE/VC had submitted detailed presentations to the committee, including 160 suggestions to bring an overarching framework on the lines of IBC. Though the Expert Committee has submitted its report, the government is yet to implement its recommendations, which have not been published as yet.

Medium-Term Reforms

Drivers of Domestic Capital, Aatmanirbharta in Finance

Domestic Capital is an important and resilient source, offering high returns to domestic investors, and an important tool of government policy. Simultaneously, PE/VC investment can be utilized to channel funds for diversification and to provide a safe and well-governed route for them. Global PE/VC funds are now earmarking a sizeable share of their capital pie for India, and over 85 per cent of funds earmarked for India are still pooled together with overseas destinations. About 60–70 per cent of foreign direct investment (FDI) comes through private equity. India therefore needs to promote its asset management sector, and encourage domiciling funds in India. To overcome the risk of dependence on foreign capital, we need to be aatmanirbhar and tap into domestic capital.

Enlarge the Mandate of Fund of Funds

There are only 6–7 institutional Fund of Funds (FoF) operating in India. This is in stark contrast with developed economies such as the United States (US), which have as many as 183 professionally managed FoF attracting institutional capital.

FoF like the DPIIT Small Industries Development Bank of India (SIDBI) and the National Investment and Infrastructure Fund (NIIF) have led to the flowering of VC funds, through proven fund managers with a 5–6x multiplier at daughter-fund levels. For example, the DPIIT SIDBI FFS has supported 108 daughter funds, creating a wave of next-generation Indian fund managers. They come with more than ₹8,686 crore committed to a combined corpus of ₹73,000 crore (12 per cent contribution). Assuming a similar equity infusion of maximum of 50 per cent from other sources, gross investment would be ₹1.5 lakh crore. Applying debt equity ratio of 2:1, this would result in investment of ₹4.5 lakh crore. Thus, FoF is creating a minimum of 2–3x effect with enormous employment and innovation possibilities.

Although large pools of domestic capital are available via pension, provident funds and charitable endowments, they are not used as investment sources in the country. The patient capital with these institutions constitutes nearly 25 per cent of GDP. We could see that DPIIT FoF was largely successful, as SIDBI was nominated to channelize as safekeeper. In the same way, the Pension Fund Regulatory and Development Authority (PFRDA) and the National Pension Scheme (NPS) may be encouraged to invite bids from professional fund managers like NIIF or SBI (State Bank of India) Capital Markets (that manage the Self-Reliant India Fund) to run a FoF. Globally, on an average, more than 10 per cent of pension and endowment funds contribute towards PE/VC funds. If Indian institutions who invest largely in government securities apportion a sliver of their total funds to PE/VC funds, they would enjoy higher returns and boost Indian enterprises (besides innovation and employment). The higher returns from AIFs would in turn help enhance the corpus every year, and help enlarge the social security network to large a number of people.

Foreign development finance institutions may also be encouraged to join local asset-management companies to set up thematic FoF structure. This may include an agriculture FoF by National Bank for Agriculture and Rural Development (NABARD); or FoFs that promote social growth or support start-ups that work on issues like water, climate change, healthcare, divyang and venture/start-up sectors with the same multiplier effect.

It was gratifying to get our voice heard and that there were two announcements. The first one was relating to thematic FoF in areas like climate change, deep tech etc., with Public–Private Partnership. The second one was about co-investment with NABARD for promoting agri-tech start-ups. There is a need to see implementation of these two key initiatives for mobilizing domestic capital with a huge multiplier effect.

Short-Term Reforms

Taxation Parity: The Need of the Hour

Investment in unlisted shares and securities should be encouraged as they provide risk capital, much needed by start-ups, to promote innovation and employment. Accordingly, from domestic risk capital providers' perspective, further measures are required in reforming the tax framework. These reforms could come through uniformity in taxing unlisted securities and public market securities. At present, the taxation system discriminates in favour of investments in the public markets rather than private investments.

Long-term capital gains (LTCG) of resident investors in the equity market (for securities held for more than a year) are taxed at 10 per cent without indexation (without a higher surcharge of 37 per cent). This is in comparison to LTCG on unlisted shares with indexation (for shares held for more than two years), or unlisted securities without indexation (for securities held for more than three years) which are taxed at 20 per cent (with a higher surcharge of 37 per cent).

While indexation is available on the sale of unlisted shares, it does not sufficiently compensate for the discrepancy in rates between listed and unlisted shares. In 2004, an exemption was introduced for listed shares to incentivize stock-market participation. This was reversed in 2018, and a lower tax rate of 10 per cent was introduced on gains during transfer of listed shares. The time has now come to take this reform a step further. Besides, it is noteworthy that foreign investors pay LTCG tax of 10 per cent even on unlisted securities. This rate is lower compared to domestic investors.

In most developed economies (including the US, the United Kingdom [UK], Germany and Singapore), taxes on listed and unlisted securities are on par. There is the need to bring not only parity in tenure but also a uniform average rate of LTCG, including surcharge on all securities. This will not lead to revenue loss. In fact, it could lead to increased collections and provide parity to investments in different asset classes by domestic investors.

It is heartening to see that this long pending demand on parity of listed and unlisted shares was partially addressed in the 2022 Budget by capping the surcharge on LTCG at 15 per cent. To encourage more flow of large sums of private money from family offices and UHNWIs (Ultra high-net-worth individual), it is but necessary to bring in parity on LTCG between listed and unlisted shares.

Domestic Listing

While pooling of domestic capital is necessary for building sustainable PE/VC ecosystem in India, it also needs to result in higher returns for Indian investors. Some of the successful start-ups chose to list overseas in pursuit of higher returns while the entire profits are made through Indian operations. It is necessary to provide an enabling environment for them to list in Indian bourses, so that the benefits of their growth reach Indian investors. Markets in India have gained maturity as seen in the successful listings of tech companies in 2021 outperforming some of the listed counterparts in the overseas markets. This dispelled the doubts in giving higher returns in India.

Exclusion of small retail investors in a market where equity participation is lower compared to global standards may not be in the larger interest of the nation. Needless to add that Mutual Funds AUM to GDP ratio (currently at 15 per cent compared to the global average of 75 per cent) is slowly growing, thanks to tech companies listing in India. The next generation's interest in such stocks would increase the direct and indirect equity exposure component in financial savings from the current level of 6.9 per cent.

Let us not repeat the ills of the past where East India Company took away $40 trillion of economic interests from India and brought down India's contribution of world trade (from more than 25 per cent in 1600 to less than 2 per cent at the time of Independence). It's time we pool the domestic capital of India, by India and for India.

THE WAY FORWARD

India has abundant patient domestic capital with various institutions. It is time to successfully channelize aatmanirbharta sources for promoting the start-ups and growth enterprises through the PE/VC ecosystem. This can be done by addressing all the aspects holistically through a harmonized and enabling framework.

14

STRATEGIC DECOUPLING AND AATMANIRBHAR BHARAT

[*]Bibek Debroy and [**]Aditya Sinha

[*]Chairman, Economic Advisory Council to the Prime Minister;
[**]Public policy professional, Economic Advisory Council to the Prime Minister

Power arises from asymmetrical interdependence.

—Klaus Knorr[1]

Suppose there is over-dependence on a single country for essential and strategic goods. In that case, even the short-term trade liberalization and apparent welfare gains for consumers end up being myopic and don't serve the country's medium-term goals. Any exogenous shock in such a setting can debilitate the supply chain and lead to a sudden price rise. Smartphones; components for smartphones and automobiles; telecom equipment; plastic and metallic goods; active pharmaceutical ingredients (APIs); and chemicals are India's essential imports from China. Looking at India's pharmaceutical industry, more than 70 per cent of APIs were imported from China. Reliance on essential goods

---

[1]Knorr, K., 'International Economic Leverage & its Uses', *Economic Issues and National Security*, University Press of Kansas, 1977, p. 102.

can have geostrategic implications in times of crisis. The problem gets exacerbated with excessive external dependence on critical infrastructures like telecom, power grids and broadband.

India's pursuit of self-reliance needs to be viewed in the above context. On 12 May 2020, Prime Minister (PM) Narendra Modi addressed the nation, saying:

> The state of the world today teaches us that a AatmaNirbhar Bharat (Self-reliant India) is the only path. It is said in our scriptures—*EshahPanthah*. That is, self-sufficient India. [...] When the Corona crisis started, there was not a single PPE kit made in India. The N-95 masks were produced in small quantities in India. Today we are in a situation to produce 2 lakh PPE and 2 lakh N-95 masks daily. [...] India does not advocate self-centric arrangements when it comes to self-reliance.[2]

AatmaNirbhar Bharat doesn't imply protectionism, isolation or autarky. One can argue that there are some similarities between AatmaNirbhar Bharat and the 'neo-mercantilist' conception of economic nationalism, which Friedrich List had advanced in the nineteenth century. Autarky is all about minimizing international linkages. Whereas, neo-mercantilism aims for outward-oriented targeted trade restrictions. The government's economic activism is aimed to make domestic industries compete on the global stage.[3] The stress is on promoting domestic manufacturing rather than just the domestic industries. There is a distinction. India aims to attract investors and manufacturers to manufacture in India. The aim is to reduce import dependence and promote

---

[2]'English Rendering of Prime Minister Shri Narendra Modi's Address to the Nation on 12.5.2020', *PIB Delhi*, 12 May 2020, https://tinyurl.com/2u2zf3b8. Accessed on 26 June 2023.

[3]Helleiner, E., 'The Return of National Self-Sufficiency? Excavating Autarkic Thought in a De-Globalizing Era', *International Studies Review*, Vol. 23, No. 3, September 2021, pp. 933–57.

exports. The logic of a market economy is to locate economic activities in geographical regions where they are most productive and profitable.[4] Production linked incentive (PLIs) schemes are doing precisely that. PLIs have aided the relocation of the manufacturing units to India. Global mobile manufacturers such as Samsung, Pegatron Corporation, Wistron Group, Foxconn Technology Group and Rising Star have set up their manufacturing plants in India. According to India Cellular and Electronics Association estimates, exports of mobiles from India in the financial year (FY) 2021–22 would be around US$5.7 billion. The quest to become aatmanirbhar by promoting manufacturing would also have multiplier benefits, such as employment and taxes paid, occurring within India and not in other countries.

INTERNATIONAL RELATIONS, CONFLICT, TRADE RESTRICTIONS AND SELF-SUFFICIENCY

Self-reliance is often seen at odds with the idea of free trade. Some have even equated AatmaNirbhar Bharat with autarky. Dating back to the seventeenth century, many thinkers have delved into national self-sufficiency. Many have made a case for autarky. Helliner analysed ideas of thinkers such as Jean-Jacques Rousseau, Johann Fichte, Mohandas Karamchand Gandhi and John Maynard Keynes. Based on this, Helliner has identified three critical ideals of autarky, namely: '(1) insulation from foreign economic influence, (2) insulation from foreign political and/or cultural influence, and (3) the promotion of international peace.'[5]

---

[4]Gilpin, R., *The Political Economy of International Relations*, Princeton University Press, 1987.

[5]Helleiner, E., 'The Return of National Self-Sufficiency? Excavating Autarkic Thought in a De-Globalizing Era', *International Studies Review*, Vol. 23, No. 3, September 2021, pp. 933–57.

India's model of AatmaNirbhar Bharat does not aim to achieve any of these objectives.

TRADE AND PEACE

The quest for aatmanirbharta should rather be seen through the lens of international relations and pragmatism. International relations are about reciprocity. So are the trade relations between any two nations. In his book, *The Wealth of Nations*, Adam Smith identified mainly two exceptions to free trade. First, specific tariff restrictions may be imposed in scenarios wherein the country's defence comes into question. For him, the defence was 'of much more importance than opulence'.[6] Second, Smith also talked about reciprocity. He advocated for retaliatory protectionism if a country imposed disproportionate tariffs on its trading partners. According to Smith, such restrictions by one trading partner would have aided in removing trade barriers by both trading partners. Retaliatory protectionism is generally imposed both by tariff and non-tariff barriers.

In some instances, trade restrictions including the non-tariff trade barriers, are not just determined by the reciprocal restrictions. A vast body of research has been done on the impact of trade on conflicts and vice versa. There is no dearth of literature that suggests that if there is mutual trade dependence between two countries, it sufficiently raises the cost of conflict between the two countries. The greater the level of economic engagement, the lesser are the chances of hostility.[7] One of the greatest liberal philosophers, Montesquieu, saw trade as a tool that resulted in peace. In his book, *L'Esprit des lois* (*The Spirit of Law*), he says:

---

[6]Smith, A., *An Inquiry Into the Nature and Causes of the Wealth of Nations*, Claredon Press, 1776, p. 464.

[7]Polachek, S.W., 'Conflict and Trade', *Journal of Conflict Resolution*, Vol. 24, No. 1, 1980, pp. 55–78.

'It is almost a general rule that wherever the ways of man are gentle, there is commerce; and wherever there is commerce, there the ways of men are gentle.' Several studies have also found that bilateral trade interdependence promotes more significantly in contiguous countries.[8]

Conversely, there is no dearth of anecdotal evidence and empirical studies claiming that trade does not necessarily lead to peace. According to Albert Hirschman, reasons for undertaking trade with a country could be both economic and political.[9] A state may choose to pursue trade relations with a political adversary to ensure economic dependence, which may, in the future help the former to achieve its political objectives. Any abrupt disruption in trade relations can be highly detrimental for the country's economy. This is at the wrong end of the trade imbalance. Hirschman and several other scholars have illustrated this using the example of Taiwan.[10] China is the largest trading partner of Taiwan. The extent of Taiwan's dependence on China is so much that if China decides to close down on the cross-strait economic relations, Taiwan will become vulnerable to a recession.[11]

One should also read a seminal paper by John Maynard Keynes titled 'National Self Sufficiency' for the *Yale Review* in 1933. This essay should be mandatory reading for those that blindly advocate for free trade or protectionism. It was written when the world saw the worst excesses of protectionism during the interwar years (1919–39). To quote Keynes:

---

[8]Lee, J., and J.H. Pyun, *Does Trade Integration Contribute to Peace?*, Cato Institute, 2020.

[9]Hirschman, A.O., *National Power and the Structure of Foreign Trade*, University of California Press, 1945.

[10]Benson, B.V., and E.M. Niou, 'Economic Interdependence and Peace: A Game-Theoretic Analysis', *Journal of East Asian Studies*, Vol. 7, No.1, 2007, pp. 35–59.

[11]Tanner, M.S., *Chinese Economic Coercion Against Taiwan: A Tricky Weapon to Use*, RAND Corporation, 2007.

I was brought up, like most Englishmen, to respect free trade not only as an economic doctrine which a rational and instructed person could not doubt but almost as a part of the moral law. I regarded ordinary departures from it as being, at the same time, an imbecility and an outrage... But it does not now seem obvious that a great concentration of national effort on the capture of foreign trade, that the penetration of a country's economic structure by the resources and the influence of foreign capitalists, and that a close dependence of our own economic life on the fluctuating economic policies of foreign countries are safeguards and assurances of international peace... A considerable degree of international specialisation is necessary in a rational world in all cases where it is dictated by wide differences of climate, natural resources, native aptitudes, level of culture and density of population. But over an increasingly wide range of industrial products, and perhaps of agricultural products also, I have become doubtful whether the economic loss of national self-sufficiency is great enough to outweigh the other advantages of gradually bringing the product and the consumer within the ambit of the same national, economic and financial organisation. Experience accumulates to prove that most modern processes of mass production can be performed in most countries and climates with almost equal efficiency.

Moreover, with greater wealth, both primary and manufactured products play a smaller relative part in the national economy compared with houses, personal services, and local amenities, which are not equally available for international exchange; with the result that a moderate increase in the real cost of primary and manufactured products consequent on greater national self-sufficiency may cease to be of serious consequence when weighed in the balance against advantages of a different kind. National self-sufficiency, in short, though it costs something, maybe

> becoming a luxury which, we can afford, if we happen to want it.[12]

In all fairness to Keynes, he had warned against self-sufficiency and economic nationalism if its goals were narrowly defined. Keynes had also delved into the idea of foreign trade and peace. He also talked about how excessive dependence on foreign countries in certain cases can be counterproductive. He suggested:

> Yet the orientation of my mind is changed… To begin with, the question of peace. But it does not now seem obvious that a great concentration of national effort on the capture of foreign trade, that the penetration of a country's economic resources and the influence of foreign capitalists, and that a close dependence of our own economic life on the fluctuating economic policies of foreign countries are safeguards and assurances of international peace… Let goods be homespun whenever it is reasonably and conveniently possible, and, above all, let finance be primarily national… A greater measure of national self-sufficiency and economic isolation among countries than existed in 1914 may tend to serve the cause of peace, rather than otherwise.[13]

Further, with regards to dyadic relationships, Katherine Barbieri explains that the interdependent dyads are more likely to enter into militarized conflicts as compared to the ones with less or minimal trade ties.[14] Asymmetrical trade between two dyads has a propensity to develop into a conflict in some instances. A thriving trade relationship between the two countries doesn't

---

[12]'Keynes, J. M., 'National Self-Sufficiency', *The Yale Review*, Vol. 22 No. 4, pp. 755–69.

[13]Ibid.

[14]Barbieri, K., *The Liberal Illusion: Does Trade Promote Peace*, The University of Michigan Press, 2005.

necessarily mean that the larger trading partner doesn't take any action, economic or military, against the other.

In some instances, some states use economic sanctions to compel the trading partner to follow a specified policy. If the specified policy is not adopted, the trading partner is threatened with curtailment of beneficial interactions with the sanctioning state.[15] China had recently imposed economic sanctions on Australia as a punishment for Canberra's insistence on investigations into the origin of the Covid-19 pandemic. Hefty tariffs were imposed on Australian barley and wine, significantly impacting the Australian industry. According to the Institute for International Trade at the University of Adelaide, Australia had to forgo export revenue of around US$4.9 billion.[16] The key commodities affected due to China's restrictions or discriminatory purchasing were frozen beef, coal, copper ores and concentrates, barley, cotton, wine, rock lobster and rough wood.

Thriving trade relations does not necessarily mean that there won't be any military conflict between two trading dyads. The Sino–Indian relationship is a good example of this. The bilateral trade between the two countries in 2021 stood at around US$125 billion. This was a 43.3 per cent increase from 2020. Despite this, there have been several incursions by China into Indian territory and unprovoked border skirmishes initiated by the People's Liberation Army. India imports about 70 per cent of APIs from a single source, i.e. from China. What if, due to some dispute, China decides to restrict the exports of APIs to India? There is always a risk of price volatility and supply disruption if the relations between the two countries sour.

---

[15]Peterson, T.M., 'Reconsidering Economic Leverage and Vulnerability: Trade Ties, Sanction Threats, and the Success of Economic Coercion', *Conflict Management and Peace Science*, 2018, pp. 1–21.

[16]Wickes, R. (et al.), *Working Paper 4: Economic Coercion by China: The Impact on Australia's Merchandise Exports*, Institute for International Trade, The University of Adelaide, July 2021.

Trade restrictions on essential commodities can eventually have national security implications. One should quote what Friedrich List, who critiqued Adam Smith's *The Wealth of Nations*, wrote in 1841:

> The imports and exports of independent nations are regulated and controlled at present not by what the popular theory calls the natural course of things, but mostly by the commercial policy and the power of the nation, by the influence of these on the conditions of the world and on foreign countries and peoples, by colonial possessions and internal credit establishments, or by war and peace.[17]

Not much has changed since 1841.

CONTOURS OF THE INDIAN MODEL OF SELF-RELIANCE

Delivering the inaugural address at the India Global Week 2020, PM Narendra Modi in July 2020 said, 'Aatmanirbhar Bharat is not about being self-contained or being closed to the world, it is about being self-sustaining and self-generating. We will pursue policies that promote efficiency, equity and resilience.'[18] India's quest for aatmanirbharta or self-reliance, thus, should be judged against India's self-interest. AatmaNirbhar Bharat should not be equated with import substitution. India already had its tryst with import substitution in the past. The highly protected (but inefficient) domestic industry because of import substitution, was disastrous for the industry itself, the economy and even for the consumers. AatmaNirbhar Bharat is not a step towards becoming a closed economy. It aims at promoting entrepreneurship and

---

[17]List, Friedrich, *The National System of Political Economy*, Sampson S. Lloyd (trans.), 1841, Longmans, Green & Co., p. 219.

[18]'Text of PM's Inaugural Address at India Global Week 2020', *PIB Delhi*, 9 July 2020, https://tinyurl.com/5228wb4p. Accessed on 17 July 2023.

innovation by removing bureaucratic hurdles. It is about attracting industries to manufacture in India. It is about building resilient supply chains. Consider the example of medical devices. More than 75 per cent of medical devices in India were being imported until very recently. The medical devices, including something like ventilators, were subjected to supply shock during the pandemic. But why wasn't it being manufactured in India in the first place? Was it because of the absence of technical know-how to manufacture this equipment? No. It was simply because the import duties were higher on raw materials/intermediate products than on the finished medical devices. Simply by addressing the issue of inverted duties, the government promoted the manufacturing of medical devices in India.

We have identified five critical aspects of the Indian model of self-reliance. First, as discussed in the previous sections, geopolitical considerations and the principle of reciprocity play a vital role in international trade. Self-reliance becomes a prerequisite if the imports are heavily sourced from a country that has revisionist inclinations. India should reduce imports from the countries with which it has active conflicts. This includes the imports of essential goods.

Second, India should be self-reliant in manufacturing goods that are solely imported from one source (be it from China or any other country). Any supply shock tends to have a negative impact on Indian consumers, as well as the industry as a whole. Third, the Indian model of self-reliance should be focussed on the manufacturing of goods that have high domestic demand. India has already launched PLIs for auto components, telecom and networking products, textiles, air conditioner components, LEDs, etc.

Fourth, the production of essential goods which are subject to supply shocks in times of crisis needs to be prioritized. For instance, before the pandemic, China was the largest manufacturer of N-95 masks. The advent of Covid-19 in China completely stopped exports of N-95 masks and PPE (personal protective equipment) kits. It was then that Indian manufacturers decided to manufacture N-95 masks and PPE kits in India. Similarly, other such goods should be manufactured in India. The supply of APIs was also disrupted due to the Covid-19 pandemic. The government has launched schemes to promote the production of APIs in India.

Finally, India should also become self-reliant in manufacturing strategic and defence equipment. The world is going through an unprecedented shortage of something like a semiconductor. They are required in the manufacturing of small LEDs for advanced weapon systems. The global shortage of semiconductors has crippled supply chains across industries. Again, India has recently launched a PLI scheme for manufacturing semiconductors in the country. The manufacturing of defence equipment is another area in which India needs to be self-reliant. India still imports more than 50 per cent of its defence equipment from Russia. The Ukraine–Russia crisis took a toll on these imports. According to SIPRI (Stockholm International Peace Research Institute), India was the biggest importer of arms from 2017–21. However, the volume of imports has been falling. Thus, the aatmanirbharta push is now showing some results.

CONCLUSION

Keeping the aatmanirbharta objective in view, India has to take two concrete actions. First, it has to invest in research, development and innovation. The absence of technological innovation will hamper the competitiveness of Indian exports. This, in turn, will hinder economic growth. If India is to compete on the global stage, it has to invest in frontier technologies. This would require a lot of investments from both the government and the private sector.

Second, India should constantly pursue the objective of getting market access for its exports. One way would be to pursue regional trade agreements, including FTAs (free trade agreements) with countries that have a demand for our exports. India's Comprehensive Economic Partnership Agreement with UAE (United Arab Emirates) and India–Australia Economic Cooperation and Trade Agreement are steps in this direction. Vietnam has successfully forged trade relations with many developed countries. It has also become an important anchor in many multinational corporations with China Plus One supply chain diversification strategy. India should take cues and actively pursue trade deals with countries that have a demand for high-value manufactured goods.

15

STOCK EXCHANGES: A VITAL COG IN FACILITATING THE VISION OF AATMANIRBHAR BHARAT

Ashish Kumar Chauhan
MD and CEO, National Stock Exchange;
Chancellor, University of Allahabad

India possesses a rich and illustrious heritage in the fields of science, mathematics, economics and governance, which continues to shape its contemporary culture and behaviour. Our ancient history dates to the flourishing Indus Valley civilization, spanning from 5000 BC to 1800 BC. Within the Vedic philosophies and scriptures lies a treasury of wisdom that holds immense value for the progress of humanity. Practices such as yoga, Ayurveda and meditation have garnered worldwide reverence—representing just a glimpse of the diverse facets of this rich heritage. However, there is an aspect of Vedic knowledge that has faded from collective memory—the principle of self-reliance, known as aatmanirbharta.

The Vedic people embodied not only robust health, innovation and intellectual curiosity but also a sense of prosperity and self-sufficiency. They maintained a confident outlook and engaged with the global community, fostering connections rather than isolating themselves. Historical records reveal that the economy of the Indus civilization thrived on extensive trade, facilitated by advancements in transportation. During ancient and medieval times, India boasted of being the world's largest economy. It commanded an impressive share of global wealth and gross domestic product (GDP), ranging from a third to nearly a half. This led to unparalleled prosperity in human history. India held a prominent position as a leading manufacturing nation until the early eighteenth century, supported by a well-developed banking system and strong merchant capital network comprising agents, brokers and intermediaries.

The Rig Veda, the primary source of knowledge about the Vedic Age, suggests that it was a cooperative society focussed on wealth creation. Even as late as the 1800s, India remained the world's largest economy and contributed to a fourth of global GDP. This surpasses the combined output of the entire European continent, exceeding Britain's economy by almost tenfold. However, the growth of trade with India, Africa and China had already started benefiting Britain. Sadly, by the time of Independence, India's share of global GDP had plummeted by over 90 per cent from pre-colonial times.[1]

CREDIT AND LENDING IN MEDIEVAL INDIA

The practice of money lending dates to the dawn of humanity, with trade, barter and rudimentary lending methods existing during the evolution of Homo sapiens. In ancient Greece one sees an organized lending system, and traces of a credit system can be found as early as the Vedic period in India. Ancient Indian texts like the Dharmashastras mentioned that lives and livelihoods with lending featured in business practices as well. Credit and lending practices during the Vedic period in ancient India were characterized by a system of trust, informal arrangements and

---

[1]Williamson, Jeffrey G., and David Clingingsmith, *India's Deindustrialization in the 18th and 19th Centuries*, Harvard University, August 2005, https://tinyurl.com/3avu89h3. Accessed on 26 June 2023.

mutual obligations within the society. While there are limited written records specifically addressing credit and lending during this period, insights can be gathered from Vedic texts and archaeological findings.

During the Mauryan period in ancient India (321–185 BC), there were significant developments in structured lending practices. The Mauryan Empire, under the reign of Emperor Chandragupta Maurya and his successors, witnessed the establishment of a well-organized systematized lending structure. Mauryan texts, particularly Kautilya's *Arthashastra*, mention various forms of loan deeds known as '*rinapatra*', '*rinapanna*' or '*rinalekhaya*'. These documents served as legal instruments that detailed the terms and conditions of loans. They provided a written record of the debt, repayment terms, interest rates and collateral. These ensured the enforceability of lending transactions. An instrument called '*adesha*' emerged during the Mauryan period, which can be considered a precursor to the modern bill of exchange. An adesha literally means an 'order' or 'instruction' directing a banker to pay the amount mentioned in the note to the holder. It facilitated the transfer of funds and acted as a form of credit instrument in trade transactions.

In this period, the well-developed banking system supported lending activities through intermediaries. Credit instruments like letters of credit were widely used by merchants, ensuring trust and facilitating trade. Payment orders known as *barattes* directed funds to specific individuals, while bills of exchange enabled fund transfers and debt settlements. Merchants played a crucial role in structured lending, given their involvement in trade and commerce. The expansion of trade networks amplified the need for structured lending practices, which contributed to the organization and formalization of lending; regulating activities; promoting trade; and fostering economic growth in ancient India.

Credit and lending practices continued to evolve in medieval

India, building upon the foundations established in earlier periods. The medieval period in India spanned from approximately the sixth century to the eighteenth century and witnessed significant developments in commerce, trade and economic systems.

One prominent feature of credit and lending during this period was the emergence of indigenous banking systems, known as *shroffs*. These shroffs played a crucial role in facilitating credit and lending transactions within local communities. They acted as intermediaries between borrowers and lenders, providing financial services such as loans, deposit-taking and money transfers.

The shroffs were often trusted members of the community, known for their integrity and financial expertise. They operated as private moneylenders and maintained extensive networks to cater to the credit needs of individuals, businesses and even ruling elites. These indigenous banking systems were prevalent across different regions of medieval India, and their operations were governed by customary laws and community practices.

Credit transactions during this period involved various types of loans. The most common form of lending was through cash loans, where money was lent for specific purposes, and repayment was expected with interest within a predetermined period. Interest rates varied depending on factors such as the borrower's credit-worthiness, the purpose of the loan and prevailing market conditions.

In addition to cash loans, there were other forms of credit instruments utilized in medieval India. *Hundi*, also known as a bill of exchange, was a widely used instrument for transferring funds and facilitating trade transactions. It allowed for the transfer of funds from one place to another, often across long distances, without the need for physical movement of cash. Hundi transactions involved parties such as bankers, merchants and individuals who endorsed and guaranteed the payment. The Hundi system played a crucial role in promoting trade and commerce during this period.

Collateral-based lending was another prevalent practice in medieval India. Borrowers often provided collateral, such as land, jewellery or other valuable assets, to secure their loans. In case of default, the lender had the right to seize and liquidate the collateral to recover the outstanding debt.

MERCANTILE TRADE USING 'HUNDIS'

The Hundi system that has been widespread for many centuries facilitates fund transfer and money remittance within India. It is internationally based on reputation and trust of individuals. The system is extensively used by traders, businessmen and communities engaged in long-distance trade and personal remittances. This is particularly present in regions such as Gujarat, Rajasthan, Maharashtra and other commercial hubs in India.

Hundi system played a crucial role during the colonial era as a financial mechanism, especially for communities with limited access to formal banking services. Its informal nature allowed for quick and convenient fund transfers, particularly when formal channels were restricted. However, the system also faced challenges. Operating outside formal regulatory frameworks, the Hundi system relied on trust and personal connections for money transfers. This made it susceptible to misuse and illegal activities like money laundering and illicit transactions.

Unlike formal banking systems, the Hundi system had limited financial accountability and documentation. This made it difficult to track funds or establish legal ownership. Funds were transferred through intermediaries, relying on personal trust, which posed security risks and the potential for fraud or misappropriation. Victims of fraud often encountered difficulties in recovering their money due to the lack of legal remedies. While effective within specific networks and communities, the Hundi system had limited reach in areas without a network of *hawala* operators. This made fund transfers less convenient for individuals in remote or less-connected regions. Currency exchange, especially for international transactions, was common within the system.

However, the absence of standardized exchange rates and transparent mechanisms could lead to discrepancies or unfavourable rates. This could potentially result in financial losses for users. The Hundi system became associated with illegal or covert financial activities, hindering its recognition and acceptance as a mainstream method of fund transfer (both domestically and internationally). Operating in a legal grey area outside formal banking regulations, it presented challenges for authorities in monitoring and controlling financial transactions. Governments implemented stricter regulations to combat money laundering and illicit activities, which affected the functioning of the Hundi system. During the period of British rule, measures were taken to discourage the use of the Hundi system and promote Western banking practices. Actions such as implementing stamp duty, regulation and licensing, and introducing the Banks Act of 1934 were employed.

As a result, the utilization of Hundis gradually declined in India as the formal banking system offered greater legal protection, transaction convenience and stability. The Hundi system remained popular in areas with limited access to banking services, where financial transactions relied on trust-based relationships.

THE ADVENT OF BANKS

The pioneering of banking in India can be attributed to the European traders who arrived during the colonial period. The Portuguese, Dutch and British played significant roles in introducing and establishing the foundations of modern banking in India. The Portuguese were the first to establish a trading post in India in the early sixteenth century and introduced the concept of modern banking, through the establishment of money exchange houses. This marked the initial steps towards the development of banking in the region. It started with the 'Madras Bank' in 1683[2], and the 'Bank of Bombay' in 1720[3]. Subsequently, the British and Indian merchants founded the 'Bank of Hindostan' in 1770. It was one of the earliest attempts to bring modern banking to India. The British East India Company also played a major role in establishing three presidency banks in the early nineteenth century: the Bank of Bengal (1806), the Bank of Bombay (1840) and the Bank of Madras (1843). These banks acted as central banks for their respective regions and played a crucial role in financing trade and commerce.

Apart from the Revolt of 1857 and the transfer of India from the East India Company (EIC) to the British Crown, 1857 also saw The Indian Companies Act. This enabled the formation of joint-stock banks in the country and helped provide a legal framework for banking institutions as joint-stock companies. The entry of the first joint bank, the Allahabad Bank, in 1865 paved the way for the establishment of other joint-stock banks. This contributed significantly to modern banking in the country.

Collectively, these factors laid the groundwork for modern banking in India. It shaped the banking landscape and facilitated economic growth and development in the country. Today, India boasts a diverse and robust banking system that caters to the financial needs of individuals, businesses and the overall economy.

ORIGINS OF CAPITAL MARKETS IN INDIA

The earliest records of security dealings in India are meagre and obscure. The EIC was the dominant institution towards the close of the eighteenth century, and business in its loan securities used

---

[2]'District Profile-2017, Chennai District', *Government of Tamil Nadu*, https://tinyurl.com/bdhncvxw. Accessed on 26 June 2023.

[3]'The Advent of Modern Banking in India', *Reserve Bank of India*, https://tinyurl.com/bdz662t3. Accessed on 26 June 2023.

to be transacted in those days. In the 1850s, the Companies Act introducing limited liability was enacted and with it commenced the era of modern joint-stock enterprise in India.[4] The 1850s also witnessed rapid development of commercial enterprise. In 1857, the first nationwide freedom struggle against the British rule occurred, which was brutally suppressed. Reverberations of the same were heard in the UK (United Kingdom) and the British government subsequently took direct charge of India. The extension of railways, introduction of telegraph and gradual improvement in the communication systems all promoted internal trade and commerce. Many new enterprises were floated and by 1860s, the number of brokers increased to 60 and they made their marketplace under banyan trees between the old fort walls in the place now known as the Horniman circle in Mumbai. Many of the original brokers came from the cotton trading business. Bombay Cotton Exchange was a force to be reckoned with in the world markets those days.[5]

During the period of the US Civil War, cotton prices moved up many times in Mumbai and consequently, the number of stockbrokers also swelled to about 200. They were treated as the privileged class. However, the end of the Civil War brought disillusionment and many failures of the enterprises floated. As the number of brokers increased, they had to shift from place to place and almost always overflowed into the streets. At last, in 1874, the brokers found a permanent place and one that they could (quite literally) call their own. The new place was aptly called Dalal Street (Brokers' Street).

The brokers organized an informal association and finally, on 9 July 1875, a few native brokers doing brokerage business in

---

[4]Majumdar, R.C. (ed.), 'The History and Culture of the Indian People: British Paramountcy and Indian Resistance', *Bharatiya Vidya Bhavan*, Vol. 10, 1951.

[5]Thomas, P., 'Report on the Regulation of the Stock Market in India', *Government of India*, 1948.

shares and stocks resolved upon forming the Native Share and Stock Brokers Association. They pledged to protect the character, status and interest of native share and stockbrokers and to source a hall or building for the members. At a meeting in Brokers' Hall on 5 February 1887, it was resolved to execute a formal deed of association, constitute the first managing committee and appoint the first trustees. Accordingly, an indenture was executed on 3 December 1887 constituting articles of association of the exchange and the Bombay Stock Exchange (BSE) was formally established.

STOCK EXCHANGE: THE EARLY DAYS

The industrial sector in India began to grow during the nineteenth century, with the establishment of textile mills, cotton factories and other manufacturing units. The cotton trade played a significant role in the early development of the securities market in India. Mumbai, then known as Bombay, was a prominent centre for cotton trading that attracted foreign investors. The stockbrokers and traders involved in the cotton trade formed the backbone of the early securities market.

As industrialization progressed, more companies started to issue securities to raise capital for their operations and expansion. The formation of a stock exchange provided a platform for the trading of these securities, enabling companies to access capital and investors to participate in the industrial growth. Establishment of stock exchanges in other major cities such as Kolkata (Calcutta Stock Exchange) and Chennai (Madras Stock Exchange) facilitated participation of a wider group. Investors could buy and sell these securities on the stock exchanges, providing liquidity and investment opportunities.

The First World War led to an increase in economic activities and industrial production in India to support the war efforts. This, in turn, led to the growth of various industries and companies and their stocks were listed and traded on the stock exchanges.

The war created opportunities for investors to participate in the growth of industries like textiles, steel, shipping and infrastructure. The outbreak of the Second World War resulted in heightened uncertainty and volatility in global financial markets, including India. But with large increase of profits due to war orders, share prices also improved. This continued until the fall of France and entry of Japan, post which restrictions had to be put in place. The post-war period once again saw growth in capital markets due to excessive optimism and a flush of money with the investors.

In 1914–15, there were 2,545 joint stock companies with total paid-up capital of ₹81 crore, and by 1939–40, the number of companies rose to 11,372 and the paid-up capital to ₹303.7 crore. By the end of Second World War in 1945, the number of companies was 14,859 with paid-up capital of ₹388.9 crores.

The Indian securities market witnessed the introduction of regulatory frameworks during this period. The Securities Contracts Regulation Act of 1956 and the Companies Act of 1956 provided a legal foundation for securities trading, listing requirements and corporate governance. In 1988, the Securities and Exchange Board of India (SEBI) was established as the primary regulatory authority for the securities market in India. SEBI's mandate includes investor protection, regulation of market intermediaries and promoting the development and regulation of the securities market. In the early 1990s, India embarked on a series of economic reforms and market liberalization measures. These reforms aimed to open up the economy; encourage foreign investment; and strengthen the securities market. It led to the establishment of the National Stock Exchange (NSE) in 1992, which introduced electronic trading and brought greater transparency and efficiency to the market. In 1996, the National Securities Depository Limited (NSDL) and Central Depository Services Limited (CDSL) were established. These facilitated electronic settlement and holding of securities.

The Indian securities market gradually integrated with global markets during the post-war period. In 1999, the Foreign

Institutional Investors (FII) category was introduced which allowed foreign investors to invest in Indian securities. Over time, foreign investment limits were increased and Indian equities were included in global indices. This attracted greater foreign participation in the Indian market. The introduction of index futures in 2000 and index options in 2001 provided investors with hedging and trading opportunities. The derivatives segment expanded to include stock futures, stock options and other derivative instruments.

The rapid adoption of technology in the Indian securities market with electronic trading platforms; online trading; mobile trading applications; and algorithmic trading gained prominence, and brought efficiency and ease of access to market participants. Also, SEBI's various measures to enhance investor protection and market surveillance such as Know Your Customer (KYC) norms, stricter disclosure requirements and surveillance mechanisms were introduced to safeguard investor interests and maintain market integrity.

The market has witnessed increased investor participation, improved market infrastructure and regulatory reforms to align with international best practices. These developments have contributed to the growth and evolution of the Indian securities market, making it one of the significant emerging markets globally.

WHAT INDIA MISSED OUT ON

Stock exchanges facilitate the flow of capital in an economy, but the initial lead achieved by nations in Europe was significant. Illustratively, the industrial revolution commenced with the invention of the steam engine, then the power loom in UK, leading to a substantial shift in the labour force from agriculture to industry. The Indian economy, barring parts of Bengal, continued to have medieval and agricultural practices as the mainstay. For the trading companies of Europe seeking to trade with disparate Indian kingdoms, it made sense to procure raw materials from

India for their already well-established industries. And with the pickup in British imports, the traditional industries in India—like weaving, carpentry, pottery and metallurgy—gradually declined, unable to compete with the lead of a century and regulations that favoured the Crown.

During the 1850s, India saw the emergence of its first engineers who were trained in colleges located in Calcutta, Madras and Roorkee. However, these colleges primarily focussed on civil engineering as the British required engineers for construction projects. It wasn't until the 1930s that the first mechanical engineers received training in India. The training of Indian electrical, chemical and aeronautical engineers was still a distant prospect. In the 1930s, a staggering 90 per cent of Indians were illiterate. This starkly contrasts with Europe's 80 per cent literacy rate and the United States' 90 per cent literacy rate.

By 1950, India had a population of nearly 380 million but its literacy rate remained low, with just about 2 million factory workers. In comparison, Britain had a population of 50 million with a literacy rate of around 90 per cent and nearly 10 million factory workers. Despite this, Britain still needed to import workers for its factories. The years of colonization had widened the chasm between British and its colonies. For the Indian subcontinent, it would have been unrealistic to bridge this gap in even half a century. The advent of the first aircraft in Europe and the US in the early 1900s had all the basic industries, the level of industrialization and the required labour force in place. This was something that India did not have even by 1950.

A UNIQUE OPPORTUNITY TO TAKE-OFF

The first Industrial Revolution began in the late eighteenth century with the steam engine and the power loom, and brought significant advancements in manufacturing, technology and transportation. India, under British colonial rule at the time, faced several challenges that hindered its ability to fully participate and benefit from this transformative period. Colonization led to the country's resources and wealth being appropriated, leading to economic drain and hindering local industrial development. Traditional Indian industries such as textiles faced stiff competition from British manufactured goods, resulting in the decline of indigenous industries.

This deindustrialisation led to limited growth in the facilitating infrastructure that other countries came to rely on, like transportation, communications and power. It also led to the second Industrial Revolution there in the late nineteenth and early twentieth centuries with electricity, mass manufacturing and new industries. India remained under British control during this period. With policy restrictions on indigenous manufacture limiting industrial capability, technological adoption and capital investment; raw material extraction remained the focal point of the British Raj.

Industrial policy post-Independence chose the path of a planned economy, with noble intentions, but led to a closed and protectionist economy that focussed on import substitution. Liberalization in the early 1990s finally saw growth in a sustained, non-volatile manner. With its economy above the US$3-trillion mark now, and still growing at nearly 7 per cent, India is in position to enter the next phase of industrialization and innovation.

TECHNOLOGY ADOPTION TO DRIVE THE NEXT STAGE OF GROWTH

As we witness the peak of the fourth Industrial Revolution, the concept of 'disruption' has become prevalent. The anticipated disruption has already become a reality. Over the past 25 years, the average Indian has experienced significant changes. The Indian economy has undergone a transformation, leading to a starkly different living environment. The shift from scarcity to abundance is apparent. Examples like Aadhaar and the India Stack infrastructure have showcased the potential of digitalization in governance, welfare delivery and payments. This has made them global exemplars of GovTech innovation. India's early adoption of stock market automation in the 1990s propelled the nation to the forefront of global stock market infrastructure automation. It also drove the development of its renowned Information Technology (IT) capabilities.

Technology has historically been the most influential catalyst for change. Technological advancements occur in waves, with each wave bringing forth new discoveries or inventions. For instance, the mastery of fire revolutionized societies. It enabled longer lives, better food and enhanced defence mechanisms. Subsequent technologies, such as the wheel and the use of tools made from bones, further transformed human existence. Societies that embraced these technologies witnessed significant improvements in quality of life, even if they didn't fully comprehend the underlying mechanisms.

In recent years, technology waves have accelerated and profoundly impacted our lives. Information technology, within a single generation, completely transformed our world. The upcoming technologies promise even more transformative changes. Societies that adapt their laws and way of life, embracing and leveraging new technologies, will thrive while those lacking flexibility may face disadvantages. The industrial revolution itself was a massive disruption, with countries either embracing it and experiencing prosperity or missing out and declining. Today, we find ourselves amidst the next Industrial Revolution which is expected to be even more disruptive in nature.

THE NEED FOR AATMANIRBHARTA

Physical labour-intensive manufacturing emerged as the key driver of economy-wide productivity growth, since the beginning of the industrial revolution. Countries in Europe, the Americas and East Asia successfully transitioned unskilled workers from rural farms to urban factories. This lead to higher individual incomes and national GDPs (gross domestic product). However, not all nations followed the path of manufacturing. In India, services now constitute more than half of the GDP while the industrial and manufacturing sectors have faced some challenges.

To address this, under the leadership of Prime Minister (PM) Narendra Modi, India has embarked on a re-industrialization programme. The introduction of production linked incentives (PLIs) aims to attract renowned global manufacturers, industry experts and high-quality long-term investments. With the availability of high-speed internet and advanced computing technology, research, design and development can happen anywhere in the world. Software has become increasingly vital in driving additive manufacturing, automating factories and facilitating the 'servicization of manufacturing' as traditional intermediaries are bypassed.

WHY INDIA CAN LEAD THE NEXT INDUSTRIAL REVOLUTION

India possesses a unique opportunity in the global landscape. With its cost advantages; a young population; a stable government; and a thriving services ecosystem, India can become a hub for rapid, scalable and cost-effective innovation that the world needs. A median age of 28 and a large English-speaking populace, places India in a pivotal role in shaping the agenda of the next global Industrial Revolution in a responsible, inclusive and scalable manner. By leveraging a combination of accelerators such as regulatory frameworks, educational ecosystems and government incentives, India can lead the fourth Industrial Revolution. It can do this while simultaneously improving the quality, equity and sustainability of its own growth and development outcomes.

In the coming 50 years, the world is poised to generate wealth on an unprecedented scale. It might even surpass the accomplishments of the past 10,000 years. Moreover, it is anticipated that 70 per cent of the jobs created during this period will be completely novel and beyond our current imagination. India, with its technologically oriented youth, will significantly contribute to both job creation and wealth generation. In many emerging technology sectors, large capital investments are no longer necessary to achieve substantial returns and generate immense wealth. This shift can be attributed to the non-linearity of payoff, where relatively meagre capital investment can yield significant results.

Unlike smaller countries, India cannot rely solely on importing technologies and business models for national-scale prosperity. There is a remarkable opportunity for Indian industries, venture investors and entrepreneurs to embrace the role of profit-maximizing agents; rewrite conventional playbooks; and establish new paradigms that utilize technology to create wealth and drive innovation.

HOW THE STOCK EXCHANGES CAN HELP

Indian households' annual savings amount to over ₹50 lakh crore or US$700 billion. Analysis of national accounts data for the financial year (FY) 2021 and savings trends for FY 2022 reveals that total household savings have consistently remained above ₹50 lakh crore, over the past two years. Given the scale of these savings, there is potential for sustained retail flows. This is considering that households save $700 billion annually while current equity flows directly through stocks (or indirectly through mutual funds and related products), representing less than one-twentieth of this amount. Bank deposits remain the preferred investment option within the financial sector, with three times the investment volume of equities.

Stock exchanges play a critical role in the global economy as they facilitate the raising of funds, both long-term and short-term, for governments and companies. They also serve as channels for directing these funds to various stakeholders within the ecosystem. The resilience of Indian markets is evident in their successful navigation through challenging periods that have affected global markets. These include the Asian financial crisis of 1998, the global financial crisis of 2008, the Covid-19 pandemic in 2020 and many smaller crises in between.

IN CONCLUSION

The fundamental role of the stock market in a nation's economy is to mobilize household savings and facilitate the raising of capital for companies. This capital enables companies to create job opportunities and contribute to overall economic growth. In line with the vision of AatmaNirbhar Bharat, the stock markets serve as a platform for corporations to raise equity and debt financing (supporting their long-term objectives). Additionally, they play a crucial role in capital formation, leading to wealth generation for investors and fostering employment opportunities within the country.

Indian entrepreneurs can consistently rely on the Indian capital markets to access capital whenever required. Embracing the call for AatmaNirbhar Bharat, the frontiers of Indian capital markets will expand significantly and assume greater importance and urgency. Indian stock exchanges will continue to be the primary drivers of capital formation, working at an accelerated pace to foster a more prosperous, confident and self-reliant Bharat (India).

India is a unique developing country with a very low per capita income but extremely highly developed and liquid capital markets, which are markets for trust. Indian markets today are touching US$3.5 trillion market capitalization and are ranked among the top 4–5 countries in the world with such market capitalization;

70 million direct unique investors; and almost 20 per cent of households directly investing in stock markets.

Other countries with 2-4-8 times (200 per cent–400 per cent–800 per cent) of India's per capita GDP have not been able to create vibrant, liquid and healthy markets like India. It can be leveraged further to help India grow and create wealth for all its citizens.

16

AATMANIRBHAR BHARAT: BUILDING WORLD-CLASS INDIAN BRANDS

Sanjiv Puri

Chairman and managing director, ITC Limited

A POWERFUL VISION

A few years ago, the Hon'ble Prime Minister (PM) Narendra Modi, gave a clarion call for building an AatmaNirbhar Bharat. This was an exhortation at par with clarion calls in history like 'Jai jawaan, jai kisaan', by former PM Lal Bahadur Shastri; and 'Give me blood, I'll give you freedom' by Subhas Chandra Bose. It was a vision that was far-sighted and transformational, setting the stage for a powerful and dynamic New India. It envisaged the creation of a powerful India where economic growth would generate and retain value for India, and bring with it social equity and boundless opportunities for the future generations.

Aatmanirbhar or self-reliant India, to my mind, is about developing capabilities that would multiply value for the domestic economy. This will be done by creating world-class products and services, that stand their ground in the face of intense competition from across the globe. The spirit of aatmanirbharta is about going 'local for global', and 'Make in India' programmes where superior and unique capabilities are developed in the country. These leverage India's deep intellectual capacity, creative prowess and innovative capabilities. In addition, self-reliance is about knowledge and collaboration from across the world to manufacture world-class Indian products, brands and services that would win consumer patronage—not only in the Indian global market but in markets across the world. Intrinsic to aatmanirbharta are thoughts, strategies and actions that support growth that is sustainable, inclusive and environmentally beneficial. It is my firm belief that AatmaNirbhar Bharat is about creating champion national enterprises, that have the singular aim of addressing national priorities and contribute towards strengthening of value-chains that foster inclusive growth.

WORLD-CLASS INDIAN BRANDS: A CRITICAL PILLAR FOR BEING AATMANIRBHAR

At the heart of self-reliance lies the ability of a nation to create brands that are best suited, first and foremost, for its own requirements and which are then gradually modified keeping the global market in mind. World-class brands elevate the standing of the nation in the eyes of others and bolsters its reputation, particularly in the economic sphere. The global economy is replete with inspiring stories of successful brands that enrich their economies in multiple ways, and bring a great deal of respect for their countries. Google and Apple in the US (United States), Samsung in Korea and Toyota in Japan are popular examples that have become household names. They achieved this owing to their innovative excellence, which has resulted in global consumer franchise, trust and respect.

Undoubtedly, brands can be one of the most important cogs in the wheel of a nation's economic journey. At a time when India's story is being meticulously shaped, Indian brands can play a significant role in creating larger national value. Champion brands serve as powerful engines that drive growth in several ways. They stimulate innovative capacity and create a culture of innovation, thereby, providing a launchpad for India's rich scientific and technological talent. Such innovative capabilities make a nation future-ready and a global player that enjoys considerable heft and reputation. Winning brands not only add to building intellectual property for the nation but lead to the creation of globally benchmarked manufacturing infrastructure, along with building valuable economic assets for the country.

Apart from supporting large-scale livelihood creation across the value-chain, successful brands can also help in anchoring the development of local entrepreneurship and medium, small and micro enterprises (MSMEs) and promote the development of the ancillary sector. This helps create robust industrial ecosystems. More importantly, for an agrarian country like India, strong brands can anchor and empower local value chains making them more competitive. This helps in uplifting some of the weakest sections in the society and supporting sustainable livelihoods. Over time, these assiduously built domestic brands will provide a powerful thrust to 'Brand India'; create a conducive environment in the sphere of perception; and put India in the orbit of nations synonymous with world-class quality of products and services. These countries include Japan, which became popular with brands like Sony, Mitsubishi, Sumitomo, Honda, Nissan and SoftBank; and Germany with brands like Mercedes-Benz, Audi and BMW.

Over the years, the absence of strong local brands in India led to the dominance of popular global brands in even the most basic products. A few domestic brands that were present, did not possess the ability to handle intense international competition. As more and more services were extended to India, it was quite understandable that owners of global brands began to seek returns for the use of their assets; be it in the form of royalty, patents, trademarks, copyrights and designs. Therefore, creation of intellectual property assets, like brands, is a vital prerequisite for attaining aatmanirbharta and enhancing international competitiveness. In this context, the clarion call for building local brands that can go global is pertinent and exhibits sound understanding of the prevalent situation and the future challenges.

I am of the firm view that a country's economic capacity is significantly enriched when its enterprises build and own internationally competitive brands. The time for creating strong Indian brands is now, and we must leverage India's strong position in the international economic platform. Frankly, the conditions could not be more favourable. India is endowed with a wide spectrum of competitive strengths in terms of intellect, spirit of entrepreneurship, conductive economic environment and favourable policy frameworks. A significant number of Indian brands are now well placed to attain a leadership position in the international markets. It is time that we seize the moment and become the colloquial 'world-beaters'.

THE INDIA PROMISE: A GROWING MARKET THAT NURTURES FMCG BRANDS

India has always been a land of infinite promise. The nation, for many years now, has been on a fast track to emerge as a formidable economic power. The Indian economy is projected to be the fastest-growing among the major economies in the financial year (FY) 2022–23. In addition, the government has undertaken path-breaking economic reforms that are bound to make India the second largest economy in the world by 2047.[1]

As one of the largest consumption markets in the world, India offers immense opportunities for fast-moving consumer goods (FMCG) brands. The Boston Consulting Group states that India's consumption market will triple by 2030; driven by urbanization, higher disposable incomes and nuclear families.[2] In a year, India

---

[1]'India to Be 2nd Biggest Economy in World by 2047: Commerce Secretary', *mint*, 3 September 2022, https://tinyurl.com/33acrasy. Accessed on 21 June 2023.

[2]Pinto, Viveat Susan, 'India's Consumption Market Likely to Triple by 2030, Says

is poised to overtake China as the most populous country in the world and is well positioned to take advantage of a favourable demographic dividend. In FY 2021, India's FMCG market grew at 16 per cent, the fastest growth compared to the previous nine years.[3] This makes the sector a significant contributor to India's gross domestic product (GDP) growth. The market is expected to increase at a compound annual growth rate (CAGR) of 14.9 per cent to reach US$ 220 billion by 2025, from US$ 110 billion in 2020. Indian packaged food market, in particular, is expected to double to US$70 billion by 2025.[4]

The Government of India has recognized the absolute need to bolster manufacturing, and for good reason, as the sector generates significant livelihood opportunities and contributes to 40 per cent of the total employment in the organized sector. Several policy interventions to support manufacturing and increase its contribution to 25 per cent of the country's GDP have been made. These include initiatives like the production-linked incentive (PLI) scheme, the Prime Minister's Gati Shakti Plan, Startup India and Digital India—all of which have the potential to transform the nation into a preferred manufacturing investment destination.

In addition to a growing market, structural drivers are also emerging that promise an exciting direction for quality Indian brands. The pandemic fast-tracked undercurrents towards greater digital adoption, better awareness, preference for trusted brands and easier access. The trends towards convenience, wellness, hygiene, safety, purpose-led brands as well as change in lifestyles will nurture innovation and agility like never before. There is

---

BCG Report', *Business Standard*, 10 March 2021, https://tinyurl.com/y459abca. Accessed on 21 June 2023.

[3]'FMCG Industry in India', *India Brand Equity Foundation*, April 2023, https://tinyurl.com/mukdn9zb. Accessed on 21 June 2023.

[4]Minhas, A., 'Market Size of Fast Moving Consumer Goods in India from Financial Year 2011 to 2020, with Forecast until 2027', *Statista*, 2 May 2023, https://tinyurl.com/yn8sez3p. Accessed on 21 June 2023.

a move from unbranded products to more quality trademarks as consumers become more brand conscious and discerning. The opportunities in the Indian market, especially for FMCG, is very exciting given the low penetration levels for quality branded products and the headroom it provides for growth relative to many other countries. In fact, rural India is seeing a huge rise in FMCG demand, and consumption too has shown positive signs. The growth in these regions is faster than in the urban areas, and is going to provide a huge fillip to the Indian consumption story. As incomes rise, and preferences for trusted domestic brands increase, greater accessibility through digital and omnichannel retail promise new horizons of growth in the future.

I strongly believe that digitalization and sustainability are the megatrends that will reshape the future in more ways than one. If there is one defining trend over the last two years, it has been the tectonic shift towards digital adoption across the country. Today, estimates suggest that India has more than a billion phone connections and more than 850 million Internet users.[5] This is along with a 60 per cent Internet penetration, emerging as one of the biggest consumers of data worldwide. India's Unified Payments Interface (UPI) has been a game changer, setting new records every passing month. More than 104 billion UPI transactions with total value of $2.2 trillion took place by the middle of 2022. It is estimated that 40 per cent of all FMCG consumption in India will be online. E-commerce share of total FMCG sales is expected to increase by 11 per cent by 2030.[6] The digital landscape for

---

[5]'Monthly Telecom Scenario, March' 23', *Department of Telecommunications, Government of India*, 2023, https://tinyurl.com/mrdhm79e. Accessed on 17 July 2023.

[6]Sun, Shangliao, 'Number of Wireless Telecommunications Subscribers in India as of September 2022, by Service Provider', *Statista*, 13 April 2023, https://tinyurl.com/4adrpxf7. Accessed on 21 June 2023; Basuroy, Tanushree, 'Internet Usage in India - Statistics & Facts', *Statista*, 22 September 2022, https://tinyurl.com/45h8chtw. Accessed on 21 June 2023; 'India Saw Record of ₹149.5 Trillion UPI, Card Transactions in 2022; This City Tops the List', *mint*, 18 April 2023,

FMCG is set to transition to smart ecosystems across every node of the value chain encompassing digital marketing, commerce, products and operations. Winning domestic brands will have to leverage the emerging digital paradigm in India to forge new growth pathways for the future.

The transformative reforms undertaken by the government also augurs well for the future of the Indian economy. The Union government's PLI scheme gives companies a major opportunity to boost exports, paving the way for the growth and success of Indian brands and products.

It is heartening that today there are committed Indian brands that have made their presence felt in the Indian market, and also in some overseas markets. Indian brands such as Amul, Adani, Bajaj, Godrej, Hero, Mahindra, Reliance, Tata have made inroads into the hearts of millions of Indian households. At ITC, we have been passionate about building 'Proudly Indian' brands like Aashirvaad, Sunfeast and Classmate that anchor sustainable value chains and delight more than 200 million households. Such unique and triumphant brands, which are now being exported to over 60 nations, contribute not only to the vision for AatmaNirbhar Bharat and 'Vocal for Local' but for 'Local for Global' as well.

For me, there are a few critical levers that are imperative to help build Indian brands that can make a multidimensional contribution to the nation's progress and inclusive growth. Let me mention them briefly.

Building Innovative Capacity for an AatmaNirbhar Bharat

It is my conviction that tomorrow's world will belong to those who are at the forefront in nurturing innovative capacity to create, own and protect intellectual capital. Winning brands and trademarks

---

https://tinyurl.com/2wr43mh3. Accessed on 21 June 2023.

drive research and innovation, to create intellectual assets that form a superior basis for sustaining competitive advantage in the long run. Lessons from successful global brands highlight their unwavering focus on constantly spurring innovation, to address the evolving needs of consumers. It is only when such innovative capacity is developed and promoted in India, that greenfield high-quality brands will be able to garner a larger share of the growing Indian global market. This will also help retain significant value in the country.

ITC's growing market for its vibrant portfolio of FMCG brands reflects the power of purposeful innovation that draws considerable strength from its research and development (R&D) facility, the Life Sciences and Technology Centre. Today, with 900 patents filed, the Technology Centre is ranked as the top private sector innovator in the country.

It is reassuring to note that the government is strengthening the intellectual property ecosystem to drive innovation in the country, and the results have been most promising. The Intellectual Property Rights Policy was adopted in 2016 and, for the first time in 11 years, the number of patents filed by Indian applicants overtook those filed by international ones in April 2022. The proportion of Indians filing patent applications in India improved to 40 per cent in 2020–21 (from 20 per cent in 2010–11), and India's placement on the Global Innovation Index rose by 35 places to 46 among 132 economies.[7]

India can further benefit in the R&D space if it can enhance its expenditure, and come on par with its BRICS (Brazil, Russia, India, China and South Africa) or ASEAN (Association of Southeast Asian Nations) counterparts. While a significant amount of R&D expenditure is with the public sector, it would also be crucially important to enlarge private sector investments in this area. India

---

[7]'Number of Patent Filings Rises to 66,440 in FY22', *The Economic Times*, 12 April 2022, https://tinyurl.com/y68febax. Accessed on 21 June 2023.

is well poised to significantly enhance its innovation infrastructure given that the nation has the highest number of universities in the world[8], and also has over 1,400 dedicated R&D centres in India. India has significant scientific talent. The speedy development of indigenous Covid-19 vaccines around the same time as the developed countries; the Green Revolution which made India food-secure; and the nation's expertise in atomic and missile space programmes are testimony to that. In fact, India has been a seat of higher learning for centuries. Today our country has published more research papers than Russia, Brazil and South Korea, demonstrating its intellectual mastery. It will be the enhancement in this innovative capacity that will help shape new dimensions of growth in the future.

Supporting Indian Value Chains

Indian brands have the potential to make a much larger and meaningful contribution by anchoring competitive and sustainable value chains. These value chains can support large-scale livelihoods and empower farmers.

It would be important to devise business models that can drive the competitiveness of value chains that it is a part of, thereby contributing to sustainable and inclusive development. For example, strengthening agricultural value chains in areas such as food processing and wood-based industries (encompassing mostly small and marginal farmers) can lead to significant transformation of the agricultural sector.

A case in point is the sustainable and inclusive model that is resident in the afforestation initiative of ITC's Paperboards and Specialty Papers Business. To enable a competitive and secure source of wood pulp for its growing paperboards business,

---

[8]'Estimated Number of Universities Worldwide as of July 2021, by Country', *Statista*, 17 November 2022, https://tinyurl.com/3sx88w9m. Accessed on 21 June 2023.

and also contribute significantly to import substitution, ITC spearheaded a major afforestation programme over two decades ago. This was based on high-yielding disease-resistant clones developed through intensive R&D and grown in degraded (and other) lands owned by marginal farmers. This initiative not only enabled the paperboards business to offer the greenest and best-quality products with a secure fibre source but has cumulatively greened over 950 acres, supporting livelihoods of nearly 175 million person-days. In addition, ITC's Mangaldeep brand of *agarbattis* (incense sticks) supports a bamboo value chain that generates significant livelihood opportunities. As per estimates domestic cultivation of bamboo for agarbattis (by substituting exports) can generate over 22 million person-days of employment per year. These examples of a sustainable and inclusive business model, anchored by B2B (business to business) as well as B2C (business to consumer) brands such as Classmate stationery and Mangaldeep, demonstrate how competitive agricultural value chains can be anchored with a larger societal purpose.

ITC, as the largest incubator of FMCG brands in India, also anchors competitive and inclusive value chains in wheat; potato; fruits and vegetables; dairy; and aqua through its foods businesses. The wheat and spices value chain is anchored by the Aashirvaad and Sunrise brands, as well as through exports. The potato value chain is driven by ITC's Bingo! Snacks; the fruits and vegetables value chain is powered by ITC's B-Natural juices, Farmland and ITC Master Chef Frozen Foods; and the dairy value chain leverages Aashirvaad Svasti Dairy Products and Sunfeast Wonderz milk-based beverages.

These examples indeed highlight the power of Indian brands contributing not only to AatmaNirbhar Bharat but to meaningfully supporting livelihoods and environmental replenishment, critical for the country's progress.

Building Competitiveness through Digital Transformation

The fast-paced adoption of digitalization and the advancement of technologies expected in the near-future can also contribute significantly to building competitiveness of Indian brands. Artificial intelligence (AI) and analytics enable businesses to understand consumer trends almost in real-time now, allowing companies to offer products and services that are best suited to the evolving demand. Competitive efficiencies are also enhanced through smart sourcing, manufacturing, marketing and distribution.

Under the present circumstances, it is paramount that Indian enterprises invest in building digital capabilities to create a connected ecosystem that drives agility, consumer-centricity and builds a future-ready enterprise that possesses the core ability to stay ahead. It is only after this that home-grown brands will be able to enhance competitiveness and gain larger market share in the increasingly global Indian marketplace. It is with this objective that ITC has increased its investments in the digital space, and we are confident about contributing significantly towards Digital India—a key element of AatmaNirbhar Bharat.

Supporting 'Make in India' with Building of National Assets

It is imperative to build strategic national assets to realize the true spirit of an AatmaNirbhar Bharat. We need assets that can anchor inclusive value chains, enable import substitution, support local entrepreneurship and MSME's, enrich environmental capital as well as support large-scale livelihoods. Manufacturing of world-class brands in the country supports the Make in India vision, and has the potential to transform India into a competitive manufacturing hub. It can also bring about superior value-capture in the economy.

Building national assets has been a priority for ITC. These have entailed significant investments, be it through our network of state-of-the-art integrated consumer goods manufacturing facilities (that produce ITC's vibrant portfolio of Indian brands) that support indigenous value-chains; strong agricultural infrastructure that empowers millions of farmers; the largest integrated paperboards business contributing to import substitution; or through iconic hotels that enrich the nation's tourism landscape. These assets will remain an enduring contribution to the Make in India vision, and to achieve the goal of building an AatmaNirbhar Bharat.

NURTURING BRANDS WITH THE PURPOSE OF AN AATMANIRBHAR BHARAT

The world today faces unprecedented sustainability challenges with climate change becoming a crisis, and livelihood generation a critical imperative for nations across the globe. With climate change the world is witnessing extreme weather events leading to colossal economic losses and food security threats. This is accompanied with fall in output in hotspots as well as supply-side disruptions of substantial magnitude. The pandemic also exacerbated the livelihood crisis, even as millions of youth entered the job market with fewer opportunities. Responsible brands cannot remain insulated from the larger social and environmental context in which they operate.

Enterprises as vital economic organs of society have the responsibility to craft purpose-led brands that can become catalysts of social change. Today, consumers are assessing and exercising franchises for brands and corporates with a larger societal commitment to walk-the-talk. Winning brands are now playing a larger role in society, by working towards creating larger awareness and action on critically important issues. These include issues like climate change, food and nutrition, mental health, diversity and inclusion. Investors too are driving enterprises towards more responsible conduct. Enterprises that foster purpose-led brands and adopt sustainable and inclusive business models will also be more competitive. They will also create enduring value for their stakeholders and the nation, in the true spirit of AatmaNirbhar Bharat.

Going forward, it is necessary to step up our collective efforts to build national enterprises, assets and brands that can power competitive, sustainable and inclusive value chains. This will play a leading role in shaping an AatmaNirbhar Bharat. The realization of this dream can indeed become a reality, as we traverse the Amritkaal journey towards India@100.

17

AATMANIRBHAR BHARAT IN CONTEXT OF IMPERATIVE FOR A NEW WORLD ORDER

N.K. Singh

Chairman, 15th Finance Commission, Government of India

The International Bank for Reconstruction and Development (the World Bank) came up in July 1944 to rebuild the economy devastated by war. It had initially lent for reconstruction and then for development projects, and much later in the 1970s for tackling social sector challenges such as poverty, health and education. It set up the International Development Association, a soft-loan window to assist poor countries. Simultaneously, the International Monetary Fund (IMF) came into existence on 27 December 1945 with the broad charter to promote international monetary cooperation. These twin multilateral institutions were the centrepiece of global response in the aftermath of the Second World War.

Apart from balance of payments support for enabling countries to meet their debt obligation, the IMF's principle objectives were defined in the charter in Article I(ii) as follows: 'To facilitate the expansion and balanced growth of international trade, and to contribute thereby to the promotion and maintenance of high levels of employment and real income and to the development of the productive resources of all members as primary objectives of economic policy.'[1]

The surveillance mechanism of the IMF centred around the mandatory annual Article IV consultations with all member states. Balance of payments support, which was to provide only temporary relief and liquidity, was invariably contingent on the fulfilment of certain conditions. This came to be popularly known as the 'conditionalities of the fund'. It is another matter that the extent to which the Article IV consultations are able to predict the emergence of incipient crises has eluded success. The conditionalities of the fund have had a mixed story. In some cases, it has put countries which have implemented them on a sustainable higher growth trajectory. In respect of others, it is debatable whether the consequential repercussions in fulfilling these conditions have brought about abiding macroeconomic stability.

Alongside that, in the United Nations (UN) family, the General Agreement on Tariffs and Trade (GATT) restructured itself into what is now the World Trade Organization (WTO). Specialized UN bodies have been established such as regional development banks like the Asian Development Bank, African Development Bank Group and European Investment Bank. The UN has expanded its family with specialized functionaries such as the International Labour Organization (ILO), United National Educational, Scientific and Cultural Organization (UNESCO) and United Nations Children's Fund (UNICEF). The UN General Assembly in some ways represented the hopes and aspirations of the world to foster long-term stable peaceful arrangements. The UN Security Council was the watchdog with enormous powers of the permanent five members—the United States (US), the United Kingdom (UK), France, Russia and China—each of which had veto powers. The electoral cycle and the membership of the UN Security Council had regional dimensions but none of the elected

[1]'Articles of Agreement', *International Monetary Fund*, 2020, https://tinyurl.com/yn78rax4. Accessed on 12 July 2023.

members have been conferred veto powers, that rests with only the Permanent Five. This infirmity, notwithstanding far-reaching global changes, has been a serious malaise in recognizing the new world.

Countries pursuing more rational economic policy along with much freer movement of trade, technology, capital and information undoubtedly brought enormous benefits in a broader sense. Global poverty dramatically changed for the better. Many have regarded this to be a miracle of the twenty-first century. Millions of people in Africa, India and China have been pulled out from debilitating poverty.

Some of these ideas had evolved earlier in the architecture, popularly known as the Washington Consensus. This term, which was first used in 1989 well after globalization had set in, was coined by the English economist John Williamson. He broadly prescribed policies for macroeconomic stabilization, progressive opening up of the economy and an increasing expansion of market forces (in the management of the domestic economy). In the earlier phase, Williamson himself liked to distinguish between origins of policy agenda and broad sense of policy in articulating 10 important ingredients in his so-called neoliberal manifestation. The term 'Washington Consensus' began to acquire a pejorative connotation relying in excessive belief in the power and role of market forces. The unexpected geopolitical developments had cast a deep shadow on the Washington Consensus.

Before we examine the ingredients of the Washington Consensus, it is important to point out that according to Joseph Stanislaw and Daniel Yergin this consensus was developed in the context of Latin America by Latin Americans. Joseph Stiglitz, an American economist, added that the Consensus was designed to respond to the real problems of Latin America. He further mentioned that it was a response to the exceedingly restrictive and draconian prescriptions of the IMF. It is another matter that Williamson himself regretted that there was an embedded diplomatic faux pas, so to say, in using the word 'Washington' rather than a general consensus.

This short paper is designed to examine the ingredients of the Washington Consensus and more importantly, to conclude that this Consensus is irrelevant. Geopolitics has evolved in a manner in which we have already commenced a new world order which is not bipolar anymore. The new world order is multipolar and its framework therefore needs to be seen in this revised context.

The Washington Consensus as originally articulated by Williamson included 10 important ingredients:

1. Fiscal policy discipline with avoidance of large fiscal deficits relative to gross domestic product (GDP)
2. Redirection of public spending from subsidies
3. Tax reform, broadening the tax base and adopting moderate marginal tax rates
4. Interest rates that are market determined and positive in real terms
5. Competitive exchange rates
6. Trade liberalization
7. Liberalization of inward foreign direct investment
8. Privatization of state enterprises
9. Deregulation
10. Legal security for property rights

What is the relevance of many of these articulated principles given rapid changes which we are currently witnessing? The new world order recognizes the historical reality that the cozy compact between the two superpowers, namely the US and the USSR (Union of Soviet Socialist Republics), was long broken. Other forces and entities had risen significantly in strength and reach. Large parts of Asia have achieved significant prosperity. The rise of China and India had, to some extent, taken the world somewhat by surprise. China itself has, in more than subtle ways, claimed that it can be a power centre on its own while exercising enormous influence over other countries through financial and security arrangements.

In the Indian context, the normalization of trade and other relationships was being taken for granted. Even with the episode of the Sino-Indian War in 1962 somewhat pushed in the background, the events of the last few years in Doklam, Ladakh and frequent and unprovoked intrusion into Arunachal have awakened India to the newly emerging geopolitical challenges. The world is wary of China's intentions for the Indo-Pacific region and even South Korea, as it aims to increase its influence there. Japan itself has been concerned that notwithstanding large investments—in trade, technology and the presence of Japanese companies in China—it must rethink the new geopolitical realities.

Along with this, the disorderly breakup of the erstwhile Soviet Union into independent states created their own unsettled problems. The Russian federation has never quite accepted whatever may have been the compulsions of the enormous economic crisis, which led to the breakup of the Soviet Union. This was, in their view, an irrational and unjust parcelling in circumscribing its spheres of influence with the creation of independent states. Europe has woken up to the somewhat hard reality of rearming itself and looking after its own security concerns and challenges, than exclusive dependence on the security umbrella of the US. The enhanced defence budget by Germany and some other west European powers reinforces the European security concerns.

This is also an Aatmanirbhar moment for India and other countries in the region. Japan, which had legislations embedded in the national psyche of never rearming itself, was forced to reconsider its defence outlay. Many developing countries in Asia and Africa have received financial support from the Chinese, with serious backing. This has resulted in higher levels of indebtedness, and the ever-mounting debt liabilities have lead to disorderly responses. Many countries have resented the pressures to reshape domestic policies, often with serious conditionalities. Recourse to multilateral institutions have not proved very successful, and the record of the fund in timely and orderly restructuring of debt has been slow and problematic.

Based on all these far-reaching geopolitical and other changes, there are six more important challenges that we must address (explained below).

Broken Psyche of GVC (Global Value-Added Chain)

The future of globalization, namely the theorem that the global value-added chain (GVC) (which emphasizes enhanced productivity and efficiency) is a path to mutual prosperity. Is this philosophy of GVC, which is at the heart of the Washington Consensus, valid anymore? The GVCs refer to international production sharing, wherein production tasks and activities are carried out in different countries. The philosophy is that irrespective of location, comparative factor advantages either in terms of raw material or skills can disaggregate the production systems in multiple ways. Given transportation efficiency, each production entity contributes to the final product and this economizes cost efficiency significantly. All this is based on the assumption of free movements of goods and services, efficient transportation system, respect for intellectual property rights and a trade regime which contributes to the final product and enhances efficiency. The quest for GVCs has been an important ingredient in the availability of global goods and services at cost-efficient prices. In the end, it is a win-win situation for all stakeholders.

However, think of an arrangement where this becomes a hostage due to geopolitics or what may be called weaponization of trade instruments. What if China and Taiwan interrupted the assured supply of chips or, active pharmaceutical ingredients (APIs) with multiplier effects? Other countries which have little options or have discontinued the production of APIs (as is the case with India) would face a crisis. The value-added chain is frequently broken in such a sequence. This becomes an inescapable necessity for the diversification of sources of supply and in no small measure self-sufficiency, implying an aatmanirbhar regime. Countries will need to reassess their external strategy by identifying critical items, areas, processes and products where investments must be encouraged and supported through regulatory and tax changes.

Weaponization of Money Disturbing Faith

On the macro side, is the future of central banking and its financial arrangements. Without commenting on the ongoing war in Europe, which India rightly has sought to end and seek restoration of peace, has caused great concerns. Nonetheless, irrespective of the ongoing war in Ukraine there has been a new demonstration of 'weaponization of money'. This fragments the global economy and makes it less efficient. Martin Wolf, the well-known economic commentator, writing on this in the *Financial Times,* has brought out that Russia held reserves worth $469 billion by its own policies to give it financial independence.[2] But the special military operations led to freezing of its own resources in dollar reserves. This has not even happened during the height of the Second World War where legitimate money and assets were frozen for countries who were at war. Russia's weaponization of its own assets and reserves jeopardizes the working of the global financial system, in a manner which had hitherto not happened. Wolf writes, 'Money is a public good. A global money—one that people rely upon in their cross-border transactions and investment decisions—is a global public good. But the providers of that public good are national governments. Even under the old gold

---

[2]Wolf, Martin, 'A New World of Currency Disorder Looms', *Financial Times*, 29 March 2022, https://tinyurl.com/4kp7zukh. Accessed on 30 June 2023.

exchange standard, that was the case.'[3] The outcome of all this is to undercut the credibility of the financial system in the way we have understood it. Alternatives like private currencies by way of Bitcoin, global currency as IMF's Special Drawing Rights or even national currency is not a substitute for large volume transactions. Going back to gold would make transactions much more onerous. Jeopardizing the hitherto acceptable arrangements by weaponizing the financial system has far-reaching consequences in the working of the global financial system.

Decline of Multilateralism

This point is on trade and trade liberalization. Are trading patterns designed to change irreversibly? Will WTO continue in some way, outlasting the quest for preferential or bilateral trade agreements? The principal instrument of devising and enforcing the rules of the multilateral trade regime rests with the WTO. However, apart from the failed Doha Development Round, many of the commitments remain unrealized. One of the creators of this institution, namely the US, decided to disempower this body by reluctance to nominate members to the Dispute Settlement Body. This diverts, in a certain sense, the legitimacy of the organization itself. In the meantime, multilateral trading arrangements are being increasingly replaced by regional trading agreements such as the Regional Comprehensive Economic Partnership (RCEP), and others besides free trade agreements (FTAs) between and among nations and regional trading blocs. The multilateral trading order needs global leadership and a fresh approach. Add to this the complication that since the bipolar world is increasingly becoming multipolar, with different regions and country with spheres of influence, its consequences are far-reaching. It undercuts the basic philosophy and rationale of the multilateral trading system.

---

[3]Ibid.

Emerging Risks of Free Flow of Investments

The next factor is the foreign investments including renewed quest for private capital. On the issue of the quest for private capital, while all counties will seek to garner the larger share, there are unsettled issues. Given geopolitical factors, the freer flow of private capital will be increasingly embroiled in multiple regulatory restrictions. Tax arbitrage, issues of respect for intellectual property rights and other ways to evade a uniform regulatory regime, creates new challenges. Along with this, the issue of respecting contractual arrangements undertaken, terms for the obligation of contract and compensating mechanism enhances risks for private capital flows.

Imperative to Have Self-Reliance in Defence

Nations have come to realize that national capability for meeting security challenges is now a historical necessity. Over a period of time, given the bipolar world, India's own dependence on Russia for major security supplies (both for the commercial war and air support) has been very significant. Of course, as far as air force is concerned, alternative sources from France were integral to its ongoing policy. In recent years, we have sought to diversify our security dependence from a single country. Given the emerging geopolitics, we have brought in new partners, particularly the US, Germany and others. The orderly transition, however, is taking time. In the meantime, the challenge of aatmanirbhar defence and improving our defence capability by attracting private capital, innovation and technologies have to be pursued with more urgency than ever before.

Compulsion to Reduce Dependence on Imported Fossil Fuels

The issue of climate change is inevitably linked with the broad issue of diversifying energy sources. Dependence on import of fossil fuel sources of energy, particularly crude oil, is a dominant feature of our economic policy. The effort to move toward renewable non-fossil fuel energy, an inescapable priority for global good, mitigates against the newly experienced shortage of oil and gas. An orderly transition and adequate financing with access to technology to renewable sources of energy has been disrupted by the ongoing war. This war has spillovers not only in other aspects of globalization, but in the disruption it may cause in the adherence of nations to commitments taken under the COP26. Issues of mitigation and adaptation, access and cost affordable technology form part of the broader debate on climate finance.

THE WAY FORWARD

Apart from the ongoing difficulties of an orderly transition to renewable fuels, managing the social disruptions in employment patterns was also an ongoing concern. The international focus on climate, climate finance and renewable energy has been rudely distracted by the new energy crisis with rising cost of oil and gas (accentuated by the ongoing war).

If humanity is to survive we need, not the Washington Consensus, but a new global consensus. We can call it the Consensus of the New Global Order. In any such arrangement, some of the concerns which have been articulated in this paper must be fully addressed. Too many contradictory forces and asymmetric obligations deter the pursuit of our objectives. Long-term development challenges of poverty, gainful employment and harnessing emerging technology remain our abiding concerns. In a very short term, AatmaNirbhar Bharat has overridden national consensus in multiple spheres. These spheres include strengthening our security, addressing our climate needs and firewalling other areas.

In conclusion, I want to recall a short piece I had written in the *Hindustan Times* in November 2021 entitled, 'HTLS 2021: Order or Disorder in New World?' It is clear that for an orderly transition, we need the following five components:

1. First and foremost, the most overarching institution of global governance, namely the UN, needs fundamental restructuring. The power and economic configurations of the world have changed immeasurably since 1945. The UN Security Council represents a segmented part of the world and must become more united.
2. Second, institutes of international governance, particularly the WTO, the IMF and the World Bank also need a basic restructuring. For instance, obscurantist practices in the World Bank like the Single Borrower Limit (irrespective of the compelling needs of national or the successive failure of Article IV consultations mandated by the IMF for advance action to focus on emerging crises with corrective steps). These have repeatedly proved inadequate to serve the basic objectives of these institutions.
3. Third, these international institutions need to restructure their lending policies to factor in the problems of climate financing. The quest for renewable energy is a compelling necessity. It needs to be accorded the requisite priority and risk mitigation provisions to harness private capital.
4. Fourth is the mergence and access to newer technology, particularly 5G, Artificial Intelligence and Internet of Things. We need to harness the technological powers for multiple areas of gainful economic activity from employment generation to agriculture, health and education, to mention a few.

5. Last but not the least, how does one address the continuing unfolding dynamics of the geopolitical crisis? The cozy compact of the North Atlantic powers of the US and Europe are in tatters. The aftermath of the breakup of the great Soviet empire has yet to see a resting point. The emergence of China has geopolitical overtones and, hopefully the quest for the peaceful rise of China will not prove elusive. Asia needs an overall system of cohesiveness, predictability and a settled order to engage in the compelling necessity of improving the quality of life of this very populous continent.

Seeking instruments of cooperation, collaboration and consensus will be a continuing challenge. In all this, there is no escape from the fundamental reality. Nations have to increasingly look inward to not pursue an isolationist policy, but to address their own security concerns and compelling necessities. Re-globalization is easier said than done. These issues need to be addressed through new forms of dialogue and institutions being restructured for facilitating consensus. Consensus building in the emerging new world order will be the central challenge.

18

LABOUR RELATIONS IN AATMANIRBHAR BHARAT

Saji Narayanan

Past president, Bhartiya Mazdoor Sangh

In a fast-moving world, everyone is struggling for existence and survival of the 'fastest' is becoming the new rule. Balance or equilibrium in life is getting difficult, as the world is catching up with chaotic trajectories. Anarchic, chaotic or uncertain behaviour spreads among economies. Sometimes, this is legitimized in the name of disruptive technologies. Chaotic theory in economics works in new economic activities like the gig, online platform, cloud working, freelance work, e-commerce, supply chain, contract labour, fixed-term employment etc. In the name of disruptive technologies and disruptive business models, a new category of workers has emerged—namely 'gig workers'.

Naturally, most people want a settled life. Traditionally, we have seen an industry run by successive generations with a tag of a reputed trademark. Today, it is propagated that the life span of an industry will be up to merely four or five years. The industry then has to diversify to another business if it wants to survive. The said temporary nature, is in short conveyed by the term 'gig'. Everything becomes transient and economics becomes an unpredictable branch of study. Now very often we hear about the terms like gig economy, gig industries, gig workers, and the like which are replacing the current economic activities. The gig workers are given excess workloads and targets, which are inhuman. They come as a part of Industry 4.0, just like the invading effect of automation. Many predict that it is going to be the new normal. The oft-repeated claim is that the gig nature of work will open up new avenues of employment. International Labour Organization (ILO) explains this type of work as 'crowd-work' or 'work on-demand via apps'.

Food delivery services like Zomato, Swiggy; or e-commerce platforms like Amazon, Flipkart etc. use gig workers. These workers cannot claim regular benefits such as minimum wages, hours of work, overtime, leave, etc., compared to most traditional permanent employees. The recent cases of many app-based businesses like Uber, Lyft, Taskrabbit, DoorDash and so on, shows that they are facing backlash. The gig workers are demanding more benefits and equal rights as full-time workers. In 2021, the United Kingdom (UK) Supreme Court has ruled that Uber drivers are workers and not self-employed as the company argued. This meant they will get legal entitlements like minimum wages, paid holidays, bonus, social security benefits etc. In 2022, food delivery service DoorDash had to reach a settlement of $100 million with its drivers as per orders of a California Federal Judge. But in March, 2023, California court said Uber and Lyft drivers can be treated as independent contractors and not as workers. In 2019, New York Court had given a similar verdict against the employees of Taskrabbit.[1] A study conducted by PayPal reveals that many food delivery boys of Swiggy, Uber Eats and Zomato

[1]Browne, Ryan, 'Uber Loses a Major Employment Rights Case as the UK's Top Court Rules Its Drivers Are Workers', *CNBC*, 19 February 2021, https://tinyurl.com/3vdmuyav. Accessed on 12 July 2023; '$100 Million Doordash Settlement Won by the Law Offices of Todd M. Friedman, P.C.', *TMF*, 16 August 2022, https://tinyurl.com/32jpf4bt. Accessed on 12 July 2023; Weissner, Daniel, 'California Court Upholds Treating App-Based Drivers as Contractors', *Reuters*, 14 March 2023, https://tinyurl.com/mrxcwsr6. Accessed on 12 July 2023.

say they have taken up the jobs only as a temporary means to support themselves till they find appropriate employment. The daily working hours for these delivery boys are atrocious, and their targets are extremely difficult to achieve. Ernst and Young study of 2017 on the 'Future of Jobs in India' found that 24 per cent of the world's gig workers come from India.

The new Code on Social Security, legislated by the Indian parliament, is the first attempt to define these types of works and bring them within the ambit of labour laws. The central government is supposed to frame social security schemes for the newly emerging categories like gig workers and online-platform workers. The major challenges in addressing them is identifying the worker, locating the related employer etc. California state has laid down the 'ABC test' to identify them. The European Union has adopted a directive on 'Transparent and Predictable Working Conditions' for such workers identified by the duration and nature of their work in a week.

The biggest crisis in India's job market is the shift that has taken place in converting decent jobs into low-quality jobs, in the name of casualization. The country is fast losing quality jobs. Most jobs, including government jobs, are gradually becoming temporary. So-called 'employees' are being converted into 'workers' or cheap 'labour'. IndiaSpend study says, more than four-fifths of the workers (around 84 per cent) are employed as casual labour in the construction sector. Nearly 80 per cent of jobs are under the contract labour system in many industries. Decent jobs—with reasonable salaries and working conditions, in the government sector—are being replaced by contract labour, outsourced workers, temporary workers, fixed-term employees etc.

India being a labour surplus country, badly needs to declare a National Employment Policy. We have to prioritize so that our reforms, technology and planning are labour-intensive and not labour-displacing ones. Hence, a total revisit of the policies and reforms is needed.

MARX'S NEGLECT OF RURAL WORKERS

Further, we witness that there has been a general neglect of rural workers. Creating classes even among workers is a defect in Western thought. Marx recognized only industrial workers as the proletariat. Agricultural workers were outside his scheme of analysis. In 1852, Karl Marx ridiculed the peasantry as a 'sack of potatoes' when peasants were passive towards his experiment of the Paris commune. Even traditional kinds of work and the concept of 'immaterial' work (like the computer, service work etc., of the modern times in the post-industrial world) were outside his view of labour. Others like artisans, peasants, shopkeepers, small manufacturers and other lower middle-class were called 'lumpen proletariat'.

Most Western economic historians have treated rural workers as either peasants or slaves. The modern capitalist system also categorizes workers with different status levels. It divides workers into classes like salaried employees, wage workers and cheap labour. This is done according to the status of wages, working conditions, job security etc. The West looks at countries like India merely as a hub of cheap labour and raw materials. Governments also have become proud of supplying cheap labour. Multinational Corporations (MNCs) engage cheap labour at the endpoints in the supply chain and demand union-free, labour-law-less workplaces. Developed countries are worried about protecting their workers, welfare and social security of workers. Whereas, developing countries are desperately waiting to supply their cheap labour to the exploitative hands of MNCs.

EXPECTATIONS FROM AATMANIRBHAR BHARAT

Because of the ideological problems of our national leaders, the unfortunate fate of independent India was to experiment with two foreign ideologies, namely: the Russian model of socialism in the Nehruvian era and the US model of capitalist Liberalization, Privatization and Globalization (LPG) reforms in the Dr Manmohan Singh era. During the first one, namely, the Nehruvian era (which continued till the 1990s), India's potential was being trapped for decades by intense protectionism. This model of socialism resulted in high unemployment, poverty, inequality, inefficiencies and a low rate of growth (which can be called the 'Nehruvian rate of growth'). It created the world's largest section of working poor, commonly called the 'unorganized sector'. India has the largest unorganized sector in the world. 93 per cent of Indian labour is in the unorganized sector. Failure of Nehruvian socialism was formally endorsed in the 1990s by none other than Dr Manmohan Singh, the then Congress finance minister. Nehru created a weak economic base. Owing to this, Dr Manmohan Singh could very easily change it into another paradigm of the American model of capitalism with its new face—globalization. But again, failure of LPG reforms was identified within a decade when its growth was recognized as a 'jobless growth'.

The two stages convey two ideologies that have ruled the world: capitalism and socialism (or state capitalism and the capitalist state). LPQ (Licence, Permit, Quota) Raj of the socialist era was replaced by LPG Raj of the capitalist era. Despite the exercise of following these adopted ideologies, India's Human Development Index has been extremely disgusting.

The biggest issue the LPG reforms have created in the labour sector is the generation of low-quality jobs in place of quality jobs. It includes the increase of casualization and the contract labour system. We find its ugly face during crisis times, and we witnessed it during the Covid-19 crisis period.

Against Nehruvian socialism, Pandit Deendayal Upadhyaya had proposed the 'Integral Human Philosophy'—a basic and universal viewpoint that applies to everything related to human and social life. Dattopant Thengadi carried forward the idea and presented the 'Third Way' in the background of Dr Manmohan

Singh's capitalist globalization. People voted for total change in 2014. The historical rise of the new government with a thumping majority in 2014 and 2019 was a clear sign of the towering expectations of the common man.

On 12 May 2020, Prime Minister (PM) Narendra Modi began the third stage in the economic history of independent India—the AatmaNirbhar Bharat, which is the swadeshi paradigm. The new way out, the ray of hope or the sudden shift manifests the aatma or soul of India. Thus, an appropriate time has arrived to deliberate changes required in various facets of national life based on Indian ethos. A thorough revamping of our economic policies should be the core of the new AatmaNirbhar Bharat. This will be the swadeshi foundation of an economic transition for the new millennium. It is not a mere economic remodelling of the country, it has many things beyond. Hence a national debate has become inevitable, probing a new paradigm of change in India. PM Narendra Modi has indicated that the real wealth creators are the labour, MSMEs and farmers as a part of AatmaNirbhar Bharat. But, AatmaNirbhar Bharat has the danger of losing its flavour and flair if it again gets trapped in the cobweb of the capitalist reforms.

Total change is what is required. The concept of development reaching the last man is called '*Antyodaya*'. The benefits of development should reach the last man. Minor programmes here and there will not be able to bring radical changes. Let us not be satisfied with anything short of total change. Nothing short of total transformation is acceptable for the poor, who strive for a better living. So, social progression has to be revolutionized. Governance for the people is to be reinstated. This is important for labour since 40 per cent of the population is labourers. So, we may have to adopt new styles and methods while going to the vast unorganized sector. Change has to be from low-quality work towards quality work or decent work as propounded by the International Labour Organization (ILO). The United Nations

(UN) has come with a proposal to eradicate world poverty through its programme of MDG (Millennium Development Goal), which ended in 2015. But it was not so successful. Hence its second phase is named SDG 2030 (Sustainable Development Goal ending in 2030). How far this will be successful is not known.

PLIGHT OF MIGRANT WORKERS DURING COVID-19

The impact of Covid-19 on the labour sector was disastrous. Job loss and non-payment of wages were at the centre of issues in the labour sector, especially for daily-wage workers. There were issues like no pay, delayed pay or reduced pay. Many industrial units reduced their workforce, and several workers were terminated. Daily wage workers, casual workers, contract workers, women workers, fishing workers, plantation workers, beedi workers, self-employed small businesses, tourism sector etc., were worst affected. In the labour sector, the 'new normal' of disrespecting international labour standards became rampant. Most of the state governments raised working hours. Suspension of labour laws; restraint on trade unions; the principle of no work no pay; engaging young workers and avoiding elders; and tendency to shift the burden of the ill-effects to the shoulders of the labour were seen.

The pandemic exposed a big migrant labour crisis in India. There was massive reverse migration of workers from urban centres to their villages and the return of foreign migrants, especially from Gulf countries. Nearly 10 million migrant labourers lost their jobs or felt insecure and neglected in the urban areas.

When migrant labourers felt insecure in the host states, a sort of psychosocial scare developed among them. In many places, agents and owners deserted them during the spread of the pandemic. They were sheltered in poor conditions without sufficient food. They felt that their love and affection lay in their beloved villages and they wanted to join their families in their native places. Wherever employers and local people cared for them well, they stayed back.

There was a massive exodus to home states from host states, where they were left in the lurch by their employers.

The villages of India received the migrant workers back and protected all of them. The migrant workers who lost their jobs in urban areas were absorbed by increased agricultural and rural activity. India is alive because of the rural economy and the poor villagers, whom our 'experts' call cheap labour. India still lives in villages. Unfortunately, they comprise the world's largest number of working poor.

'INDUSTRIAL FAMILY'

The model that the Indian paradigm depicts to the whole world on almost all types of human and social relations is the 'family model'. It is the most successful model human history has ever seen. The family model sees our nation as *Bharat Mata* (Mother India). The problem of atrocities on women can be addressed if every other woman is considered as a mother (*matruvad para dareshu*). International relations are based on *vasudhaiva kutumbakam* (the world is one family). The human relationship with nature is also based on the Atharv Veda's concept of Mother Earth (*Prithvi mataram*) and *putroham prithivya* (Earth is our mother and we are her sons). From its inception, the Bharatiya Mazdoor Sangh (BMS) has been proposing the concept of 'industrial Family' in employer–employee relations (as propounded by Dattopant Thengadi). This is in opposition of the master–servant model of the West or the class antagonist model of the communists.

Made in Japan: Akio Morita and Sony is a famous autobiography of Akio Morita, the founder of Sony Corporation, which is often treated as a textbook of industrial relations in Japan. The book reiterates 'to create a family-like feeling' between management and employees as the secret of the success of his industry. He explains: 'The most important mission for a Japanese manager is to develop a healthy relationship with his employees, to create a family-like feeling within the corporation, a feeling that employees and managers share the same fate.' This accepts the Indian family concept and rejects the Western 'master-servant' model.

Japan is supposed to have an ideal industrial relations system. There, both management and workers dedicate themselves to the development of their industries and nation. Japan which was destroyed in the Second World War, within 10 years rose from the ashes and regained its glory to become the most industrialized nation. This was mainly because of its peculiar culture of industrial relations. Thus, work culture is not about worker's culture alone; it is also about the employer.

Industrial relations cannot be just a bundle of laws and rules. Thus, like any other human relationship, industrial relation is a question of culture or attitude—or the work culture. A new industrial culture needs to be created. The concept of HR (human resources) also looks at labour merely as a 'resource'. Hence HR should be 'human relations' and not 'human resources'. The name of the basic labour law of India, the Industrial Disputes Act, is rightly replaced recently by the name 'Industrial Relations Code'. Tripartism should give way to the concept of 'three social partners'. They are not 'parties' but 'partners'. 'Industrial harmony' is a positive term compared to the term 'industrial peace'. A balance between the rights of the employers and the employees has to be achieved, the latter being the more disadvantaged class. This will erase the relevance of all adversarial theories in the labour sector.

Karl Marx believed in a constant class struggle based on dialecticism to bring change. Capitalism also believes in the struggle for existence and competition. But Indian ethos believes in cooperation and co-existence of all. Confluence and not conflict will bring success. We do not believe in class interests and conflicts, but we stress on human brotherhood. Instead of the slogan, 'workers of the world unite', BMS has made the clarion call: 'workers, unite the world'. So, BMS rejects violent revolution and opts for *navothan* (renaissance), not *kranti* but *samkranti*. Indians always like value-based change. This is a positive indication of movements like that of BMS, that believe in values. Our pace of social progression has to be accelerated. This is the real *Bharat Mata pooja* (worshipping of Mother India) that we can do.

IS THERE AN END TO STRIKE?

India has seen militant trade unionism in the 1970s and 1980s. Strikes and lockouts were a common feature. Since the 1990s number of strikes have been considerably reduced. But after 2010, strike days have come back and the nation witnessed two successful national level strikes in 2012 and 2013. This was when all trade unions in India participated. Now the question that arises is, is there an end to the method of the strike? The answer is, there should be a self-restrictive and effective redressal mechanism to render strikes superfluous. In Japan, employers show a high level of work culture and thus, strikes are almost unnecessary. Even token protests by workers there are earnestly honoured. In the present Indian scenario casualization is increasing, job security is becoming a foregone dream, labour unrest is growing and responsible trade unions have no effective and alternate method of redressal. However, BMS believes that strikes should always be the last resort.

SHARING SURPLUS VALUE WITH SOCIETY

Surplus value is the excess labour produced by the worker, in excess of the wage he earned. Marx borrowed the labour theory of surplus value from classical capitalist economists like Adam Smith and David Ricardo. In capitalism, this excess goes to the hands of capitalists as profit. This is the exploitation of the toils of labour, resulting in the impoverishment of the workers. Capitalism thrived on extracting surplus out of natural resources and human labour. For the capitalist, labour is only a commodity that can be calculated in terms of money.

Whereas in India's traditional labour culture, profit is to be enjoyed by the capital investor, labour and society together—not merely by the individual like in capitalism or by the state like in communism. *Rashtra hita, udyog hita aur mazdoor hita* (The welfare of the country, industry and labourers) have to go together. Guru Golwalkar's (Guruji) vision about the role of society in sharing surplus value has been expanded by Dattopant Thengadi in *The Third Way*: 'Surplus value of labour belongs to nation.'

While considering the interest of the industry and workers, no one should lose sight of the interest of the society. Hence, every collective bargaining agreement between employer and worker should take care of the interest of the society as well. This is our national commitment. Therefore, Dattopant Thengadi says that 'collective bargaining' of two parties should be replaced by 'national commitment' of both the partners. Industry and labour are two wings of our national bird, which has to fly to ambitious heights. Every social organization, including trade unions and employer organizations, has to work in tandem with the nation's interest (especially in an unprecedented crisis period). In the same way, every issue related to labour should be consulted in a tripartite forum to find solutions. Jointly, we can succeed.

WAGE-LED GROWTH

In this era of globalization, the section which has got the worst treatment is the labour. The share of real wages of workers has failed to increase commensurately with the share of other factors of production; especially capital, causing severe hardships for the labourers in general. It may be noted that between 1990–91 and

2018–19, the share of wages in net value addition of registered manufacture sector has come down from 25.6 per cent to 16.9 per cent. Whereas, the share of profits has gone up from 22.1 per cent to 43.6 per cent during the same period. As India is making strides towards self-reliance, it is natural for labour to get better treatment than what was meted out to them in the past.

In the mad rush for growth, we have forgotten the economics of the development of the last man. Education, health, minimum wages and food security (including price stability) are the four pillars for empowering the marginalized sections of India. Radical improvements in these aspects can revolutionize over six lakh villages in rural India. Every citizen should get the opportunity to manifest their personality.

Empowering people economically by increasing their purchasing power can be achieved by a 'wage-led growth' or people-centric growth, and not a market-centric growth. Growth in real terms is related to the wage of workers. An increase in wages means an increase in the purchasing power of the people, which in turn will strengthen the market and the economy. It acts like a cycle. Proper implementation of minimum wages can revolutionize the standard of living of the majority of the population. However, the concept of fair wages and living wages are still out of our discussion.

INDUSTRY AND LABOUR

40 per cent of the total population is working population. They, along with their family of children, women and older people, comprise more than 85–90 per cent of the population. That means labour welfare and development is almost equal to national development.

For the first time, the industry now realizes the importance of interstate migrant workers (whom many considered India's 'cheap labour'). Industrialists openly said, without workers, the industry cannot survive.[2] Hitherto it was propagated that workers cannot exist without industry. Migrant workers got new respect when they were called 'guest workers'. Such a name has found a place in dictionaries and encyclopaedias. Thus, once again, it was proved that the idea of 'industry versus labour' of communists or 'industry minus labour' of capitalists could not succeed. The concept of 'industry AND labour' is the basis on which a nation can excel in the era of AatmaNirbhar Bharat.

---

[2]Malik, Faisal (et al.), 'Reverse Migration, Dip In Output Spell Tough Times for Industries', *Hindustan Times*, 16 May 2020, https://tinyurl.com/nu7dynte. Accessed on 30 June 2023.